MADNESS, BETRAYAL AND THE LASH

The Epic Voyage of
Captain George Vancouver

The EPIC VOYAGE *of*
CAPTAIN GEORGE VANCOUVER

STEPHEN R. BOWN

Madness,
BETRAYAL
and the Lash

Douglas & McIntyre
Vancouver/Toronto

Douglas & McIntyre Ltd.
2323 Quebec Street, Suite 201
Vancouver, British Columbia
V5T 4S7
www.douglas-mcintyre.com

Library and Archives Canada Cataloguing in Publication
Bown, Stephen R
Madness, betrayal and the lash :
the epic voyage of Captain George Vancouver / Stephen Bown.

Includes bibliographical references.
ISBN 978-1-55365-339-4

1. Vancouver, George, 1757-1798. 2. Northwest Coast of North America—
Discovery and exploration—British. 3. Explorers—England—
Biography. I. Title. II. Title: Epic voyage of Captain George Vancouver.
G246.V3B69 2008   910'.92   c2008-901631-9

Editing by John Eerkes-Medrano
Copy editing by Iva Cheung
Jacket and text design by Jessica Sullivan
Front jacket illustration by John Horton
Back jacket portrait, believed to be of Captain George Vancouver
© National Portrait Gallery, London
Printed and bound in Canada by Friesens
Printed on acid-free paper that is forest friendly (100% post-consumer
recycled paper) and has been processed chlorine free.

We gratefully acknowledge the financial support of the Canada Council for
the Arts, the British Columbia Arts Council, the Province of British Columbia through
the Book Publishing Tax Credit, and the Government of Canada through the Book
Publishing Industry Development Program (BPIDP) for our publishing activities.

Contents

⸺◈⸺

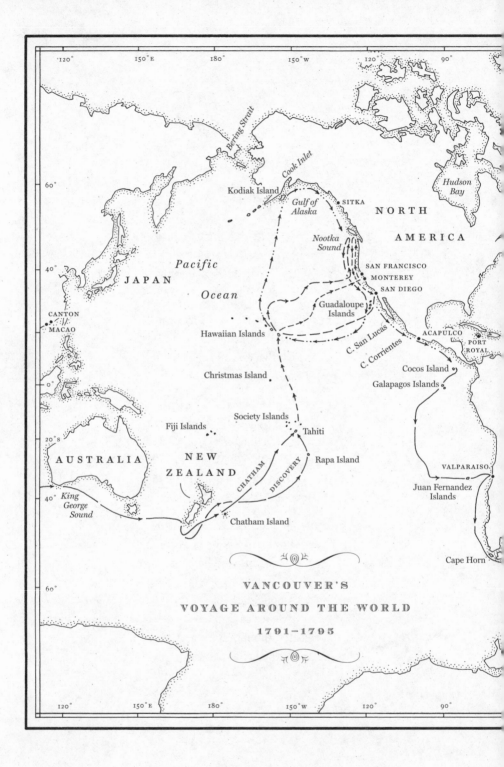

120°   150° E   180°   150° W   120°   90°

60°

Bering Strait

Cook Inlet

Kodiak Island

Gulf of
Alaska   SITKA

NORTH

Nootka
Sound   AMERICA

40°   Pacific

JAPAN   Ocean   SAN FRANCISCO
                                    MONTEREY
                                    SAN DIEGO

CANTON   Guadaloupe
MACAO   Islands

Hawaiian Islands   C. San Lucas   ACAPULCO
                                                        PORT
                                    C. Corrientes   ROYAL
0°
                                                        Cocos Island
Christmas Island   Galapagos Islands

                    Society Islands
Fiji Islands   Tahiti
20° S
                    NEW   Rapa Island
AUSTRALIA   ZEALAND   VALPARAISO

40° King   CHATHAM   DISCOVERY   Juan Fernandez
     George   Islands
     Sound
                         Chatham Island

Hudson
Bay

Cape Horn

60°

VANCOUVER'S

VOYAGE AROUND THE WORLD

1791–1795

120°   150° E   180°   150° W   120°   90°

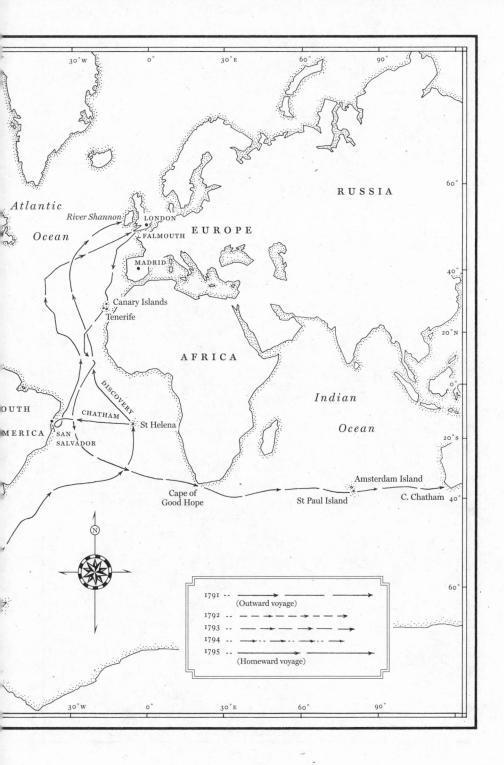

30°W 0° 30°E 60° 90°

Atlantic

Ocean

River Shannon

LONDON

FALMOUTH

EUROPE

RUSSIA

60°

MADRID

40°

Canary Islands

Tenerife

20°N

AFRICA

DISCOVERY

Indian

OUTH

CHATHAM

St Helena

MERICA

SAN

SALVADOR

Ocean

20°S

Amsterdam Island

Cape of

Good Hope

St Paul Island

C. Chatham 40°

60°

1791 --	
	(Outward voyage)
1792 --	
1793 --	
1794 --	
1795 --	
	(Homeward voyage)

30°W 0° 30°E 60° 90°

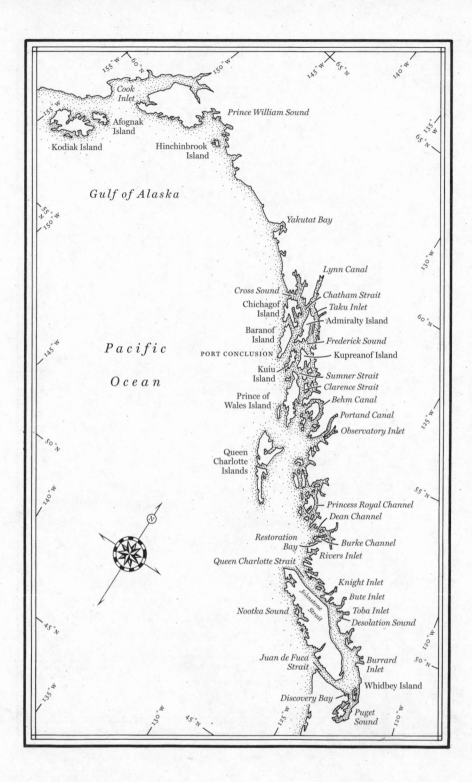

Cook
Inlet

Afognak
Island

Hinchinbrook
Island

Kodiak Island

Prince William Sound

Gulf of Alaska

Yakutat Bay

Lynn Canal

Cross Sound

Chatham Strait

Chichagof
Island

Taku Inlet

Admiralty Island

Baranof
Island

Frederick Sound

PORT CONCLUSION

Kupreanof Island

Kuiu
Island

Sumner Strait

Clarence Strait

Prince of
Wales Island

Behm Canal

Portand Canal

Observatory Inlet

Pacific

Ocean

Queen
Charlotte
Islands

Princess Royal Channel

Dean Channel

Restoration
Bay

Burke Channel

Rivers Inlet

Queen Charlotte Strait

Knight Inlet

Bute Inlet

Nootka Sound

Johnstone Strait

Toba Inlet

Desolation Sound

Juan de Fuca
Strait

Burrard
Inlet

Whidbey Island

Discovery Bay

Puget
Sound

Prologue

◄ ◆ ►

THERE ARE NO people in view. I'm standing on a small, pebble-strewn beach bounded at each end by giant rock outcroppings and hemmed in by a wall of mighty cedar trees. It is cold and raining. Mist clings to the treetops and obscures the surrounding mountains. The waves gently curl in towards my boots, so I step back, leaving a boot print in the pebbles. The beach is deserted and unremarkable, indistinguishable from thousands of other tiny, stone beaches along the rugged coast of the Pacific Northwest. I turn and walk through the drizzle, scramble over the rock outcropping and return to the larger beach and the grassy clearing above it. The clearing is the only level ground on this narrow spit of land that juts south from Nootka Island.

From my vantage point in the clearing, I now see two very different aspects of the same ocean. On one side of this narrow finger of land lies the open Pacific, its wild waves rumbling ominously with white-caps before they crash into the shore. The other side is as calm and placid as a lake, the finger of land subduing the rough water and creating a snug shelter. The boat I arrived on is moored here on the calm side, in Yuquot or Friendly Cove, where dozens of ships once sought shelter. For a brief period in the late eighteenth century, this remote and lonely spot on the southern tip of the largest island west of Vancouver Island was one of the most important and talked-about places in the world: more than a thousand people lived here. The deserted beach I strolled on so recently had commercial storage sheds and workshops that, although primitive, serviced activities that changed the course of empires. The grassy clearing at one time supported dozens of enormous cedar longhouses of the Mowachaht people and, during another, briefer time, a Spanish settlement and garrison—the northernmost outpost of Spain's vast American empire.

In the late 1800s, after centuries of European naval exploration and particularly after the three great voyages of Captain James Cook, most of the world's coastline, apart from its Arctic and Antarctic coasts, was reasonably well charted. The other remaining blank spot was the Pacific coast of North America. In the wake of Cook's hasty voyage along this coast in 1778 came a discovery that would dramatically change the course of history: sea otter pelts, which were worth a fortune in China. Within a few years, dozens of American and British ships were cruising the coast in search of the velvet booty. It was also somewhere along this vast unexplored coast that armchair geographers had decided to place the elusive western end of a northwest passage connecting the Pacific Ocean to Hudson Bay or to a great inland sea in the uncharted continental interior. Pacific North America was a wild card in the game of empire, a tectonic struggle for global supremacy between the nations of western Europe. Controlling the Pacific coast, or at least preventing others from controlling it, was suddenly very important. Spain claimed the territory outright as part of its New World empire and forbade any trespassing, a claim based on the historical precedent of the Treaty of Tordesillas, signed in 1494. Britain maintained that the seas should be open to every nation for trade and commerce. These two views were of course incompatible.

The stakes were dramatically upped in the summer of 1789, in Friendly Cove in Nootka Sound, when a Spanish captain captured several "trespassing" British trading ships and sent their officers and crews to Mexico as prisoners. The Spanish seizure of British ships and property incited a patriotic outcry in England—after Captain Cook's glorious navigation and charting of the Pacific, people asked, how could the Spanish dictate where British ships could sail and trade? Slogans were chanted, the rhetoric escalated, troops and warships were mobilized. The clash brought two great empires to the brink of war. The reluctant and temporary peace that followed inspired one of the great eighteenth-century voyages of exploration, an epic adventure that was to last nearly five years and change the histories and geographies of Spain, Russia, Britain, Hawaii, the new republic of the United States of America, the yet-to-exist country of Canada and dozens of First Nations.

In 1790 the British government commissioned two small ships, *Discovery* and *Chatham,* to circumnavigate the world, sail to Friendly Cove and meet with a Spanish representative to ratify the terms of a boundary agreement between the two empires. The British leader of the expedition was also commissioned to do something far more daunting and ultimately far more important: complete a detailed nautical survey of the uncharted coast from California to Alaska, settling the issue of the legendary east-west passage south of the Arctic, and compile a detailed report on the region, its peoples and its resources. What was its potential as an outpost of the British Empire?

Mapping a place is the first step to controlling it. For Britain, staking a claim to this distant but strategically important region, the unknown western coast of its sole remaining North American colony, was vital. If ignored, this coast was likely to fall under the control of potentially hostile foreign powers. For a commander, completing the exploring and charting of Pacific North America was a prized commission, a chance to make one's mark as an explorer and navigator. But the young captain chosen for the plum appointment, although experienced, had inherited a major prejudice: a deep skepticism about the existence of a northwest passage, variously known as the legendary Great River of the West, the Strait of Juan de Fuca or the Strait of Anian. He felt that the fabled sea route was a mere chimera for hopeful but deluded traders. The young captain also harboured within himself the kernel of an illness, not yet evident but growing daily like a cancer—an illness that would drive him into uncontrollable rages that left him humbled, shamed, exhausted and bedridden. The captain's fraying temper left him ill-equipped to deal with a belligerent and obnoxious midshipman and led to a violent conflict that had terrible repercussions.

The leader of that incredible voyage was a thirty-three-year-old, upper-middle-class Royal Navy officer, a protege of James Cook and one of the finest hydrographic surveyors of his time. His life would end not long after he returned to London, after being humiliated, professionally blacklisted and lampooned in the press for his alleged misdeeds on the far side of the world. He should have returned a hero, for he was one of the great mariners of all time, but instead he died in obscurity. The details of his epic voyage were lost amid the slander and innuendo propagated by his aristocratic enemies and in the din of cannon fire: Napoleon had just begun ten years of military adventuring, and Britain was suddenly overtaken by patriotic—and military—fervour. The young captain, George Vancouver, could neither defeat his enemies at home nor compete with Napoleon's exploits. But he may, in the end, have earned a more honourable place in history.

PART I

SCIENCE
and
DISCOVERY

ONE

A Hero Returns

———◄ ◈ ►———

ON JULY 12, 1771, a tiny, battered ship slipped up the English Channel and anchored at the Downs, a sheltered area of sea a little north of Dover. Several men clambered over the gunwales and down into a waiting longboat and were rowed to shore. The ship was unceremoniously guided by a pilot up the Thames for repairs and refitting in London, where the crew would be paid off. It was an unremarkable and somewhat deflating conclusion to one of the greatest marine voyages of all time. No one yet had any knowledge of the tremendous and world-altering accomplishments of the ship's forty-two-year-old lieutenant, James Cook, during his three years of exploring and charting the far side of the world. Word travelled quickly. First the Admiralty, then the people of London and then all of Britain and Europe in turn heard the astonishing revelations of this first of Cook's, and Britain's, voyages of science.

A slim, distinguished man of ordinary parentage but extraordinary nautical skills and determination, James Cook had accomplished far more than the Admiralty had expected of him. His orders had called for him to explore the South Pacific, but no one imagined that Cook would be so thorough. He had landed at and charted Tahiti and the adjacent Society Islands, rediscovered New Zealand after Abel Tasman's little-documented voyage fifty years earlier, sailed around both the North and South islands, proving their disputed insularity, and charted 2,400 miles of New Zealand's coast. He had also cruised along the east coast of Australia and charted it. He had discovered entirely new land masses and brought back previously unknown, intriguing and potentially valuable plants and animals. The grand three-year adventure presented Britain with a great deal of new information about the world's geography and peoples and celestial knowledge useful for navigation. The expedition's botanist and naturalist—the young aristocrat Joseph Banks—displayed countless new specimens of plants and animals. The world would never be quite the same: this voyage set in motion a flurry of similar expeditions from Britain, France and Spain to discover, explore and take possession of overseas land before the end of the century.

Most of the fame of the voyage initially went to Joseph Banks, thereby bolstering the scientific credentials of the voyage and over-shadowing its less illustrious but more pragmatic purpose: to counter French expansion and extend Britain's imperial arm into the Pacific. Extending imperial aims was a surreptitious activity in this remark-able era. The success of and the publicity given to the glorious voy-age of "Mr. Banks" was a feather in Britain's cap, bestowing national prestige in a brief era of international peace, when competition was scientific rather than military. Banks's and Cook's findings were pub-lished and graciously shared with the rest of Europe as a gesture of camaraderie and mutual friendship.

By the time Cook's journals were published several months later, after being nipped and tucked and enlivened by an editor, the expe-dition's fame and celebrity had spread to its commander: Cook, the lower-middle-class upstart, a Scottish migrant labourer's son who first went to sea on North Sea coal ships, was lionized in the parlours of the distinguished and fashionable. Cook was one of the few sailors in the Royal Navy's history to rise through the ranks, be granted a commission as an officer and then command an expedition of great importance and high profile.

Tall and stern, with a natural sense of command and charisma, rough around the edges and only rudimentarily educated, Cook became a national hero, the embodiment of all that his ambitious and outward-looking nation aspired to be or imagined itself to be. Cook was the idealized symbol of Great Britain: bold, fearless, curious, wise, meticulous and generous in victory but, above all, unequalled in the magnitude of his accomplishments.

For one inspired and adventurous fourteen-year-old boy, Cook's return was a call to action, to live a life of adventure, travel and danger rather than follow the predictable, stable and dull road that his upbringing might suggest. Like thousands of others in the wake of Cook's epic circumnavigation and the optimistic age it ushered in, George Vancouver dreamt of sailing to the farthest reaches of the globe to see wonders that Europeans had never seen before. Several months after Cook's return, rumours began to circulate about the possibility of a second, even greater and more demanding voyage to the South Seas, to be led by Banks and Cook. The young Vancouver knew he wanted to be part of that voyage.

George Vancouver was born on June 22, 1757, in King's Lynn, Norfolk, an ancient seaport about one hundred miles north of London on the North Sea at the mouth of the River Ouse. He was the youngest of six children born to John Jasper Vancouver and Bridget Berners. His mother was of a respected Essex and Norfolk lineage. Her father had been the sheriff for the region. His fortunes had declined, and he had moved to King's Lynn from his estate at Wiggenhall St. Mary, a few miles south of the town. When she wed, Bridget Berners was, for the time, the advanced age of thirty-two. John Jasper Vancouver was descended from the ancient, titled Van Coeverden clan of Overijssel, in the eastern Netherlands. The Vancouvers were landowners whose connection with King's Lynn resulted from trade and land reclamation: the area's low-lying fens and marshes were similar to the terrain of the Netherlands, and the drainage and land-reclaiming work, involving dikes and drains, was done primarily by Dutch engineers. Vancouver's great-grandfather, Reint Wolter van Coeverden, was likely the first to extend his business and move his family across the sea when he married Jane Lillingston in 1699. Their son, Lucas Hendrik, married an Englishwoman named Sarah, of unknown surname, who was Vancouver's grandmother. By the mid-eighteenth century she is recorded as dwelling in King's Lynn, as part of a possibly significant

Dutch minority. Her son was John Jasper. George Vancouver was well aware of his Dutch ancestry; when he was naming geographical features in Alaska in 1794, he named Point Couverden "after the seat of my ancestors."

John Jasper was an important man in King's Lynn. In addition to holding several other official positions, he was the deputy collector of customs. George Godwin, Vancouver's first biographer, wrote in *Vancouver: A Life* that John Jasper "was a small man, very active in the Tory interest, and contemporary political satires lampoon him as 'Little Van,' but without malice." The customs position was granted by Sir Charles Turner, a powerful local Tory and one of the greatest landowners in the region. The post was one of prestige and political influence. Although Turner held the customs sinecure, he delegated the actual work to John Jasper, who was wealthy but not aristocratic.

George Vancouver grew up in a large, extended family that enjoyed reasonable wealth and status in their town. They lived, according to Godwin, in "a large house set snugly in a well-matured garden of pear and apple trees; while in the big yard on the east side of the house stood a roomy stables." He and his older brothers, John and Charles (possibly twins), probably attended the King's Lynn Grammar School, where they learned the rudiments of mathematics and English composition as well as French and Latin, skills that were of great help to Vancouver in his career in the Royal Navy. George's mother died in 1768, when he was only eleven years old, and his father was left to raise the family with the help of his grandmother Sarah. Although George was partially raised by his three older sisters—Bridget, who was at least six years his senior, Sarah and Mary—it was with his brothers Charles and John, barely two years older than he, that he maintained the strongest relationships throughout his life—a life in which he seldom returned to King's Lynn for any significant length of time.

King's Lynn was a thriving and important port. Servicing Europe and five inland counties of eastern England, it was the fifth greatest port in terms of custom duties in all of Britain. Its harbour was cluttered with ships; its streets were crowded with carts hauling goods to and from the docks and enlivened by the antics of tattooed and pierced-eared sailors, and occasionally by the violence of press gangs securing "recruits" for the navy. The greater world was evident in King's Lynn, and the dozens of ships in the harbour were the tangible vehicles that communicated with that world. They arrived and departed daily from Europe and beyond. The commerce of the world passed through the busy harbour, as did the news of the world, including, very quickly, news about the exploits and discoveries of Cook's voyages.

VANCOUVER CAME OF age during a remarkable era in human history. The late eighteenth century offered a rare window of peace, a temporary lull in the epic struggle between France and Britain for global pre-eminence. The Seven Years War had ended in 1763, and the American Revolution and Napoleonic Wars were still years in the future. The happy coincidence of this cessation of the warfare that had plagued Europe for centuries, of the Age of Enlightenment, when reason and science and learning were emerging after centuries of fragmentation, and of improvements in naval technology was changing the lives of people worldwide. It was the beginning of an age that would witness revolutionary discoveries in medicine, science, technology and politics.

In the late eighteenth century, the focus of geographic and scientific exploration was the Pacific Ocean. Centuries of voyages by the Portuguese, the Spanish and more recently the commercially aggressive Dutch had contributed to an ever-expanding horizon. The earth was known to be a globe, and its circumference was reasonably accurately known—having been painfully revealed at the cost of thousands of mariners who had sailed blindly into the unknown and never returned. They had been smothered in the surf, broken on jagged spires of rock, swamped by monstrous waves and lost at sea because they had no accurate charts, no accurate method of navigation and no fresh food, and the last of these problems led to the most dreaded of maritime diseases: scurvy. Cook, among others, had made great strides in preventing scurvy and in perfecting recently discovered methods for navigating by calculating longitude at sea.

This spirit of fraternity in scientific inquiry masked an intense struggle: the European powers were currently fighting not for military supremacy in the late eighteenth century—although that struggle would come again all too soon and occupy much of Vancouver's career—but for cultural supremacy, as embodied by recent discoveries in science, natural history, geography and ethnography. The entire world was now Europe's playing field. By learning more about the world and unravelling more of nature's secrets, a nation gained prestige. France had already sent out Compte Louis Antoine de Bougainville on a world-girdling expedition of science and discovery, and Britain had funded several lesser voyages before Cook's. Spain had sent, from Peru, two ships that had visited Tahiti. But it was James Cook who set the new standard for scientific voyages.

One of the great geographical mysteries of the age—the talk of armchair geographers, the idly curious and high-placed officials in national governments—was the existence of the "great southern continent" described by the Greek philosopher Claudius Ptolemy around AD 150 in his renowned tome *Geography*. While working at the library · of Alexandria, Ptolemy had created a great chart of the world, a chart that incidentally did not include North or South America or the Pacific Ocean. But in the obscure southern hemisphere he placed the mysterious land mass whose possible existence would haunt European explorers, map-makers and cartographers more than a millennium and a half later: *Terra Australis Incognita*, the unknown southern continent. The original inspiration for this idea sprang from the ancient Greek belief in the perfect balance and symmetry of the world. Ptolemy was certain that a southern land equal in size to the known northern lands had to exist, because a lopsided and ill-shaped earth was an affront to divine perfection. This land was all fabrication, of course, based on an odd theory and unsubstantiated travellers' tales, but Ptolemy drew this southern continent with the same confidence that he described the more tangible civilizations of the Mediterranean.

Ptolemy's *Geography* is the high-water mark of ancient knowledge about the earth. Less than a century after Ptolemy's time in Alexandria, the city's famous library fell on hard times, and the efforts of western geographers and astronomers to decipher the mysteries of the size and shape of the earth took a thousand-year hiatus. On several occasions during its five-century reign as the world's foremost intellectual storehouse, parts of the library's collection were burned, and political unrest around AD 270 destroyed much of the library. It struggled on for another hundred years, but in AD 391 the remnants of this great centre of learning were plundered by Christian mobs. The scrolls were burned, and the building was converted to a church.

The problems of Alexandria were symptoms of a much larger political malaise throughout the Roman Empire. The destruction of the museum and library coincided with the fragmentation of Roman central authority and a decline in trade, travel and prosperity. During the era of uncertainty that followed the collapse of the Roman Empire, scientific inquiry into the shape of the earth and its unknown regions was not a priority, and Europe's intellectual focus shifted to a preoccupation with the ethical and spiritual world. Map-makers no longer attempted to accurately represent the geographical features of the world but produced simplistic and stylized route maps for pilgrims. This intellectual regression was in stark contrast to the flourishing of Islamic culture during much of this period. After the rise of Islam in the late seventh century and its military expansion throughout the Middle East, North Africa and Spain, the work of many ancient Greek philosophers was rediscovered, translated and in some cases improved upon by Arabic scholars.

Ptolemy had the great luck that his two major works, *Almagest* and *Geography*, were translated into Arabic while the work of many others was lost. The reintroduction of Ptolemy's works to Europe from the Middle East more than a millennium later had a profound effect on the burgeoning Renaissance in Italy and, later, in all of Europe. His opinions of the ancient Greek philosophers acquired an importance that exceeded that of all others. The world according to Ptolemy became the accepted truth, and *Terra Australis* was part of Ptolemy's truth.

In the eighteenth century, one of the foremost experts on the mythical southern continent was a wealthy and influential Scottish armchair adventurer, Alexander Dalrymple. After studying ancient texts and consulting the most accurate maps of the day, Dalrymple asserted that the earth was unbalanced. In 1767 he announced that the existence of the southern continent was beyond question: a continent "was wanting on the South of the Equator to counterpoise the land to the North, and to maintain the equilibrium necessary for the Earth's motion." The world needed a large land mass in the southern hemisphere to prevent the earth from spinning lopsidedly and shaking itself apart. The land mass had to be of "greater extent than the whole civilized part of Asia, from Turkey eastward to the extremity of China." Surely more than fifty million people lived there, making the as-yet-unexploited trade potential of the region truly immense. "The scraps from this table," Dalrymple claimed, "would be sufficient to maintain the power, dominion and sovereignty of Britain, by employing all its manufactures and ships." Dalrymple wanted to ensure that when this fabulously wealthy and vast continent was discovered and regular trade was established with Europe, Britain—rather than France or Spain—derived the greatest commercial benefit: a continuous stream of raw materials to fuel Britain's manufacturing industry. A new source of trade was an important consideration for Britain at this time because of the growing agitation in, and the quarrelsome disobedience of, the American colonies.

Locating this potentially valuable southern continent had been one of the prime objectives of Cook's first voyage, and it would continue to be an important objective of his proposed second voyage. When both Cook and Banks proclaimed their doubts that the southern continent existed, Dalrymple claimed that Cook should have sailed farther south and that if he had, he undoubtedly would have discovered the elusive continent. He claimed that Cook was derelict in his duty by not pushing farther south beyond New Zealand, 46 degrees south latitude. But in all the public debate no one seems to have voiced the seemingly commonsense observation that a continent so far south would hardly be the balmy temperate counterpart to Europe but rather the wind-blasted, snow-drenched equivalent of the Arctic. Or to have drawn the other obvious conclusion: that a land so endowed with the fruits of temperate bounty and populated with industrious multitudes had never been encountered before, despite centuries of European trade with the Indies and nearly every other region of the globe; surely, during this centuries-long commercial circus, someone would have mentioned this great land and its peoples? Nevertheless, politics and curiosity provided the political and scientific clout needed to secure funding for another voyage whose objective was to prove or disprove, once and for all, the existence of this mysterious land.

All of Britain was caught up in the spirit of the latest voyage. What new secrets about the world would be revealed? For the boy from

King's Lynn, this great undertaking would be the auspicious beginning of a remarkable career. When news of the voyage became known
competition was fierce to gain a position on one of the two ships, the
Resolution and the *Adventure*. Outfitting the ships became a major
public attraction with, as Cook noted, "scarce a day past on which she
was not crowded with strangers who came on board for no purpose
other than to see the ship in which Mr. Banks was to sail around the
world." Most of the publicity was for "Mr. Banks's voyage," but with the
publication of the *Journals* from his first voyage Cook himself began
to enjoy a modest amount of celebrity. Thousands of people wanted to
be part of the next history-making expedition. It would surely bring
glory and secure one's career to be part of such famous exploits. One
young midshipman, John Elliott, who managed to secure a berth for
the voyage wrote in his memoirs that the general understanding was
that "it would be quite a feather, in a young man's Cap, to go out with
Captn. Cook, and it required much Intrest to get out with him."

Interest—not ability, qualifications or experience—was the time-
honoured criterion for obtaining the most-sought-after positions and
promotions in the Royal Navy. Both Cook and Banks were inundated
with letters from important people passing on requests regarding
their friends and relations. Vancouver must have had the advantage
of strong influence to be selected, likely through his father's connections to Sir Charles Turner, a political ally of John Montagu, Earl of
Sandwich, the recently appointed First Lord of the Admiralty and one
of the originators of the voyage. This was remarkable luck, and Vancouver's family celebrated when the letter assigning him to the voyage arrived. He joined the ship's muster on January 22, 1772, and soon
afterward boarded a ship for the first time in his life. His fellow midshipman John Elliott described him in his memoirs as "a quiet, inof-
fensive young man."

Fourteen-year-old George Vancouver, already motherless for three
years, had now joined the Royal Navy for a world tour with Britain's
master mariner. It was the end of his youth and of his life ashore. He
would be at sea for nearly four years and was on his way to becoming
one of the most travelled men in history.

TWO

With the
Master Mariner

⊷ ◈ ⊶

WHEN HE JOINED the Royal Navy, George Vancouver was not merely choosing a vocation—he
was choosing a new way of life and a new fam-
ily. He undoubtedly had an inkling of what his career choice entailed,
given his father's contacts with the maritime world of King's Lynn,
and he was likely not suprised to hear that Cook planned to be away
for three years or more. Life in the Royal Navy was hard and it was
one that carried a great chance of death by misadventure or horrible disease, but it was also a life in which, if he survived, Vancouver
would see the world in an era when travel was difficult, dangerous and
impossible for the average person. The only way to cross the seas was
by sailing ship, and unless one was fabulously wealthy one had to join
the navy or, less glamorously, the merchant marine. Vancouver chose
to become a man of action—an adventurer and an explorer rather
than a sedate clerk, solicitor or agent. He would have stories to tell:
of dangers overcome, of comrades who died, of strange peoples and
strange places. The Royal Navy was a common career choice for the
younger sons of the nobility or the well-to-do merchant class. In his
upbringing and temperament, Vancouver fit nicely within this group.

Although the life of a sailor was often, to use John Locke's phrase,
"nasty, brutish and short," at least the life of a naval officer had the
advantages of better food, better living conditions, better pay and far

greater prestige. Vancouver enlisted as an able seaman, but he was actually on the officer track and was a junior midshipman in training, essentially an apprentice for a commission in the Royal Navy. The pay was low, and his father covered most expenses associated with his learning before the voyage. Vancouver would have to serve at least six years at sea, including two years as a midshipman, before he would be eligible to write his examinations for the rank of lieutenant. He had a lot to learn, and he would have a long wait to become a true officer, with responsibility for commanding others, but the task was made easier by the fame and profile he gained in his first appointment.

On Cook's ships the young gentlemen and boys were expected to learn all the ropes, and not just figuratively. Cook tolerated no slackers; he took a serious interest in the education of his young charges. John Elliott recalled, "In the Early part of the Voyage, Captn Cook made all us young gentleman, do the duty aloft the same as the Sailors, learning to hand, and reef the sails, and steer the ship, exercise Small Arms & thereby making us good Sailors as well as good Officers." Midshipmen both worked with the crew and attended classes in academic fields of study. Cook was particularly insistent that his young gentlemen learn navigation and charting. On board to help teach them the art and science of navigation, mathematics and astronomy was William Wales, a prominent scientist and future member of the Board of Longitude. Years later, Vancouver remembered Wales fondly. In 1793 he named a point of land in Pacific North America "after my much-esteemed friend Mr. Wales, of Christ's Hospital; to whose kind instruction, in the early part of my life, I am indebted for that information which has enabled me to traverse and delineate these lonely regions."

When Vancouver was first rowed out to the *Resolution* in the spring of 1772 and clambered up the ship's rope ladder to stand on the gently swaying deck, he could be forgiven for feeling dismayed at the size of his home for the next three years. Like Cook's previous ship, the *Endeavour,* the two ships Cook selected for his second voyage—the *Resolution* and *Adventure*—were squat, inelegant northern colliers rather than impressive ships-of-the-line or sleek frigates. Little more than thirty feet wide and about one hundred feet long, the 463-ton

Resolution had a ship's company of 111 men. The slightly smaller, 336-ton *Adventure* housed 81. These ships were small even by Royal Navy standards.

Like the rest of the crew, midshipmen lived a harsh life of infrequent sleep, foul food and little privacy, even on Cook's ships. The young gentlemen dwelt below the waterline in a bleak, fetid and crowded communal compartment, shielded from the bulk of the crew by a mere canvas flap. But they were kept continuously busy and spent little time there. Cook's voyages were unusual not only in the nature of their mission but also in the attention the captain paid to the health of his crew.

Vancouver's introduction to the naval world was not standard, either. Before he even set foot on a ship, he was travelling down a different path than other midshipmen entering the Royal Navy at the same time, and his future career and accomplishments spring directly from this fateful and fortuitous beginning as a young gentleman with Cook.

Cook's first voyage had pushed the limits of what was believed to be possible by surpassing the legendary sixteenth-century voyages of Ferdinand Magellan and Francis Drake in both distance travelled and duration. The plan for his second voyage was even more daring: to circumnavigate the globe in a high southern latitude, farther south than anyone had sailed before, in order to prove or disprove once and for all the existence of the mysterious *Terra Australis*. These audacious objectives were made possible only because of recent advances in marine technology. By the mid-eighteenth century, a sailing ship was an incredibly complex machine that could harness the power of the wind to propel hundreds of men and thousands of tons of equipment and provisions for months at a time across any ocean. In addition to the technological advances, at the start of Vancouver's career two other innovations were then being perfected that would change ocean travel forever: a method for accurately locating the position of one's ship at any moment, according to the coordinates on a map, and a practical solution to the dreaded mariners' disease, scurvy.

Calculating longitude is the key to navigation and charting. It was a problem that had vexed cartographers since the time of the ancient

Greeks. In the eighteenth century, two new methods for calculating longitude at sea made Cook's voyages possible. The first was John Harrison's creation of a chronometer that would retain its accuracy on ships. Chronometers work by keeping time at a specific location—Greenwich time became the standard—and comparing it with local time, which was determined by observing the time the sun was at its highest point in the sky with a sextant. By comparing the time differences between the two points with the prior knowledge of the speed of the earth's rotation, a navigator could calculate the distance from Greenwich. Harrison's innovation tremendously improved the accuracy of navigation and marine cartography.

The second newly developed method for determining longitude at sea was known as the comparison of lunar distances. This method, which used the motion of the moon's orbit of the earth as a clock, required a detailed compendium of observations of the moon at Greenwich. The mathematical calculations required for celestial navigation were incredibly complex, requiring competence in geometry and trigonometry as well as the use of precision instruments for measuring the angles of the moon, stars and sun. George Vancouver excelled at navigation: persnickety attention to detail and a preoccupation with the tedious minutiae suited his personality, and he could be finicky and easily angered when others did not meet his exacting standards. Thus, when the *Resolution* and *Adventure* proceeded south into the Atlantic, James Cook knew more or less where he was going and could calculate where he was at any time on the trackless expanse of the ocean.

The second major barrier to long-distance sea travel that Cook had overcome on his first voyage was the disease known as the scourge of the sea and bane of mariners—scurvy—which resulted from a lack of vitamin C in the diet. Fresh food was not always available in the eighteenth century, especially during the winter months. There was no method of preserving food other than drying or salting it, nor were there quick and efficient ways to transport produce from the countryside to the cities and ports. For most people, fresh food was uncommon and malnutrition was rife. At sea the problem was even more significant. Scurvy was responsible for more deaths at sea than storms, shipwreck, combat and other diseases combined. Historians have conservatively estimated that during the Age of Sail (from the sixteenth to the nineteenth centuries), more than two million sailors perished from scurvy. The disease was present on virtually every major voyage of discovery, including those of Jacques Cartier, Vasco da Gama and Francis Drake.

Scurvy is a hideous and frightful affliction in which the body's connective tissue degenerates. Psychological symptoms such as melancholy, moroseness, listlessness, lack of motivation and unusual fatigue precede physical manifestations such as weakness, lack of coordination, easy bruising, aching joints and swelling in the extremities. Later, the gums swell and become spongy and blood-soaked, the breath becomes foul and the skin becomes ill-coloured, sallow and rubbery. Internal hemorrhaging causes purple splotches on the skin and under the eyes. Once-healed broken bones eventually come apart, leading to a slow, agonizing death.

The usual pattern was that after several months on a diet of salt pork and biscuit, the crew sickened and grew weaker, with many expiring in misery before the brave commander—himself little better than a lethargic, zombielike creature with blackened gums and open sores—steered the ghost vessel to a port. There it remained for many weeks while officers scoured the town and countryside, desperately seeking men to fill the empty hammocks of the ship.

Seeking a scientific explanation for, and a solution to, scurvy was a fashionable concern of eighteenth-century physicians. On his first voyage Cook had devised a practical solution, although his feat was obscured by the fact that dozens of his men perished in Batavia (now Jakarta) from other diseases. Fortunately for Vancouver, Cook did not plan on letting anyone perish from the grey killer at sea on his second voyage—even though he had no idea how to cure it, apart from trying every known method then in fashion. The young Vancouver witnessed first-hand how Cook managed to keep his ship free of the affliction: infusions and "inspissations," tinctures and concoctions of wild grasses, roots, bulbs and foreign fruits. Every evening the mess tables aboard Cook's ships were laden with trenchers of sloppy fermenting cabbage blended with tantalizing ingredients such as wild celery and scurvy grass. "The Sour Krout the Men at first would not eate," Cook sagely noted in his journal, revealing one of his leadership secrets, "until I put in practice a Method I never once knew to fail with seamen, and this was to have some of it dress'd every Day for the Cabbin Table... whatever you give them out of the Common way, altho it be ever so much for their good yet it will not go down with them and you hear nothing but murmurings gainest the man that first invented it; but the Moment they see their Superiors set a Value upon it, it becomes the finest stuff in the World and the inventor a damn'd honest fellow."

Confusion abounded as to which antiscorbutics of the dozens that Cook employed were the most effective. The controversy chiefly existed between wort of malt, a sort of de-alcoholized beer that had no effect on scurvy whatsoever (but enjoyed the institutional support of many influential scientists), and rob of lemons and oranges, a concentrated citrus juice preferred by, among others, the Scottish physician James Lind. The story of scurvy offers a fascinating look into the politics, fashions, personal conflicts and science of the Age of Sail. A universally agreed-upon practical solution to scurvy—a daily ration of lemon juice—was not implemented in the Royal Navy until 1795. Cook's voyages, and later Vancouver's, could never have succeeded without their captains' uncommon preoccupation with preventing scurvy.

AFTER DEPARTING BRITAIN, the *Resolution* and *Adventure* spent the years between 1772 and 1775 scouring the South Pacific for the mysterious and elusive *Terra Australis*. Summers were spent probing the fringes of the frightening, ice-bound Antarctic without sighting the continent. The ships spent the winters, when Antarctic voyaging was impossible, skirting the tropical South Pacific and cruising the South Indian and South Atlantic oceans. The two ships completed a circuit—a circumnavigation as close as possible to the South Pole between 55 degrees and 60 degrees south—in a manner "as to leave not the least room for the possibility of there being a continent, unless near the pole, and out of reach of navigation."

It was rough going at times, as the ships plunged south into "Lands doomed by nature to perpetual frigidness," according to Cook, "never to feel the warmth of the sun's rays; whose horrible and savage aspect I have not words to describe—such are the lands we have discovered; what then may we expect those to be which lie still farther to the south?" The young assistant naturalist, George Forster, later commented: "Our southern cruises were uniform & tedious in the highest degree, the ice, the fogs, the storms and ruffled surface of the sea formed a disagreeable scene, which was seldom cheered by the reviving rays of the sun; the climate was rigorous & our food detestable. In short, we rather vegetated than lived; we withered and sacrificed our health, our feelings and our enjoyments to the honour of pursuing a track unattempted before." During these tedious days Vancouver learned the tricky operations of a sailing ship, and he excelled at the difficult mathematical calculations needed for navigation.

On January 30, 1774, just as the crew were fearing the worst, as the biting winds shrieked in the rigging and the *Resolution* bobbed in the monstrous waves like a toy in a tub, the ice growling as they pushed through it, Cook ordered his ship about. He could safely go no farther, and he reasoned that it would be irrelevant if he could sight land here—it would certainly be of little immediate value even if it could be reached, and it was unlikely to be inhabited by the millions of people that Dalrymple had stridently argued must exist. Young Vancouver, however, still possessed some pluck and energy despite the gloomy prospect: he dashed to the front of the ship, scrambled out on the bowsprit, surrounded by "impenetrable mountains of ice," and stretched into the sky waving his cap and wildly yelling, *"Ne Plus Ultra!"* He had gone farther south than any man, including Cook. It was a story Vancouver liked to tell years later.

As the *Resolution* cruised home Cook wrote, "Thus I flatter myself that the intention of the voyage has, in every respect, been fully answered; the southern hemisphere sufficiently explored, and a final end put to searching after a southern continent," both praising himself and smugly answering his critics who doubted his earlier claims. "I have now done with the Southern Pacific Ocean," he noted with satisfaction and perhaps a little wistful regret, "and flatter myself that no one will think that I have left it unexplored; or that more could have been done, in one voyage, towards obtaining that end, than has been done in this." The *Resolution* and *Adventure* returned to Britain in July 1775, having lost not a single man to scurvy during the entire voyage. It was an unprecedented feat.

Three years aboard the *Resolution* provided Vancouver with a unique and enlightened environment in which to learn the formative skills of a mariner, an environment not available anywhere else in the navy at that time. Not only was the lad coming of age as a sailor on an exploring expedition instead of on a commercial ship or a traditional Royal Navy vessel on routine patrols, but he was also seeing how a ship could be organized and run as practised by Cook, the most forward-looking and enlightened commander of his era. Cook was not interested in the hidebound traditions that had tethered ships and crews to centuries-old practices; his concern was getting the job done. If something worked, he kept it; but if it did not, he discarded it without regret. This unusually progressive attitude and an ability to conceive of unconventional solutions were qualities that Cook imparted to his midshipmen, in addition to teaching them the practical skills of a competent seaman and officer.

Cook was a superior leader and mentor, and for three years young Vancouver witnessed at close quarters decision making and command by a true master. Cook knew how to get the best from a crew, how to make difficult decisions and how to plan months ahead, taking into account weather, possible disasters and food supplies. Most importantly for exploration, Cook remained flexible in his approach to difficult and life-threatening situations—canvassed his crew's opinion and calmly evaluated danger and outcomes. Vancouver witnessed and experienced Cook's devotion to the health of his crew, knowing that the success or failure of the enterprise depended upon it. Not surprisingly as a result, Vancouver venerated Cook.

In July 1775, when Vancouver stepped ashore in Britain, he was no longer a boy but a young man nearly eighteen years of age. He had been places and seen things very few people had even dreamt of. He had sailed around the world, probed the ice-bound fringes of Antarctica, visited South Africa, New Zealand and numerous islands of the South Pacific, including Tahiti and the Society Islands, witnessed a ritual cannibalistic feast, endured blasting hurricanes and frostbitten limbs, stood in awe beneath towering ice castles and dined for weeks on putrid, weevil-infested biscuit. He had seen men die by misadventure and had witnessed flogging, the brutal corporal punishment then common in the Royal Navy, little knowing that Cook's ship was a bastion of enlightenment and sanity compared with the disease-riddled floating coffins that were the rule at that time. He had also met and communicated with many people of foreign and often alien cultures that would fascinate him his entire life.

When he returned to King's Lynn to regale his family with tales of his adventures, he was stunned by the news that his father had died over two years earlier. No mail had been sent to or received from the far side of the world. Vancouver was now not only parentless, but his years away had left him permanently unmoored from the rhythms of life ashore. He was disconnected from his family and former friends not only by time but also by experience. Although he could boast of circumnavigating the globe with Cook, a routine life in King's Lynn— a life like the one his brothers and sisters were leading—was forever lost to him. The navy was his family now.

IN 1775, AFTER COOK's triumphant return from nearly seven years of explorations on the far side of the globe, the aging mariner enjoyed widespread fame and admiration. King George III awarded him a royal coat of arms; the Royal Society presented him with the Copley Gold Medal for his defeat of scurvy; prominent men of science and lords of the Admiralty invited him to their homes; he gave orations on his scientific and navigational observations to learned societies. He had challenged and triumphed over England's rigid caste system. Now at the height of his fame, Cook should have been contemplating retirement from a dangerous and unpredictable life. But he was unable to rest on the laurels of his success. He still yearned for the open sea and the thrill of discovering unknown lands, encountering unpredictable situations that made him feel alive. So he leaped at the chance to lead a third voyage into the unknown—this time, the unknown west coast of North America.

Cook's quest on this voyage would be nothing less than to discover the fabled Strait of Anian or Strait of Juan de Fuca, the rumoured waterway through North America. If it provided a shorter route for ships to travel from northern Europe to the Orient, it would be a vital component of any European plan for global maritime dominance. The mythical strait might lie anywhere along thousands of miles of uncharted coastline. Europe's knowledge of North American geography west of the Mississippi and the Great Lakes at this time was vague at best and sometimes bordered on fanciful speculation. Some French charts, such as the Bauche-Delisle map from 1750, showed not the Great Plains and a series of mountain ranges but a vast inland sea occupying what is now the western United States and Canada. The renowned navigator Juan de Fuca, Greek by birth but working in the service of Spain, claimed to have discovered the western exit of the waterway and followed it through to the Atlantic Ocean two centuries earlier. The most recent Russian charts depicted Alaska as an island and showed a clear western entrance to a polar sea. In short, Europeans may as well have been discussing the geography of the moon. Tackling this greatest of geographical mysteries would provide a grand conclusion for Cook's already illustrious career. Who more deserved the accolades of this final great discovery?

In the mid-1770s the Spanish mariners Juan José Pérez Hernández and Juan Francisco de la Bodega y Quadra had navigated the coast and claimed the region for Spain. They had, however, sailed north from Mexico, not from Europe, and left no permanent settlements or trading outposts. Indeed, they left no public record of their voyages. Although these voyages were secret, the entire region from California to Alaska was claimed as part of the territory of the Spanish Empire. At the same time, Russian maritime traders were slowly creeping eastward along the Aleutian Islands, in the wake of Vitus Bering's 1741 voyage, but they hadn't yet moved south along the mainland.

In the interior of the continent, eastern North American fur traders had not yet pushed their trade routes across the Great Plains, let alone penetrated the snowy ramparts of the Rocky Mountains or the endless series of other mountain ranges extending west to the Pacific. No one had yet crossed the continent by land. (Alexander Mackenzie would be the first to cross the continent from east to west in 1793.) At the time of Cook's third voyage, the Hudson's Bay Company consisted of a string of isolated forts along the gravelly shores of Hudson Bay, and the North West Company was a loose conglomerate of Montreal traders that did not begin pushing west until the late 1780s. Although many independent fur traders flourished in the old northwest and the Mississippi basin, the trading frontier would not extend west of the Continental Divide for decades. The Pacific coast of North America was only accessible to ships that navigated the treacherous, storm-plagued Horn of South America or flung themselves east across the vast and capricious expanse of the Pacific Ocean.

Vancouver must have proven himself, in Cook's eyes, to be suitable for the quarterdeck in both knowledge and discipline. The famous captain, who had his pick of the nation's best mariners for this third voyage, promoted Vancouver to junior midshipman in the *Resolution*'s consort ship, the smaller *Discovery*, under the command of Captain Charles Clerke on a voyage that would irrevocably change both Vancouver's life and the history of the world. The two ships began their voyage in July 1776.

Cook led the two ships, with 191 mariners in total, down the estuary at Portsmouth into the English Channel and then the Atlantic. The ships sailed south around Africa, wound their way through the Indian Ocean and made the first recorded landing of Europeans at Hawaii before nearing the misty shore of Oregon almost two years later, on March 7, 1778. In the rolling sea just off the cape that Cook named Foulweather (the name remains), Cook stood on the pitching deck and strained to glimpse the land through the chilly haze. But he could discern only patches of dark green forest and the crest of mountain peaks above the fog, before gales and squalls drove his ships from the shore. Cook kept the bobbing ships clear of the treacherous coast to avoid hidden shoals and sunken rocks. In averting a potential disaster, however, he missed the mouth of the Columbia, the most important river in the region.

Unaware of the oversight, Cook continued floating north, nodding his ships along a coast deeply indented with winding fjords that led back into the mountains. Again the ill-named Pacific lashed the wind-blown ships, and in the appalling squall the famous Strait of Juan de Fuca slipped by, out of view, in the night. Annoyed with his Russian map, which clearly showed the inlet, Cook scrawled in his journal: "It is in the very latitude we were now in where geographers have placed the pretended Strait of Juan de Fuca, but we saw nothing like it, nor is there the least probability that iver [*sic*] any such thing existed." He named the headland Cape Flattery—after "a small opening which flattered us with the hopes of finding a harbour"—a timeless monument to the great mariner's error.

During the storm the main mast of the *Resolution* had splintered with a sickening crack, and Cook ordered his battered vessels north along the coast of what would later be known as Vancouver Island searching for a sheltered inlet where the crew could repair the damage. A few days later he spied a large bay and steered his ships through the narrow channel into a small sound. The weary sailors scanned the wild, misty shore that rose steeply in lumpy hummocks, covered with a canopy of drooping, impenetrable foliage and monstrous trees, searching for a spot to furl the sails and drop anchor. Without warning, over thirty cedar-plank canoes were launched from the beach. As the canoes approached the ships they began circling, while a figure in one of the canoes stood in the prow gesticulating in a frightful manner. "He worked himself into the highest frenzy," Lieutenant James King of the *Resolution* recorded, "uttering something between a howl and a song, holding a rattle in each hand...taking handfuls of red Ocre and birds feathers and strewing them in the Sea." Thus were Cook and his companions officially welcomed to Nootka Sound, an inlet destined, for a brief time, to be the most important location in western North America.

The people Cook encountered, the Mowachaht, lived in large communal longhouses crafted from split-cedar planks. In front of the community, carved poles were aligned on the beach. Called Yuquot ("where the winds blow") by the Mowachaht, the place was named Friendly Cove by Cook because of the reception he received. Perhaps 1,500 people lived seasonally in the village, dispersing during the winter into a dozen smaller villages deeper in the inlet. They possessed elaborately carved masks and had intriguing rituals and songs, but these were not enough for Cook to overcome his eighteenth-century prejudices. Although generally open-minded to foreign cultures, he

nevertheless found the people to be dirty, noisy, primitive and generally unimpressive. Their most endearing traits, in Cook's view, were
that they were friendly and unthreatening. But he was annoyed at
their tendency to take things from the ships without permission. In
contrast, Vancouver and several other of Cook's officers were fas-
cinated with foreign cultures. Vancouver had a natural facility for
languages, and he learned words from the native peoples whenever
possible. Observing the curious and unusual activity of the Europeans
and their enormous ships was a young man named Maquinna, who
was destined to become both a powerful figure in the history of his
people and a shaper of the global events unfolding in Pacific America.
He and the young midshipman Vancouver would have further dealings when they were older and in positions of responsibility more than
a decade later.

When the Mowachaht, holding up giant, brown oval furs, cedar
masks and fish, paddled around the ships the sailors quickly brought
out their stakes for the barter and rowed to the pebble-strewn shore
in front of the unusual dwellings. The Mowachaht were particularly
eager to trade their luxuriant sea otter pelts for iron goods such as
blades and chisels—so eager, in fact, that the mariners stripped their
ships of metal and filled their hold with furs. But for Cook, the people
of Nootka Sound and their pelts were merely a curious diversion. He
never imagined that these beautiful furs might spark a global trade
war. After the mariners had felled a massive fir and stripped the bark
and branches to construct a new mast for the *Resolution*, the duty-
minded Cook, not to be deterred from his glorious objective, ordered
his ships north to find the elusive Strait of Anian. He had been in
Friendly Cove for about a month.

During the next few months Cook's two ships followed the coast
north as far as the Aleutian Islands before being pushed back by
a twelve-foot-high wall of bluish pack ice sluggishly descending
from the Bering Strait. They had poked into many of the inlets and
waterways along the wild coast, but each foray had been stopped
by impassable mountains or slowly slithering glaciers that calved
gigantic bergs into the dark water. Cook was satisfied that the Strait
of Anian might only exist in the far north. He had done all he could,

under less-than-favourable conditions, before abandoning his melancholy task. Disgusted once again with the inaccuracy of his Russian nautical chart, he scrawled in his journal that it was "a map that the most illiterate of seafaring men would have been ashamed to put his name to." The young Vancouver witnessed it all and no doubt formed his own opinions of the raw unexplored coastline as he sailed past in the *Discovery*.

Fleeing the dreary chill and choppy grey waves of the Arctic, the *Resolution* and *Discovery* hoisted their sails and turned south to Hawaii for what their crews hoped would be a period of rest and recuperation. Settling in for a leisurely winter, Cook intended to return the following spring for a final foray into the Bering Strait. But although he was nearly a demi-god to his crew and young officers, Cook had been slowly cracking under the strain of command and an unknown illness. He was morose, irritable, occasionally depressed and short of temper, unpredictable and losing his usually good judgment. His deteriorating mental state led to an increase in violent outbursts and punishments. The incidence of flogging on his ship, the *Resolution*, was double that of his previous voyages. Vancouver, however, because he was serving on the consort ship *Discovery*, missed seeing the decline of his mentor.

At Hawaii on January 26, 1779, Vancouver joined an exploration party of seven crew members that Cook ordered to explore the interior of the island and perhaps to climb the great "Snowy Mountain," Mauna Loa, that rose into the sky in the distant interior. The explorers were unarmed and unafraid of the helpful Hawaiians on the island, but lacking knowledge of the land they became tangled in the luxuriant undergrowth as they bushwhacked their way inland. Cold nights, steaming hot days and a lack of clean water drove them back to the shore after only four days, before they had even ascended the lowest incline. They abandoned their quest and left the mountain unconquered.

After spending nearly a month moored in Kealakekua Bay enjoying the Hawaiians' hospitality, the *Resolution* and *Discovery* departed— only to return after several days because of a damaged mast. This time, for reasons unknown to them, their reception was chilly. Tension and trouble were in the air. When a Hawaiian stole some tools from the *Discovery* on February 13 and began paddling his canoe back to the shore, the ship's master, Thomas Edgar, Vancouver and two mariners jumped into a cutter and rowed furiously to catch the pilferer. They were unarmed. In an ensuing melee involving a group of Hawaiians, Vancouver proved his bravery and vigour in defending Edgar from attack. "He [his assailant] most certainly would have knocked me off the rock, and into the water," Edgar wrote of the event, "if Mr. Vancouver, the Midshipman had not this Inst Step'd out of the pinnace between the Indian and me, & received the Blowe, which took him on the side & knocked him down." Vancouver then defended the boat from capture, taking several blows from stones and clubs before the small party escaped and rowed to safety. The rapidly deteriorating relations between the peoples did not augur well for the future.

The next morning, Cook flew into a terrible rage when he discovered that a valuable boat had been stolen from the *Discovery* during the night and ordered his ships to fire at and blast any Hawaiian canoes in the bay. He then led a heavily armed party to shore to seize the Hawaiian king, old Kalaniopuu, and hold him as a hostage for the return of the boat. Here Cook realized his situation was not good. A large crowd gathered and refused to let the king depart. Following Cook's order, the ships had fired at a canoe and killed an influential chief. The news had now reached the agitated crowd, and Cook and his men, surrounded by several thousand angry islanders, retreated to the beach. From the deck of the *Discovery*, Vancouver heard the crack of gunfire and the chanting of the mob and saw the smoke and the wild mob press close to Cook and his men on the beach. The crowd surged forward, while the marines fired another volley. Cannon shot from the *Resolution* raked the beach as the cutters closed on the outnumbered shore party. When a warrior jabbed a spear into Cook's thigh, Cook fired his pistol into the crowd and ordered his men to "take the boats." But it was too late. The islanders stabbed Cook repeatedly, and he went down in the surf. Four marines were also killed, many of the crew were wounded, and seventeen Hawaiians were also wounded in the violent clash. Cook's remaining men fled to their ships, leaving the bodies of their comrades behind. In the confusion and chaos,

Vancouver and the others learned the fate of their commander only when the cutters rowed back to the ships in a panic.

On February 15, Captain Clerke put Lieutenant King and midshipman Vancouver in charge of five boats of heavily armed mariners to search for Cook's body. When the boats neared the shore, Vancouver and Clerke negotiated for the return of their dead. Vancouver entreated the Hawaiians to return Cook's body, something they could not immediately do; it had been carried inland and would be returned the following day. The sailors returned to the *Resolution* and anxiously waited. The next morning, a sympathetic Hawaiian priest canoed out to the ship and dropped on the deck a bloody sack containing a chunk of Cook's thigh and other body parts. Lieutenant King observed that the man "seemed rejoiced to see Mr. Vancouver... who best understood them." Vancouver learned that Cook had been dismembered and parcelled out to various chiefs, who intended to ceremonially roast his body, eat his heart and conceal his bones about the island. A few days later a few more of Cook's remains—a bit of his skull, hands, arms and thigh bones—were delivered in a solemn ceremony to the British.

How did such warm relations sour so quickly? No journal account of Vancouver's views has survived, so we can only infer his feelings at having his revered mentor killed by a friendly people who intrigued him. Those feelings must have been very mixed.

Charles Clerke assumed overall command of the two ships, but with Cook dead there was little enthusiasm among the crews to continue the quest. They sailed north from Kamchatka through the Bering Strait the following spring but encountered the same problems with pack ice as they had the year before. They retreated and sailed for China and home, returning in October 1780. Vancouver had been at sea for nearly eight and a half years. Now twenty-three years old and ever earnest and career minded, he rushed as a matter of priority to the Admiralty to apply for his examination for lieutenant. He heard news of his success on October 19. A few days later his ship was paid off, and he went on half pay while he awaited his next commission. It was with pride that he returned to King's Lynn to visit his brothers and sisters. There he regaled them with tales of his four years of adventuring on the far side of the world and delivered the astonishing account of Cook's death. He was the toast of the town, but he was quiet and meticulous and never a braggart.

With the American War of Independence in its fourth year, Vancouver did not need to wait long ashore for a commission in a warship—a posting that would prove very different from the enlightened voyages of science and discovery he had enjoyed during his years with Cook. But unknown to Vancouver or anyone else at the time, Cook's final voyage had set in motion events that were rapidly bringing Pacific North America into the political and commercial orbit of western Europe.

THREE

The
China Trade

———◈———

IN AN ICE-CHOKED fjord in Alaska's Prince William Sound, about 60 degrees north latitude, a ship lay immobilized near a log cabin on the stony shore. Unrigged and draped in canvas sails, the ship had not moved for several months. It was the beginning of winter in 1786, and the mariners now realized the nature of the problems they faced. They began to weaken and became morose and listless, lying in their hammocks and bunks in the dreary interior of a ship that was "covered an inch thick with a hoary frost" despite the constantly smouldering coal fires. Soon their gums began to swell and turn black and spongy, and their teeth wobbled and fell painfully from their mouths when they tried to take a bite of food. Their joints ached, and their skin turned sallow and dry. By early January 1787, at least twelve men had advanced scurvy and four had died. February brought no respite. Dozens were so ill they could not roll from their hammocks. They lay, befouled and hopeless, gently swaying in the dim clammy stench of the interior of the ship.

The leader of the expedition, John Meares, was one of the few lucky enough to remain strong. He dragged the lifeless bodies, frozen stiff and with distorted grimaces exposing their ruined gums and teeth, across the ice and through waist-deep snow to the wind-lashed shore. "The sledge on which we fetched the wood was their hearse," Meares recorded, "and the chasms in the ice their grave." The moans of the dying formed a terrible dirge throughout February and March. By April, dozens had perished miserably, and their ordeal had not yet ended.

Meares was a young British lieutenant in the Royal Navy who had been retired onto half pay a few years earlier. At the end of the American War of Independence, he had made his way to India in a search for prospects. He had begun his adventure optimistically in the spring of 1786, securing financing and partners to sail to Pacific America in order to acquire sea otter pelts with two ships, the two-hundred-ton *Nootka* and the smaller *Sea Otter*. Neither the voyage nor the profits proved as easy as Meares had supposed, and his men grew irritable during months of sailing along the uncharted, fog-drenched chilly coast. Fearing that his men would never return to America if he sailed to Hawaii to overwinter with such a meagre supply of sea otter pelts, Meares made the bold and ultimately disastrous decision to hunker down in Prince William Sound, in order to get an early start to the trading season in the spring.

Twenty-one of his men—more than half of Meares's total crew—perished before the survivors were rescued in mid-May 1787 by rival traders in two ships, captained by George Dixon and Nathaniel Portlock. These traders were also half-pay Royal Navy men, officers who had sailed on Cook's voyage, and slightly older shipmates of Vancouver's on the *Discovery*. Unlike Meares, they had wisely decided to winter at Hawaii. They charged Meares dearly for their aid and supplies but, taking pity on him and his despondent men, lent him two able-bodied seamen to help sail his ship—so many of Meares's men had perished from scurvy that the survivors would have been unable to sail away. The unlikely groups of English mariners spent a month repairing and refitting their ships together, caulking seams, untangling rigging and stowing ballast. Just before they parted company, Portlock presented Meares with a document demanding a bond of £1,000, to be forfeited if he should ever be caught sailing along the coast again.

Portlock and Dixon held licences; Meares did not. The East India Company had a monopoly on all British trade in China, and the South Seas Company controlled all trade in the South Pacific, as well as on the coast of North America. Between them, the two companies jealously defended their exclusive rights to all British commerce in these regions. They brought the full force of the law to bear in their threats: any non-licensed ships found on the coast, like those of Meares's expedition, could be captured as a prize, according to British law. Meares scowled and scrawled his name on the bond document; he had no choice. Then he ordered the sails set, and he slunk out of Prince William Sound. He steered south to Hawaii and then west across the Pacific to convey the dispiriting and mournful news to his business partners in the Bengal Fur Company.

But he did not despond. Meares, a flamboyant, handsome man with flowing locks, finely arched eyebrows, an aquiline nose and full lips, was a charming rogue destined to play a volatile and key role in the history of the region. He was persuasive, with a talent for the loose interpretation of prior discoveries and place names, and a powerful writer who never let truth get in the way of his version of the story. The following year he was back on the coast with two ships flying under Portuguese flags of convenience, which would avoid the strictures of the British trading monopolies. He had learned from his mistakes and was impressed with the necessity of a permanent and secure location for wintering on the coast.

MARINERS NEEDED GOOD reasons to risk a treacherous voyage around the world in a creaking, rat-infested ship on trips that routinely lasted over two years, and merchants needed good reasons to risk their hard-earned investments. Pacific North America was of particular concern: it was a land without clear boundaries on any known map, and no merchant ships had yet sailed here. Sea otter pelts, however, provided the necessary inducement for risky voyages. Gregarious and community oriented, sea otters lived close to shore all along the Pacific coast from northern California to Alaska, preferring the rocky shoals of the outer coast.

The coastal people were more than willing to hunt sea otters for trade purposes, if the price was right. So eager were the people of Nootka for the products of European industry—glass and metals such as lead, tin, pewter, copper and brass, but especially iron—that

Cook's sailors had traded away their own buckles and buttons, nails and knives, to satisfy the insatiable demand. "Before we left the place, hardly a bit of brass was left in the ship... whole suits of cloathes were stripped of every button," an astonished Cook recorded at the time. What the people at Nootka had to offer in exchange were the large, dark sea otter pelts—six feet by three feet of soft fur. Beautiful though these pelts were, at the time no one on Cook's voyage suspected their value.

Making their way home after Cook's death, the *Resolution* and *Discovery* stopped in Canton for provisions, and the mariners made another astonishing discovery. Since 1685, the British East India Company had held a monopoly on British trade at Canton, a congested port along the Pearl River Delta in the South China Sea. It was the centre of the extremely profitable opium trade with India and the port of entry for a good portion of the furs procured in the wilds of North America by Russian traders. When the weary seafarers wandered through the crowded markets to flog their Nootka furs they were stunned by the rate of exchange. According to one sailor, "The Chinese [are] very eager to purchase them and give us from 50 to 70 dollars a skin... for what we bought with only a hatchet or a Saw." They loaded up on Oriental luxuries—teas, spices and silk—normally the fare of wealthy landowners, merchants and other discriminating nabobs. Many of the bewildered mariners, having got rid of their ragged, rotting clothes, strutted about the decks of their ships "eked out with the gaudiest silks and cottons of China."

When the sailors realized the value of the sea otter pelts, pressing on to Britain became the last thing on their mind. Their initial profit was as high as 1,800 per cent. "The Rage with which the seamen were possessed," reported Lieutenant King, "to return to Cook's River [Cook Inlet], and, by another cargo of skins, make their fortunes, at one time, was not far short of mutiny." Nevertheless, home to Britain they went (at the urging and threats of the officers), where they quickly spread the news of their fabulous discovery among sailors in the taverns of dockside London. Fortunes could be made, they claimed, in the misty land on the far side of the world, one of the most inaccessible and least-explored regions on the globe.

They had realized the alchemist's dream: tin, lead, copper, brass and iron could be transmuted into gold. Word travelled far, and it travelled fast. Before Cook's journals and logs from the voyage were posthumously published in 1784, the first of many merchant ventures launched flotillas of eager traders to the Pacific coast of North America. Until this time, only the Russians, trading from isolated forts along the shores of the Alaskan fjords, were trading furs for the exotic luxuries of Cathay. The most enduring legacy of Cook's fateful search for the Strait of Anian was not his sketchy charting of the coast. It was his discovery, however inadvertent, of a new source of wealth that increased the political and economic value of the region to European nations. Cook had also discovered the Hawaiian Islands, midway across the vast Pacific Ocean, which provided an ideal base for refitting and provisioning. Although Spain officially claimed the entire coast as part of its huge New World empire (an empire that at this time included most of Florida, Texas and California as well as most of Central and South America), it was primarily the Russians, Americans and British who stood to gain the greatest value from the sea otter trade. And it was the merchants of these three nations who directly challenged Spanish sovereignty in Pacific North America.

IN THE 1780s, it seemed that Spain and Russia would be dividing the coast between themselves. Neither the British nor the French had any presence in the region, and the United States was still fighting for its independence. Russian fur traders began frequenting the west coast of North America soon after Vitus Bering skipped east along the northern rim of the Pacific for Alexander the Great in 1741, and Spanish traders were shipping sea otter pelts from California west to the Philippines. Then came Cook's voyage and the increased British interest in the vast territory. With the end of the American War of Independence in 1783 and the resulting general demobilization within the Royal Navy, thousands of competent naval officers were placed on half pay with no immediate likelihood of receiving a new commission. As well, a depression in New England after the war left plenty of American merchants and ship captains, shut out of commerce with Britain, looking for new overseas markets. Pacific America quickly became a magnet for unemployed British and American mariners desperately seeking a means of making a living in the post-revolutionary world.

The first privately financed American commercial voyage to reach Pacific North America was led by Captain James Hanna, who sailed from Macao in 1785 with about thirty men in a single-ship prosaically named *Sea Otter*. They traded iron bars for furs at Nootka and returned safely to China. Hanna's voyage was followed in the next year by several others with the same idea. Also in the summer of that year, Compte de la Perouse led a French scientific and exploratory voyage that departed from Brest. A semi-official British commercial enterprise departed London the same month, organized by the politically connected Richard Cadman Etches. His two ships were commanded by Dixon and Portlock, two experienced officers familiar with the region. Etches had grand ambitions: to establish two permanent trading posts on the northwest coast, at Nootka Sound and Prince William Sound, and to have a fleet of ships scour the coast for furs and scurry back and forth between China and Nootka. Etches used his influence and clout, including the enthusiastic support of Sir Joseph Banks, to secure official licences from the two British monopolies that had legal rights to the trade—the East India Company and the South Seas Company.

Officials of the East India Company, easily granting a licence to themselves, organized a two-ship expedition from Bombay to Nootka in 1786. It was also in 1786 that Meares's Bengal Fur Company had sent the *Nootka* and *Sea Otter* on their disastrous voyage, overwintering in Alaska. A total of seven ships were in the sea otter fur trade that year, and the trade saw an ever-expanding number each year thereafter. With numerous ships in the coastal trade named either the *Sea Otter* or *Nootka* or some variation thereof, the imagination used in naming them was not of a high order even if the commercial concept that motivated them was brilliant. The traders were practical people on a prosaic mission. The China trade in sea otter pelts was a grassroots enterprise begun for the most part by small entrepreneurs rather than by an organized and centrally planned government initiative. European governments, however, were eventually dragged into the politics of the situation by a series of improbable, though in hindsight entirely predictable, events.

Because of Etches's political influence in Britain, soon many grandiose plans sprang forth for this little-known and not very well understood region. Realizing the difficulty British merchants faced because
of distance and restrictive trade monopolies, Etches argued for the
abolition of those monopolies. He claimed that if anyone was free to
buy or sell anything they wanted on both sides of the Pacific, the trade
"would progressively and prodigiously increase." But Etches obeyed
the monopoly regulations even while lobbying to have their rights cur-
tailed. He also had an eye to securing political control over the region
for the long-term benefit of British commerce, and for his own benefit,
naturally. He wrote to Banks, who had publicly supported the establishment of a penal colony in New South Wales (the first Botany Bay
fleet sailed in 1787) that Pacific America should also be considered a
possible location for a convict colony. The expense would be minimal,
Etches claimed, when the convicts were set to work in the fur trade;
furthermore, hogs and fresh food could be transported from Hawaii,
in a simple compact triangle of trade similar to the impressively profitable slave trade then operating in the Atlantic. He also wrote to Banks
that "a small arm'd vessel commanded by a Lieutenant" could patrol
during the construction of the buildings, and that would then "make a
regular survey of the whole of the Coast..." The historian F.W. Howay
has suggested that this recommendation was the germination of the
concept for Vancouver's voyage a few years later. Even though none of
his plans was ever adopted as official British policy, Etches was drawing attention, and in high political circles, to this distant region with
an as-yet-undeveloped trade network. Others soon took up the cause.

Alexander Dalrymple, the same man who had years before strenuously argued for the existence of a great southern continent, now
turned his attention to Pacific America. In early 1789, he published
a short pamphlet with a mighty name: *Plan for Promoting the Fur
Trade and Securing It to This Country by Uniting the Operations of
the East India and Hudson's Bay Companies.* His plan was based on a
solid knowledge of the budding trade and included excerpts from the
journals of the principal and pioneering captains. Dalrymple certainly
had no intention to limit the monopoly powers of the East India Company, free trade then being a novel and daring, even suspect, notion.
He wanted to increase British monopoly power by amalgamating the

two mighty British monopolies and tying them more securely to the country's national objectives. His pamphlet contributed to a public awareness of opportunities in a region of the world where the commercial patterns were not yet set. The China Trade was still mostly a matter of commercial potential, but because of public interest in the complex web of expanding international trade in the late eighteenth century, the workings of this trade triangle could be understood and appreciated. The China Trade potently blended heroic adventure with nationalism and commercial profit. The amount of money actually made from selling sea otter pelts was minimal from a British national perspective, however lucrative it was to individual traders. But for Britain after the American Revolution, the Pacific coast of North America was the unexplored shore of its sole remaining North American colony. For the Americans, the west coast offered an opportunity to use their massive merchant fleet. Opening trading there would stimulate their economy and provide geographical information about the west coast at the same time. "Upon the whole," wrote Dalrymple, "I am afraid that if something is not done and that immediately, this Valuable Branch of Commerce will be lost to this Country and in Consequence of that Loss the Traders both from Hudson's Bay and Canada will find themselves in a bad Neighbourhood" when they went searching for a Pacific outlet for the furs taken from the interior of the continent.

Penal colonies, permanent trade settlements, fleets of ships servicing the whole coast, the entire lucrative business sewn up by two of Britain's greatest monopolies—these grand schemes no doubt seemed perfectly sensible while one was sipping brandy, relaxing in a comfortable leather armchair in front of a cozy fire on an English estate; but they did not hold up quite so nicely in the chilly drizzle of the dreary forests of Pacific North America while negotiating with natives who did not speak English, could be hostile to strangers and had no respect for the power of the British king. Neither Etches nor Dalrymple seemed to take any notice of Spain's claim to sovereignty over the region or to the activities of the Boston merchants who, recently freed from British rule, paid no attention to restrictive trade covenants. Nor did they appear to be concerned about the expanding Russian presence or the natural sovereignty and autonomy of the people who already lived there.

Meanwhile, in China, Meares schemed. Recovering from the humiliating and disastrous expedition in which most of his men had died from scurvy and all the invested capital was lost, he somehow interested new partners and enlisted more men to join him for a second expedition. Meares's velvet tongue and the money being made by other captains was enough to inspire them. Because only British enterprises were subject to the restrictive licensing fees and arrangements of the British monopolies, Meares decided that his ships would not, in fact, fly the British flag. He registered them under a Portuguese flag of convenience. In 1788, in preparation for his second voyage to Pacific America, Meares, the erstwhile Royal Navy lieutenant, secured some Portuguese partners and papers proclaiming his ships to be sailing out of Macao. Meares himself would ostensibly be in the employ of a Portuguese captain, so long as it suited him. Although Meares's expedition was only one of dozens of new enterprises drawn to Pacific North America by the scent of easy money in the depressed economy, his actions were to have a dramatic influence on future events.

In early 1788 Meares, Portuguese papers in hand, sailed two ships, the 230-ton *Felice Adventurer* and 300-ton *Iphigenia,* east across the Pacific to Nootka Sound. The ships separated, and while the *Felice* cruised along the Alaskan coast trading for furs the *Iphigenia,* loaded with construction materials and a crew of fifty Chinese labourers, proceeded to Friendly Cove in Nootka Sound. "In a short time the ship was surrounded with a great number of canoes," Meares recorded, "which were filled with men, women and children; they brought also considerable supplies of fish, and we did not hesitate a moment to purchase an article so very acceptable to people just arrived from a long and toilsome voyage." The whole village came out to see the newcomers and witness the return of a local chief named Comeckla, who had made the voyage to China the year before and now returned in triumph. Comeckla "set off with a flaunting cockade" around the shore, displaying his numerous copper wares. A great feast was arranged featuring a local delicacy, whale. Several days later, the two most prominent local rulers of the sound, Maquinna and Callicum; a chief of the Mowachaht, arrived in twelve war canoes, each rowed by about eighteen men chanting a "sonorous melody" and "cloathed in the most beautiful skins of sea otter, which covered them from their necks to their ankles. Their hair was powdered with the white down of birds, and their faces bedaubed with red and black ochre, in the form of a shark's jaw, and a spiral line, which rendered their appearance extremely savage."

Maquinna, son of the chief also named Maquinna and the same young man who observed the arrival of Cook's ships a decade earlier, was according to Meares "of middle size, but extremely well made, and possessing a countenance that was formed to interest all who saw him." A powerful chief, Maquinna had grown rich controlling and manipulating the trade in Nootka Sound, which had emerged as the primary summer haven and rendezvous of the sea otter traders. After presenting Maquinna with a gift, Meares, according to his own testimony, began "most readily" negotiating for a parcel of land along the shore for his enterprise. Although Maquinna later denied that he had permanently given or sold to Meares anything apart from a temporary residence, such distinctions were easily overlooked by Meares, who tended to view the world as he wanted it to be.

Along the shore, a slight distance from the village of Yuquot, Meares's Chinese artisans promptly built a two-storey dwelling and a workshop surrounded by a rough palisade with a small cannon. It was close enough for easy communication but distant enough not to interfere with the daily activities of the village, and it was sheltered from the wind with a clear stream and had good access to hunting and berries. They then began work on a small ship for the local trade, the first European-style ship constructed on the Pacific coast, aptly named the *North West America*. Meares then began cruising for furs in the *Iphigenia*, passing through dangerous heavy swells and fog along the rock-bound coast nearly as far south as the Columbia River, before returning and anchoring in Barkley Sound, named the previous year by the British trader Charles William Barkley. He also negotiated with Chief Wickaninnish at Clayoquot Sound for the right to trade in the south.

When the *Iphigenia* returned to Friendly Cove, the newly built *North West America* was ready for launching. Meares spied an approaching ship on the misty horizon, and the *North West America* sallied forth to lead the vessel to the safety of the harbour. It was the *Lady Washington,* commanded by Robert Gray, a one-eyed Boston trader who had rounded Cape Horn with the consort ship *Columbia* "under the patronage of Congress to examine the Coast of America, and to open a fur trade between New England and this part of the American Continent... to enable them to return home teas and China goods."

The ships traded and congregated in Nootka throughout the season, with Meares slyly attempting to dissuade the Americans from pursuing the trade: "All the time these Gentleman were on-board," wrote Robert Haswell of the *Lady Washington,* "they fully employed themselves fabricating and rehursing vague and improvable tales relative to the coast of the vast danger attending its navigation or the Monsterous Savage disposition of its inhabitants adding it would be maddness in us so weak as we were to stay a winter among them." Meares disingenuously informed Gray that he and his ships had not collected even fifty sea otter skins the whole season, which Gray considered a "notorious falsity."

All of Meares's ships flew Portuguese flags, a fact Meares later denied when it became politically expedient that he be regarded as a British operation. His enterprise was truly an international undertaking, with a Portuguese licence, using Chinese labour to trade with coastal natives and shipping directly to China, with provisions and winter harbour courtesy of the Hawaiians. Not much of it was actually British, apart from the nationality of the captain, although it would come to be seen, by a masterful trick of public relations, as nearly an extension of the British crown—one of the essential tendrils of the empire, a strand of the commercial web that kept Britain propelling itself towards global dominion. Meares returned to China in the *Felice,* while the *Iphigenia* and *North West America* wintered in Hawaii. Maquinna's people made their annual migration to the sheltered waters farther inland. Gray wintered at Friendly Cove, then proceeded to China and continued west until he returned to Boston, becoming the first American to circumnavigate the world. Thereafter, Gray made yearly voyages to Pacific North America, and he was present on the coast when history was redirected, not once, but twice.

By 1789, after nine years of not commissioning any voyages north of California, Spain realized that events were rapidly ushering in a new era, that mere claims to prior discovery or ancient papal treaties were not sufficient to exercise control over the region. Two Spanish ships were sent north to inspect the Russian outposts in Alaska. The expedition was commanded by Esteban José Martínez Fernández y Martínez de la Sierra, a forty-six-year-old junior officer who assumed command of the expedition when the senior officer was ill. This seemingly minor change in command would have far-reaching implications. Martínez was a brash and inflexible man, eager for advancement but with a reputation for poor judgment. An ardent patriot and believer in Spain's irrefutable right to rule the entire coast, Martínez, while visiting Russian outposts along the Gulf of Alaska, secretly performed six ritual acts of formal possession: going ashore, planting a flag or cross and making a formal pronouncement that the land now belonged to the king of Spain. In one instance he performed the ritual barely out of sight of a large entrenched Russian settlement in Unalaska, after dining with its leader, Potap Zaikov, and learning of the future plans for Russian expansion along the coast. Zaikov had informed Martínez that his plans included the occupation and fortification of Nootka Sound.

Upon returning to San Blas naval base, Martínez sent a report to the Spanish viceroy of Mexico, Manuel Antonio Flores Maldonado Martínez Angelo y Bodquin, relating the distressing news: the Russians believed they had a strong claim to the Alaskan coast based on the explorations of Bering and Alexei Chirikov in 1741, and they were planning to expand to Nootka to counter the British trading there. Martínez urged Spain immediately to "occupy the said port [Nootka] and establish a garrison in it" to forestall both the Russians and the British. He did not yet realize that American traders were also arriving on the coast in numbers. Viceroy Flores, galvanized into action by this alarming news, ordered Martínez to prepare two ships, the twenty-six-gun frigate *Princesa* and the slightly smaller, sixteen-gun *San Carlos*, for another expedition. Within a month and a half of Martínez's return, the two ships sailed north for a showdown.

In the winter of 1788–89, Meares, seeing the future and sensing an opportunity, merged his ostensibly Portuguese operations with

Etches's licensed British enterprise. Their merged business, the Associated Merchants of London and India Trading to the Northwest Coast of America, sent two ships under Captain James Colnett with dozens of Chinese labourers to build an elaborate permanent factory at Nootka, with the intention to dominate the trade and squeeze the others out. It was to be "a solid establishment, and not one that is to be abandon'd at pleasure." Hoping to secure future government support, Meares and Etches planned to name it Fort Pitt, after Prime Minister William Pitt, although without his consent or knowledge. A base, or "factory" in the eighteenth-century terminology, was vital as a place of repair and security for weary crews. It would be essential to the stability and profitability of a far-flung trading enterprise, since the distance west across the Pacific to China was ten thousand miles, and Spanish ports were generally closed to foreign ships.

In addition to being the wettest place in North America and one of the wettest in the world (annual rainfall on western Vancouver Island is as much as 3,300 millimetres, or 130 inches), the region's tricky currents and frequent fog made for extremely treacherous sailing. The west coast of Vancouver Island later became known as "the graveyard of the Pacific" because of its dozens of shipwrecks. Friendly Cove, sheltered from the open ocean, inhabited by peaceful, friendly people and midway between the Spanish and Russian habitations, was the ideal location not just for the sea otter trade but also as a beachhead of empire.

By 1789 the sea otter trade with China was busy. The west coast swarmed with merchant ships from Britain, Spain, Russia and the new nation of the United States, all anxious for a share of the newfound wealth. As many as twenty-five merchant ships traded along the bewilderingly intricate, island-studded coastline each year, scuttling in and out of the thousands of secluded inlets, handing over metal utensils to native traders and stuffing shiny pelts into ships' holds. Also each year, they were hauling west across the Pacific upwards of 15,000 sea otter pelts. The trade grew increasingly violent as conflicts among various native peoples and the traders led to murders, reprisals and the threat of further violence. The China Trade had become a true international game in an ill-defined no man's land. Without enforceable rules, laws or customs it was sure to run into problems. Who could control and regulate the extremely valuable commerce? The traders certainly were not intending to regulate and police themselves.

These captains of the China Trade were a somewhat incestuous gang. Most of them were loosely connected in some way, and their allegiances were fluid and malleable. These British and American merchants, ex–Royal Navy officers, current officers and alumni of Cook's voyages, as well as Spanish navy officers, Russian traders and indigenous hunters and chiefs, were all pursuing the velvet booty. They were compelled by economic necessity, greed and politics to congregate in Pacific North America in a volatile mélange of competing interests, interpersonal relations and national allegiances. The lives of many of the early Spanish, British and American captains who were active along the Pacific Northwest in the 1780s—particularly Gray, Bodega y Quadra, Martínez, Menzies, Meares and Maquinna—were intertwined, and their careers and activities set in motion the events that would redirect the course of George Vancouver's life and ultimately transform the commercial and political future of the entire region.

Despite Cook's voyage of discovery and the secret voyages of the Russians and Spanish, the geography of the coastline of Pacific North America was not very well understood. It might conceal any number of potentially valuable waterways, inlets or eastward-leading channels that could prove to be of great value to nations with a territorial interest in the interior of the continent. But to exercise control over this coast its geography would have to be understood and an imperial presence established.

When Viceroy Flores put Martínez in command of a sensitive political mission in the spring of 1789, it signalled trouble. Martínez's instructions seemed innocuous enough: to firmly but politely assert and claim Spanish sovereignty and to prevent others from trading with the natives along the coast and from using Nootka Sound as a base. He was to treat "their commanders with the politeness and kind treatment which the existing peace demands... without being led into harsh expressions which may give serious offence and cause a rupture." But the instruction was the spark that ignited the tinder and set ablaze the inferno over the sovereignty over distant Pacific North

America. Martínez was an abrasive commander, proud of his heritage and interested in making a name for himself. When news of his ill-conceived, brash and autocratic actions at Friendly Cove trickled in, the astonished eyes of European politicians and citizens alike scanned globes and charts and narrowed in on a seemingly insignificant inlet on the sparsely inhabited and poorly charted coast on the far side of the world.

the GATHERING STORM

FOUR

In the Caribbean

———— ◈ ————

IN DECEMBER 1780, after only two months of shore leave on half pay at the conclusion of Cook's ill-fated third voyage, George Vancouver received new orders to join the sloop of war *Martin* as lieutenant. With this promotion, he entered an entirely different world from the one he had grown used to—a world where the life of the average sailor was little valued and Cook's enlightened attitudes were disregarded under the rigid demands of a mighty military struggle. He was now an officer in the Royal Navy during a war, not a midshipman on a leisurely scientific and exploring voyage.

One of the first things Vancouver noticed when he boarded his new ship was the yawning social gulf between the lower deck, as the non-commissioned officers and regular sailors were called, and the quarterdeck, as the officers were known. For the former to disobey the latter was the cause of the frequently administered violent punishments. The gulf mirrored the extent of social stratification in British society at this time. Well-off or aristocratic individuals never found themselves on the lower deck; they were trained, as Vancouver was, for command. Conversely, it was impossible for a regular, able-bodied sailor or non-commissioned officer to cross over to the quarterdeck. Social background, education and wealth distinguished the two groups so completely that even when they were crammed together on a tiny ship for months at a time, they never spoke socially or shared free time. But a huge social gulf could also exist between the members of the quarterdeck. At the lower end were those like Vancouver, a member of the well-off upper-middle class—a prominent, respected but untitled family—and at the other end, the rarefied upper nobility. Shipboard, however, these social distinctions were subordinate to the Royal Navy's own hierarchy, at least in theory.

The *Martin* spent the next year patrolling the North Sea and escorting convoys between British east coast ports and Belgium. The war was not going well for Britain: the American colonies had secured France and Spain as allies, while Russia, Sweden, Denmark and the Netherlands had joined together to organize the Armed Neutrality. By the time Vancouver joined the *Martin*, the American War of Independence had evolved into a full-scale European war, and the American colonies had so many European allies that the Royal Navy found command of the sea difficult to maintain. In October 1781 the British army surrendered to the Americans at Yorktown, virtually ending the war in the United States, although a formal peace was not signed until 1783.

Early in 1782, while peace was being negotiated, the *Martin* was ordered to cross the Atlantic to the Caribbean, where the French and Spanish fleets congregated and thus one of the main theatres of war for the Royal Navy. From Port Royal, Jamaica, the *Martin* was sent to patrol and garrison the remote and sparsely populated Swan Island, but when it arrived the crew discovered that the island had already been attacked by a Spanish fleet. Most of the population had been seized by the Spanish and taken away as captives. On the disheartening return voyage, however, the ship's lookout spied a sail on the horizon. The *Martin* gave chase and soon caught the other ship. It hailed the captain, who "answered he came from Carthagena bound to the Havanna," Vancouver wrote in a journal entry. "Capt. Merrick then desired him to shorten sail immediately. He answered he would, but he fired a broadside at us which we immediately answered & both ships kept continually firing for near two hours."

It was Vancouver's first and only full battle at sea. The ships shuddered with the deafening blasts of cannons that lobbed hot iron balls at each other, pounding into the wooden walls and sending splinters flying through the interior decks. Acrid smoke clogged the air, enveloping the ships in a blinding cloud and stinging the crews' eyes. Men screamed in pain and excitement, their ears ringing from the thunderous explosions, and blood ran across the deck. After several hours of combat, darkness fell and the ships broke off their fighting. During the night the Spanish tried to flee, but the *Martin* kept close, and in the first light of the morning they resumed the battle until the Spanish ship lowered its colours and surrendered.

The carnage from the battle was indescribably terrifying, especially to Vancouver, who had never seen this sort of action before. Exhausted, blood-soaked surgeons sawed off limbs, gouged splinters and musket balls from whimpering victims, and slathered salve onto horrible burns. The moaning of the dying and wounded was only slightly ameliorated by the relief of the survivors. But Vancouver was unwounded. The *Martin*'s captain sent a prize crew aboard the battered and mangled Spanish ship, and they sailed back to Jamaica.

A few months later, Vancouver was promoted to junior lieutenant of the *Fame*, a much larger seventy-four-gun ship with a company of about six hundred mariners. His duties were routine; he learned the skills of a more senior officer, such as navigating, taking the wheel on watch and striving to keep his ship in the close formation of the fleet. It was on the *Fame* that Vancouver was introduced to unsavoury aspects of life at sea that he had never encountered with Cook or on the smaller *Martin*. The ship had been severely damaged in the recent Battle of the Saints, and many of its crew had been killed. Dozens were still recovering from their injuries. Typhus raged on board, killing dozens more during Vancouver's first few months aboard. He recorded in his sketchy professional journal at least one death from yellow fever, typhus or scurvy every day or so.

Life in the Royal Navy at that time could be harsh to the point of absurdity, and Vancouver had been shielded from the worst of it during his first years in the service. Poor food was the first non-negotiable aspect of employment in the Royal Navy. Although Vancouver would have been used to poor food, Cook's strenuous efforts to procure fresh vegetables alleviated this problem. James Patton, a surgeon on Cook's second voyage, remarked that "our bread was... both musty and mouldy, and at the same time swarming with two different sorts of little brown grubs, the *circulio granorius*, (or weevil,) and the *dermestes paniceus*... their larvas, or maggots, were found in such quantities in the pease-soup, as if they had been strewed over our plates on purpose, so that we could not avoid swallowing some of them in every spoonful we took." Depending on the season, the conditions could have been much worse on a larger ship like the *Fame*. The only means of preserving food were salting, drying or pickling; the first two, however, were difficult at sea because of the ever-present dampness.

Although Cook had devised a practical solution to scurvy and Vancouver was well aware of how Cook had done it, the horrible disease was still rampant in the Royal Navy, particularly in the Caribbean when Vancouver returned to service in 1780. Part of the problem was that, unlike the situation on a voyage of exploration and discovery, in which the captain had a great deal of latitude in setting standards for hygiene and diet, serving on a warship, especially one on active duty, allowed very little room for deviation from orders. A warship could not just go to harbour or send a boat ashore whenever the captain or surgeon decided that fresh food was needed. It might be awaiting battle orders, be carrying out a vital patrol of a channel or be engaged in a close blockade of an enemy port. Thus, although it might be close to the source of fresh food and water, it lacked the capacity to obtain these necessities without endangering an operation. Vancouver knew what to do to lessen the ravages of scurvy, but as a junior officer he was powerless either to change the hidebound traditions of the Royal Navy or to temper the inflexibility of military operations.

Aboard the *Fame*, up to a third of the sailors had not joined the ship's company by choice. Everyone aboard Cook's voyages had been chosen, perhaps even by Cook himself, though perhaps occasionally with the nudging or encouragement of superiors. Cook's crews were in good health and were eager and interested in being on the voyage. Apart from the usual disagreements and grumbling that were to be expected when hundreds of men were crammed together for months at a time, contentment and conviviality existed among Cook's crews. In contrast, on a warship like the *Fame*, many of the sailors were rounded up by a press gang, against their will, and either had no skills at sea or were in poor health, or both. Sometimes they were sick, malnourished, diseased, elderly or infected with typhus. Ill-suited to their new careers and lives, resentful and bitter, press gang recruits brought disease and a sour attitude onto the ship. This situation in turn led to a morose neglect of duty or, worse, hostility, which resulted in violent punishments to compel the sailors to do the captain's bidding.

The simmering resentment of pressed sailors, combined with the horrible living conditions on board and the stress of war, ensured that violence was common. It was an age of severe punishments, and the captain was a virtual dictator while at sea. Even minor crimes such as theft were dealt with harshly, usually by flogging with the dreaded cat-o'-nine-tails. Other crimes were treated much more seriously. Showing disrespect for a superior officer, drunkenness and neglect of duty, even by accident, could result in a sailor's being tied to the main mast and lashed on his bare back at least a dozen times, perhaps as many as a hundred times if the infraction was serious or deliberate. Occasionally men died from their punishment.

Certain transgressions were treated very seriously, because one person's negligence might result in serious damage to the ship or injury to or the death of others. Violent punishment varied in severity from ship to ship. Because there were no standard regulations for punishment, individual captains wielded arbitrary power over their crew. Some captains earned a reputation for brutality and erratic violence, and some undoubtedly took perverse pleasure in lashing and beating sailors far beyond what was necessary. Others, fortunately, preferred less cruel types of punishment. One of the lesser but common punishments was "starting." If an officer, taking his cue from the captain as to necessity and severity, felt that a sailor was moving too slowly or displaying signs of belligerence or disrespect, he would reach out and smack the offender with a cane. Ships peopled with convicts and pressed men had far greater incidents of lashing and starting, no doubt creating a tense and gloomy atmosphere and eroding the men's morale.

The filthiest slums of the largest cities were more sanitary than the lower decks of large ships during the Age of Sail. British naval commander Frederick Chamier wrote in *Life of a Sailor* of his first days on a ship in port as a young midshipman at the end of the eighteenth century: "Dirty women, the objects of sailors' affections, with beer cans in hand, were everywhere conspicuous: the shrill whistle squeaked, and the noise of the boatswain and his mate rattled like thunder in my ears; the deck was dirty, slippery and wet; the smells abominable; the whole sight disgusting."

Vancouver was also astonished at the filth he saw on the *Fame;* it was the antithesis of Cook's regimen of cleanliness and order. Cook was incredibly clean, and Vancouver was to become nearly compulsively so as a shocked reaction to life on warships after nearly a decade of being accustomed to something entirely different. The bowels of a warship were clogged with refuse, trash, decaying flesh, buckets of urine, excrement and vomit. The holds were populated with vermin, festering and spoiled provisions and, sometimes, rotting corpses awaiting burial. Sea water continuously leaked in through cracks in the planking, turning the ship's ballast of gravel or sand into a noxious slurry. There was no ventilation below the waterline, and as a result the bilge became so polluted and foul with gases that descending into the hold was dangerous. The vapours could leave a man unconscious if he breathed them for too long.

The overcrowding, poor food and filth on sailing ships contributed to something else Vancouver had not encountered during his years at sea: endemic disease. The standard ship-of-the-line during the eighteenth century was rife with contagious and diet-related diseases that contributed to an incredible death rate among sailors and sometimes crippled the ship—even entire fleets. Because of the high mortality rates, navy ships were oversupplied with men whenever possible.

The sheer variety of the endemic diseases that afflicted mariners in the eighteenth century was incredible. Many sailors suffered from more than one disease, and physicians found it difficult to accurately separate the symptoms of one disease from those of another. Niacin deficiency caused lunacy and convulsions; thiamin deficiency caused beriberi, with symptoms similar to scurvy, and vitamin A deficiency caused night blindness. Syphilis, malaria, rickets, smallpox, tuberculosis, yellow fever, venereal diseases, dysentery and food poisoning were routine. Next to scurvy, typhus was the most common affliction.

Spread by infected lice in the frequently shared and rarely cleaned bedding, typhus was so common on ships that it was known as "ship's fever" or "gaol fever." "Raw sailors and unseasoned marines are often the occasion of great sickness in fleets," wrote contemporary naval surgeon James Lind. He observed that most fevers seemed to derive from men living in "nasty, low, damp, unventilated habitations loaded with putrid animal steams" (for example, prisons and ships). "This fever," he claimed, "was caused by the infected clothing of these pressed men, such mischief lurked in their tainted apparel and rags, and by these were conveyed into other ships."

The physician Sir Gilbert Blane wrote extensively of the disease problems of the Royal Navy, particularly of the West Indies fleet in the early 1780s—the same years Vancouver was in the Caribbean. In his *A Short Account of the Most Effectual Means of Preserving the Health of Seamen,* Blane strenuously advocated for many of the practices common on Cook's ships and familiar to Vancouver: improved shipboard cleanliness, the washing of sailors' clothes and bedding, the inclusion of as many fresh foods as possible and citrus juice in the sailors' diet, and the seemingly obvious recommendation that feverish and infectious sailors should be removed from ships and taken to hospitals to prevent disease from spreading. In the West Indies in 1780 the death rate from disease, primarily scurvy and yellow fever, was an astonishing one in seven. "Crowding, filth, and the mixture of diseases, are the great causes of mortality," Blane observed dryly.

The stifling Caribbean heat and humidity made life even more unbearable and dangerous for sailors. "In consequence of what they undergo," Blane wrote in the 1790s, "they are in general short lived, and have their constitutions worn out ten years before the rest of the laborious part of mankind. A seaman, at the age of forty-five, if shown to a person not accustomed to be among them, would be taken by his looks to be fifty-five, or even on the borders of sixty." Undoubtedly the tropical conditions took their toll on Vancouver's constitution as well.

BY JULY 1783, the *Fame* was back in London and Vancouver was placed ashore on half pay. He waited anxiously for his next posting. The general demobilization at the end of the war made securing a commission difficult, and as a result many sailors and officers joined the merchant marine. Others flocked to distant, unexplored Pacific America, lured by the rumours of wealth to be had trading for sea otter pelts. But Vancouver remained in Britain, waiting for a new assignment in the Royal Navy. He had decided to devote his career to the navy and would not lower his standards to work elsewhere just for money. His time ashore dragged on for a year and a half. Peace could be hard on professional soldiers and sailors. There is no record of what Vancouver did to pass the time; he never mentioned it, and no record of his activities survives, but he probably rode the coach to King's Lynn to visit with family there or saw friends in London.

Having sailed so long with Cook, however, Vancouver had an uncommon set of skills in navigation and hydrography. He was not overlooked for long. In November 1784, a year after Cook's journals were finally published, Vancouver's connections and reputation secured him a posting as third lieutenant on the *Europa,* a mid-sized ship of fifty guns, leaving for Jamaica as the flagship of Rear Admiral Alexander Innes. Innes's peacetime squadron consisted of only two ships, which alternately spent their time patrolling or anchored in Port Royal, showing the flag. It was not a very exciting assignment, and there was little active service: Vancouver made one voyage to Cartagena but otherwise cruised nearby islands for smugglers. In mid-1786 a new commander-in-chief for the West Indies, Commodore Sir Alan Gardner, arrived in Port Royal. It was a fortunate event for Vancouver, now about thirty years of age and an established lieutenant. If not for powerful connections or a patron, his career would have become stalled; to hope for promotion would have been foolish. But the West Indies Station had the best possibilities for promotion— mainly because diseases killed off so many men, including officers.

The West Indies Station was the most notoriously disease-ridden posting of the Royal Navy, and Port Royal was known as "the graveyard" because so many sailors perished there from typhus, dysentery and scurvy. But ambitious young officers would sometimes sign on below their rank in the hope that the death of a superior would result in their promotion—assuming that they themselves lived. There is no evidence that Vancouver decided to come to Port Royal for this reason, but he was well placed to take advantage of deaths in the service. Not only was he competent and trustworthy, but he had a lot in common with his new commander.

Gardner was a progressive commander for his era. Like James Cook, he was devoted to the health of his crews, not just because he felt they deserved it, but because a strong and healthy crew improved the fighting and sailing strength of the ships and squadron. Rather than uphold ancient traditions that were proving ill-adapted to the increasing ship size and duration of voyages in the eighteenth century, Gardner was receptive to new ideas. He ordered sauerkraut and other antiscorbutics to be available as part of the regular diet for his crew and strove to keep his ships as clean as possible. Essentially, he followed the practices advocated by Cook and more recently by Blane.

Although a gulf existed between Gardner and Vancouver in terms of hierarchy, duties and social background, Gardner's officers spent many an evening sipping port in the captain's cabin, sweltering in the oppressive heat, perhaps hearing Vancouver relate tales of his and Cook's voyages to Antarctica and Pacific North America. Gardner's interest and zeal in adopting many of Cook's and Blane's disease-reduction practices may even have originated with Vancouver and his close experience with them.

In 1787, Gardner received orders to survey Kingston and Port Royal harbours, and Vancouver was the natural choice to organize and carry out the work. This assignment was part of the Admiralty's new efforts to improve hydrographic information about key harbours around the world. Vancouver had done this very sort of work for Cook. During the summer hurricane season European warships had habitually sailed north to New York or other similar ports to escape the storms, but after the American Revolution this option was closed to the Royal Navy. Making accurate charts of other harbours was vital to the ships' safety. Vancouver carried out the surveys in small boats, tracing the entire coastline of Jamaica while taking measurements from the shore and depth soundings of the sea floor.

Being always close to shore carried the unfortunate risk of placing Vancouver and his men closer to disease-carrying mosquitoes. The evidence points to Vancouver having contracted some form of illness, probably malaria, while completing the survey. Vancouver was absent from the survey on two occasions, in March and July of 1788. There was also a note in the ship's log that he "returned in the yard schooner" at the end of May, a euphemism for sick mariners returning to ship from a hospital ashore. The medical historian Sir James Watt has written that although there is no official record of Vancouver having an illness, the absence of such a record would not have been "unusual, for an officer's absence was not officially recorded until it extended to six weeks or more."

The marine survey was a difficult and specialized job, but Vancouver performed his duties with thoroughness, vigour and ability. He was singled out for promotion and became a favourite of Gardner, who gave him an escalating series of responsibilities. On November 24, 1787, Gardner promoted him to second lieutenant, and only a few months later, on February 13, 1788, he again promoted Vancouver, to first lieutenant, a position that essentially made him second in command.

The nearly five years that Vancouver spent on the *Europa* were nevertheless a tedious string of months stuck in the stifling humidity and oppressive heat of Port Royal, engaged in routine and uneventful cruises around the Caribbean. If not for leading the small-boat surveys of Kingston and Port Royal harbours, he would have accomplished nothing to distinguish himself. But these were generally happy times. The work was not stressful, the marine survey helped break the tedium and the officers were excellent. Vancouver was a good lieutenant and mentor to younger officers, and he formed a bond with several of them that would last the remainder of his life.

His survey companion, the newly joined ship's master Joseph Whidbey, was an older man in his mid-thirties who had begun his career two decades earlier as an able seaman. Coming from a lower social class, he rose through the ranks. He was obviously highly skilled, given that he was employed during the peace, but he was not a commissioned officer—nor would he ever be, unless he demonstrated the talents of James Cook and had equally good fortune. As a ship's master he was rather a specialized non-commissioned officer who could sail a ship and navigate but never make important decisions. Laconic, patient and quietly competent, Whidbey worked well with Vancouver for three years and often in close quarters. He was a steadying influence, and although he had no formal education he had an intensely practical mind and a great interest in science and mathematics.

And fortunately there were others Vancouver could count on. Peter Puget was a young midshipman who worked under Vancouver for four years. Of Huguenot background and with a family banking enterprise in London, Puget seems to have made an unusual career choice in the Royal Navy. Vancouver, however, taught him navigation and thought well of his ability and potential. The meticulous Joseph Baker, from the Welsh border country, served for several years on the *Europa* as a midshipman. He and Puget became lifelong friends. Zachary Mudge served on the *Europa*'s home voyage for several months as a junior lieutenant. Mudge came from a distinguished Plymouth family; his father was a renowned physician and was associated with the powerful Pitt family. All three of these gentlemen were teenagers when they served on the *Europa,* and all went on to have distinguished naval careers—Puget and Mudge eventually became admirals.

The *Europa* arrived in Plymouth in September 1789, and Vancouver was paid off after a voyage of service lasting nearly five years. His time on half pay, however, was short. Within a few months, his friend and patron Sir Alan Gardner was appointed one of the Lords of the Admiralty. This board of directors of the Royal Navy was responsible for setting policy and procedures and coordinating the deployment of ships and special expeditions. Gardner proposed that Vancouver be appointed first lieutenant under Captain Henry Roberts, another alumnus of Cook's last two voyages, for an interesting voyage that would require Vancouver's precise set of skills. The freshly built HMS *Discovery* was readying for a voyage of exploration in the South Atlantic, either in the vicinity of West Africa or the southern whale fisheries, when events in Pacific America intervened. Suddenly Vancouver's career and life took a drastic turn.

FIVE

The Nootka
Sound Incident

———◄ ◈ ►———

A N ENGRAVING OF the incident shows two small boats abutting each other in choppy water near a rocky shore. A man wearing buckled shoes, tight, light-coloured hose and a long-tailed jacket perches on the edge of one of the boats. He is attempting to maintain his dignity while the hands of an unruly mob grasp at his arms and shoulders. An unshaven man in a pointed cap points a pistol at his back. On the other boat an officer in full military regalia and cocked hat waves his arms like a conductor, grimacing as he commands his sailors to action. A cloud of smoke provides a backdrop to the melee while four or five sailing ships lie at anchor with furled sails. Such drama! Such pathos!

This 1791 London engraving purports to show the unjust seizure of Captain James Colnett and the crew of the *Argonaut* by the Spanish commandant Esteban José Martínez, at Friendly Cove in Nootka Sound, in early July 1789. Titled *The Spanish Insult to the British Flag at Nootka Sound*, it was intended to inspire a patriotic outcry against imperial Britain's erstwhile enemy, imperial Spain. Actual events, although not quite so dramatic, were about to provoke an international war between the two greatest naval superpowers of the day.

When Martínez sailed north from San Blas, Mexico, to Nootka Sound in the spring of 1789 he carried detailed instructions. Despite the long list of contingencies, some ambiguity remained about how he should respond in a few key circumstances, such as what to do if no one listened to him. Censured in the past by his commander for poor seamanship and command, he had seen his youth slip away plying the coastal waters along Mexico and California on routine voyages. Forty-six years old and an ardent nationalist, Martínez was still young enough to harbour career ambitions. Finally he had been given charge of the previous year's voyage to Alaska, and this voyage had led to his command of the current expedition to Nootka—by default, as a result of the accidental illness of the preferred commander.

In a portrait from this period in his life, Martínez appears as a slim man with a receding hairline. His hair is pulled back and clubbed in the fashion of the time. His pinched mouth, indecisive chin and long nose are balanced by serious, intelligent eyes and large, straight eyebrows. It is his posture that is most distinguishing. Whereas the subjects of nearly all other naval portraits of the time hold their arms close, their hands relaxed, firmly grasping an appropriately themed prop such as a nautical chart, telescope or cocked hat, Martínez's hands flutter nervously over a partially unravelled parchment scroll on his desk. Overall, his portrait conveys the image of a bank manager explaining to a customer why he is ineligible for a loan.

In Martínez's defence, his orders, though voluminous and seemingly detailed, were admittedly rather vague, as if the governor, Viceroy Flores, thought he could absolve himself of responsibility through the sheer quantity of the writing. Martínez, for example, was to explain the Spanish position "with prudent firmness... but if, in spite of the great efforts, the foreigners should attempt to use force, you will repel it to the extent that they employ it, endeavouring to prevent as far as possible their intercourse and commerce with the natives." What if they didn't use force, yet still refused to accept Spanish authority? Flores gave Martínez some helpful suggestions about the type of arguments to offer to any British captains in case of a dispute. "To the English," he suggested, "you will demonstrate clearly and with established proofs that our discoveries anticipated those of Captain Cook, since he reached Nootka, according to his own statement, in March of the year 1778, where he purchased the two silver spoons which the Indians stole from yourself in 1774." Indeed Martínez and other Spanish mariners had cruised the coast years earlier than Cook had, but these voyages had been kept secret in an attempt to conceal the region's economic possibilities. Despite the bluster of historical foundations for sovereignty, Spanish officials knew full well that patrolling and keeping non-Spanish ships from visiting thousands of miles of unexplored, uncharted coastline far to the north of their own Pacific settlements would be nearly impossible. Spain's secret had been so well kept that British mariners believed that Cook was the first to sail these waters.

Flores was also aware of the growing threat to Spanish sovereignty posed by the merchant fleet of the newly independent New England colonies, whose ships were also frequenting the coast of Pacific America. "In case you are to encounter this Bostonian Frigate," he wrote to Martínez, "this will give you governmental authority to take such measures as you may be able and such as appear proper, giving them to understand, as all other foreigners, that our settlements are being extended to beyond Prince William's Sound, of which we have already taken formal possession, as well as the adjacent islands." So much writing, so much detail, so much ambiguity—one almost pities Martínez. He could use force against Russian and British ships, but only if they used force against him first. He had to stop the ongoing sea otter fur trade—something that would not go over well with the British, Russian and American traders who had invested in the enterprise. Nor would it endear him to the native peoples who were eager participants in the expanding commerce. With the Boston ships he could be more lenient, although what exactly did "such as appear proper" mean?

GENERATIONS OF HISTORIANS have sifted through pages of conflicting testimony on the actual events at Friendly Cove in the summer of 1789. "Affected by interest, coloured by partisanship, distorted by emotion—such they undoubtedly are," wrote Derek Pethick in *First Approaches to the North West Coast;* "but it is not always easy to determine the exact places where these all too human failings exert their influence. We must thread our way as best we can."

Martínez's two ships, the *Princesa* and *San Carlos,* hoisted their sails in San Blas and cruised north on February 17, 1789. Martínez was aboard the *Princesa*, with ninety-one crew and fifteen soldiers for a new garrison, while the *San Carlos* was captained by Gonzalo López de Haro with seventy-three crew and sixteen men at arms. Commodore Martínez sailed his twenty-cannon ship into the quiet waters of the sound on May 6. The *San Carlos* had not yet arrived. When his ship drew near to the cove and slowly entered the secluded waters, Martínez was surprised to see other ships at anchor: Friendly Cove was a busy place. In addition to the dozens of cedar canoes and the hundreds of people in Yuquot village, several European-style ships were there.

The summer of 1789 promised to be a profitable one for the European and American mariner merchants who had been slowly learning the intricate geography of the coast as well as the customs and language of the people while solidifying their trade contacts. Two American ships had even wintered along the blustery shores of Nootka Sound. Robert Gray's *Lady Washington* had already left for a trading expedition along the coast, while the *Columbia* still lay at anchor.

The *Iphigenia*, part of the Meares-Etches conglomerate, was also in port. Meares himself had remained in Macao for the season. At first Martínez was friendly, inviting the captain to dine aboard the *Princesa*. Later they both dined aboard the *Columbia* and then again both aboard the *Iphigenia*. When the *San Carlos* arrived with its additional men and guns on May 13, however, Martínez—perhaps bolstered by the presence of additional troops, perhaps fearing for his job as a result of being overly friendly to foreigners—became suspicious of the *Iphigenia*, flying the Portuguese flag but with the obviously British commander and crew. The next day he gruffly demanded to see the *Iphigenia*'s papers and then, citing an irregularity, claimed that the papers called on the fur trader to capture Russian, British and Spanish ships and sail them to Macao as prizes, and to punish the crew as pirates. Martínez ordered the officers arrested and took a detailed inventory of their ships' provisions and supplies. He then informed them that only "a scarcity of men" prevented him from seizing the *Iphigenia* as a prize and demanded that the captain sign a bond forfeiting his ship and contents unless he immediately departed Pacific America for China. After his men had been imprisoned on the Spanish ships for two weeks the captain signed the paper, and he and his officers were released. At the end of May, the *Iphigenia* sailed out of the harbour, with a promise to depart for Hawaii or China—but instead, it sailed north to continue trading.

A week later another ship belonging to the Meares-Etches enterprise, the *North West America*, the consort ship to the *Iphigenia* that had been on a trading cruise, sailed into Friendly Cove. Inexplicably, Martínez promptly seized it, imprisoned the crew as pirates and plundered the cargo, including 215 sea otter skins. He then changed the ship's name, placed a Spanish crew on board and ordered them to continue to trade for the season. Oddly, the "scarcity of men" that prompted him to release the *Iphigenia* seems not to have been a problem when seizing the *North West America*.

Meanwhile, Martínez ordered the construction of a fort at the entrance of the harbour. It was to include barracks, workshops, a bakery and gun emplacements with ten cannons; clearly this was to be an imposing structure. On June 15, another ship belonging to the Meares-Etches conglomerate, the *Princess Royal,* approached Friendly Cove. When the ship was anchored safely, Martínez sent a note informing the captain that Spain now controlled Nootka Sound and demanding to know the reason for his visit to Spanish territory. The captain replied that after the long and dangerous Pacific crossing the ship needed repairs and fresh water and that it would depart as soon as possible. Martínez agreed and did not seize the ship. On June 24, he felt comfortable in formally claiming the terrain of Nootka Sound for Spain in a pompous and entertaining affair, no doubt observed by the bemused villagers of Yuquot. "Then the chaplains and friars sang *Te Deum Laudamus,*" Martínez recorded, "and the canticle having been concluded, the commander said in a loud voice: 'In the name of his majesty the King Don Carlos III, the sovereign whom may God keep many years, with an increase of our dominions and Kingdoms, for the service of God, and for the good and prosperity of his vassals... I take, and I have taken, I seize, and I have seized, possession of this soil, where I have at present disembarked...'" He then drew his sword and waved it imperiously towards the trees and the hills, flicked some stones on the beach and the fields and shouldered a large cross. Followed by his two ships' armed crews marching in line, chanting and singing, Martínez planted the cross in a suitable spot and piled stones around the base to secure it. The terrain was now the possession of imperial Spain, at least as far as the Spanish were concerned.

On July 2, Martínez graciously allowed the *Princess Royal* to depart unmolested. So far, he had behaved erratically, not really disobeying his orders but not really adhering to them either. He vacillated, alternately seizing ships and releasing them, or ignoring them altogether (as he did with the series of American ships that frequented the harbour). It was not the behaviour of a man in charge of the situation. The situation grew more complicated as the weeks passed, and events spiralled out of Martínez's control.

The same day that the *Princess Royal* departed Nootka Sound, Captain Colnett, the thirty-eight-year-old veteran sea otter trader and Royal Navy lieutenant who had sailed with Cook a decade earlier, arrived from China in the *Argonaut*. The *Argonaut* was the most important ship in the Meares-Etches enterprise, carrying three years of supplies, frames for another small ship and Chinese labourers to begin work on the permanent factory. Colnett was the most senior commander in charge of the entire operation in Pacific America. As the *Argonaut* approached land, Colnett observed in the distance the *Princess Royal* sailing north, but unable to contact the other ship, Colnett assumed all was well as he approached Friendly Cove. Soon, two small launches approached from the shore. One carried Martínez, who proudly stood on the prow and tried to persuade Colnett that the two Spanish ships in the cove "were in great distress from want of provisions and other necessaries and urged the English commander to go into port in order to supply their needs, inviting him to stay for some time." Colnett suspected a ruse and, when he hesitated, Martínez pleaded with him that "if I would go into port and relieve his wants I should be at liberty to sail whenever I pleased."

Against his better judgment, Colnett entered Friendly Cove. When he offered his supplies, Martínez delayed and then demanded to see the *Argonaut*'s papers. Colnett's men rowed him over to Martínez's ship. In the great cabin of the *Princesa* the two men argued over the sovereignty of the coast. Colnett claimed that Cook was the first explorer on the coast. This did not impress Martínez, who had sailed into Nootka Sound with Pérez four years before Cook. Each of these men gives a slightly different account of events in his reports and diaries, but both men were full of pride and righteous indignation, made bold and rude by fear of failing in their duty. Historian Barry Gough, in his book *The Northwest Coast*, writes: "These two antagonists at Nootka Sound make a curiously well-matched pair of agents provocateurs. Both were unbridled patriots. Both possessed a boundless attachment to duty in the names of their respective kings and countries. Both had a tendency to be heavy-handed." And they were on a collision course. Martínez claimed that Colnett's hand strayed to his sword as they argued and called him a "God damned Spaniard." Colnett claimed that Martínez refused to even read his ship's papers before declaring them to be forgeries and then ordered his men-at-arms to burst through the cabin door and seize Colnett from behind, clubbing him to the floor and sending a boarding party to take control of the *Argonaut* and arrest the other officers. After plundering the *Argonaut*'s provisions and trade goods, Martínez captured the astonished and outraged crew. Pacific America was the domain of imperial Spain, he claimed, and the British were trespassing.

Martínez feared that if he allowed the *Argonaut* to leave the harbour, Colnett would voyage along the coast a little before unloading his supplies and constructing a fort or factory. He would then be held accountable for disregarding his instructions to "prevent as far as possible their intercourse and commerce with the natives." His career, so recently taking a turn for the better, could grind to a halt. Once resolved on his course of action, Martínez herded the British mariners into the holds of various ships and ordered them to be transported south to Mexico. Meanwhile Colnett, seeing his fortune being destroyed and feeling unjustly a target of aggression "from the effects of despair or madness," tried to "throw himself into the water through one of the port-holes in his cabin" and escape, or drown trying. After attempting to leap from the railing of the ship, he was restrained and then locked up below deck.

Remaining consistent in his erratic application of his mandate, Martínez continued to ignore several American vessels trading in the same harbour throughout the summer. Although these ships were equally pushing an agenda of free trade, they made no attempt to establish a permanent base. Some British captains claimed Spanish and American collusion against them, and Martínez placed some American officers on the captured British ships that then sailed on trading expeditions for him. But the American traders were generally neutral to European imperial struggles, and were most interested in securing the best deal for themselves. They had just fought a brutal war to free themselves from the British yoke and would have been all too happy to profit from British misfortune at the hands of the Spanish.

A few days later the *Princess Royal* returned to the cove, after its captain had promised to leave the coast altogether. Martínez seized it, and his crew plundered its goods and imprisoned its sailors. Meanwhile, Maquinna's ally, Callicum, was irritated by Martínez's heavy-handed trampling of indigenous authority in Nootka Sound and decided that he favoured the British over the Spanish. He swore at the Spanish commander, and when his words were translated, Martínez fired his gun in the air to frighten Callicum. One of Martínez's men, believing that his commander's gun had misfired or missed, pulled his pistol and shot Callicum, killing him. Maquinna and his followers, fearing more violence, fled to their village at Tahsis, a safe distance from Friendly Cove.

Martínez ordered the captured British ships, under Spanish officers, to begin the long southward voyage to San Blas loaded with prisoners while he and his ships remained in the cove. At the end of July, however, Martínez received new orders to abandon everything at Friendly Cove, including the fort, gun emplacements and buildings, at the end of the summer. This development came as a shock and a disappointment to the commander, who was revelling in his new purpose and in the ascendancy of his career, and who planned on a lengthy sojourn defending Spain's right to the entire coast. As he was readying to depart at the end of October, Martínez suddenly changed his cautious and neutral approach to the American traders. He captured the small ship *Fair American* and her five sailors and then fired at another American ship, but he did not give chase. When he departed he brought the Chinese workers with him to the naval base of San Blas, arriving in December.

Soon after reaching San Blas, eight British sailors died from the poor food and muggy air. The others were moved to a higher location farther inland. Here they were generally treated well and given freedom to wander the town while they awaited news of their fate. Captain Colnett, having recovered from his "despair or madness," met the newly appointed naval commandant for San Blas, Juan Francisco de la Bodega y Quadra. There he busied himself writing letters to the British ambassador in Madrid, calling for his and his men's release and the return of their property. Colnett did, however, note that "since my first arrival in New Spain, myself, officers and crew have been treated with all humanity and kindness and every attention paid them; in the day they have the liberty to go where they please."

By the fall of the year, the busy coves of Nootka Sound had grown quiet again. Maquinna and his people, onlookers to the European conflict, once again had the waters and shores to themselves. But while Nootka was silent and emptied of the characters who had violently clashed over the summer, the repercussions of their actions were being felt halfway around the world, in Europe.

IN THE SPRING OF 1789, other events dovetailed with those in Nootka Sound to highlight the growing conflict between Spain and Britain, caused by their wildly divergent philosophies regarding world trade and freedom of passage. For centuries Spain had pursued a policy of excluding all foreign ships from trading at New World ports, a policy that resulted in countless voyages of privateering, smuggling, piracy and endless conflict among the European nations. For several years British ships had been roving the South Atlantic and South Pacific oceans to hunt whales, for their valuable skins, blubber, bone and oil, and seals, which were common along both the southeastern and southwestern coasts of South America. For this industry to thrive, it was vital for the ships to have bases and safe harbours in which to refit and resupply. The whalers were grudgingly willing to avoid any Spanish settlements, in accordance with the wishes of the Spanish government, but they wanted to be free to sail along the long, uninhabited coastlines and to establish bases there.

Around the time that Martínez was arriving in Nootka Sound, two whaling ships sailed into Port Desire on the coast of Patagonia to hunt for seals and recuperate from a long voyage at sea. Three Spanish ships, including an armed frigate, also entered the secluded waters. They ordered the British whalers to leave the inlet and the entire coast and confiscated nearly seven thousand seal skins. When the British ships returned to London in the fall, they complained to their government; the news of Martínez's seizure of British ships at Nootka Sound had not yet reached Britain.

In the fall of 1789, Vancouver had returned from duty in the Caribbean and prepared to join a scientific and exploring voyage under the command of his former shipmate Captain Henry Roberts. The objective of the expedition was to scout bases in the South Atlantic for the whaling industry. Vancouver was to be first lieutenant on the newly built 330-ton merchant ship, named *Discovery* after Cook's ship. Sir Alan Gardner "mentioned me to Lord Chatham and the Board of Admiralty; and I was solicited to accompany Captain Roberts as his second," Vancouver proudly noted. "In this proposal I acquiesced, and found myself very pleasantly situated, in being thus connected with a fellow traveller for whose abilities I bore the greatest respect, and in whose friendship and good opinion I was proud to posses a place... I had no doubt that we were engaged in an expedition, which would prove no less interesting to my friend than agreeable to my wishes." In the stultified formal language of the era, this was as close to expressing exuberance as Vancouver was capable of. Essentially he wrote that Roberts was a respected friend and mentor who shared with him the bond of being a Cook alumnus, and that they would be launched on a fascinating and exciting adventure to distant lands they had visited when they were younger. With their shared experience, camaraderie and respect for each other's abilities, the shipmates from Cook's voyages seemed to be a clique in the navy. Since, for the most part, Cook chose only good men, there was good reason for them to consider themselves part of an elite group.

Roberts and Vancouver came aboard the *Discovery* in early January 1790 and spent a couple of months fitting out, provisioning and readying the new ship for sea. Late in January the first news of the troubles at Nootka Sound trickled in: a British ship had been seized in unknown circumstances. Although this was an unwelcome addition to the news about the Spanish harassment of whalers on the South

American coast, the matter did not seem overly significant. But during the next several months more details of the Nootka Sound incident became known, and Spain's blanket claims to all uncharted and unoccupied coastline became the issue. The Spanish ambassador in London, rather than apologizing or offering an explanation or indemnification for the seized ships, called British ships in the North Pacific "interlopers" and appeared astonished at the lack of recognition of Spanish sovereignty over the region. He reminded British authorities that it had been discovered by Pérez four years before Cook and claimed, "His Majesty flatters himself that the Court of St. James will certainly not fail to give the strictest orders to prevent such attempts in the future."

In response, the expedition plans of Roberts and Vancouver were altered to include a new destination and to provide an impressive show of imperial power. Verbal protests to Spain through diplomatic channels secured no assurances that British ships would be permitted to sail unmolested in the Pacific, so the new plan was to outfit a squadron of ships to protect British interests in Pacific America. In March, Roberts received new instructions that the *Discovery* would be joined by the much larger forty-four-gun frigate *Gorgon*. They were to sail to Australia, pick up about thirty men-at-arms, some settlers, officers and convicts (who would be pardoned in exchange for their participation as settlers), proceed to the Sandwich Islands (as the British then referred to Hawaii) or Tahiti, and rendezvous with another frigate, the *Sirius*. The three-ship squadron would then proceed to the Pacific Northwest of America to establish a new colony: "such a settlement as may be able to resist any attacks from the natives, and lay the foundation of an establishment for the assistance of His Majesty's subjects in the prosecution of the fur trade from the N.W. coast of America." The voyage was to be organized and launched in secret so that the base would be completed before Spain knew of it; the destination was to be north of Friendly Cove, so as not to directly confront any Spanish fortifications there.

The Admiralty still believed in the possibility of a Northwest Passage, so the orders for the squadron called on them to "examine the whole of the coast Northward from the Latitude of 51 degrees, to Cook's River [Cook Inlet], which is in the Latitude of 60 degrees, and South from the Latitude of 49 degrees, to Cape Mendocino in the Latitude of 40 degrees, carefully examining such Rivers or inlets within the said limits, as you shall judge likely to afford a communication with the interior part of the Continent." If this extremely valuable passage did exist, Britain did not want Spain to control its western exit. A Hudson's Bay Company expedition from Canada was to depart overland, across the unknown western tract of the continent, at the same time.

Although "nautical surveys" were a key component of the proposed expedition, particularly for the *Discovery*, the squadron was also given latitude to defend British interests with force and to resist any Spanish claims to sovereignty. It was to defend British rights to "a free and uninterrupted intercourse with the whole of the American Coast lying to the North of the Latitude of 40 degrees, except such parts as may be actually settled and occupied by any other European power." Although the crews were not to provoke "Subjects of His Catholic Majesty," if attacked they were to "endeavour to destroy or capture the Vessels making such attack." For Vancouver, this new twist on his orders provided an exciting, dramatic assignment, with some potential to distinguish himself, in addition to making it possible for him to return to the places he had first explored a decade earlier with Cook. And he could reacquaint himself with the peoples and cultures that had intrigued him earlier. The enterprise was an early example of Britain's plans for using state power to nurture and secure domestic commercial interests around the globe.

In April 1790, the *Discovery* was within weeks of sailing when Meares disembarked in London from his whirlwind voyage. His arrival was to change a great many things. The orders for the three-ship expedition to assert Britain's imperial interests in Pacific America were never sent, and the ships never left port. Meares brought his version of the events at Friendly Cove: not one but four British ships had been seized, and the Spanish seemed not to be backing down from their blanket claim to sovereignty over the entire coast of Pacific America.

WHEN JAMES COOK sailed into Nootka Sound in 1778 in the *Resolution* and *Discovery*, the dozens of people paddling around the ships in cedar canoes gesticulated with their hands and shouted, *"Itchme nutka, itchme nutka.*" What they were saying was, "Go around" or "Make a circuit" as they tried to explain that Yuquot or Friendly Cove was actually on an island within Nootka Sound and that the ships should go around to the other side, to the peaceful waters of the village of Yuquot. Cook misinterpreted their instructions and thought they were shouting the name of their home, and the name stuck. Nootka soon came to designate all the coast between San Francisco Bay and the Bering Strait, and this larger definition was the focus of the international attention in the late eighteenth century. Although Friendly Cove was a beautiful harbour, a respite from the rugged, wind-lashed west coast and ideally situated for a central base of operations, the struggle between Spain and Britain concerned the entire coast, not just the inlet. The historian Barry Gough writes in *The Northwest Coast* that "by using a crowbar at Nootka Sound, Britain hoped to pry open the sealed doors of the Spanish American trade. Nootka was not an end in itself but a means to something much larger."

In the eighteenth century Spain rigidly adhered to a world view that meshed nicely with the historical precedent stemming from the birth of its empire in the late fifteenth century. A few months after Christopher Columbus returned from his epochal voyage across the Atlantic in 1492, Pope Alexander VI proclaimed "by the authority of the Almighty God" that the Spanish monarchs Ferdinand and Isabella and their heirs in perpetuity were to have the exclusive right to travel, trade or colonize the new lands, and forbade "all persons, no matter what rank, estate, degree, order or condition to dare, without your special permission to go for the sake of trade or any other reason whatever, to the said islands and countries after they have been discovered and found by your envoys or persons sent out for that purpose." With the stroke of a pen, Alexander VI created an imaginary dividing line that ran down the middle of the Atlantic Ocean, through the poles to the far side of the earth, where no European since Marco Polo had ventured. All territory east of the line was to be Portuguese, and all territory to the west was to be the sole domain of Spain. The punishment for violating the papal proclamation was excommunication.

At the treaty signed in the Spanish town of Tordesillas in 1494, Spain and Portugal affirmed the papal decree but moved the line of demarcation between the Spanish and the Portuguese halves of the world several hundred miles farther west, placing an as-yet-undiscovered Brazil in the Portuguese half of the world and the as-yet-undiscovered western coast of South and North America in the hands of Spain. By the late eighteenth century, though, the moral and political force of the Treaty of Tordesillas had been seriously eroded: not only were the nations of Europe religiously divided after the Protestant Reformation, but Spain no longer had the military strength to enforce its claims. The ancient treaty, however, still formed the foundation of Spain's blanket claims to sovereignty over the entire Pacific coast of the Americas. During Martínez's ceremonial appropriation of Nootka Sound for Spain in 1789, he invoked the papal bull as the moral authority for his territorial claim: "by reason of the donation and the bull *Expedio Notu Proprio* of our Most Holy Father Alexander VI, Pontiff of Rome, by which he donated to the Most High and Catholic Monarch Ferdinand V and Isabel his spouse... one half of the world by deed made at Rome on the 4th day of May in the year 1493, by virtue of which these present lands belong to the said Royal Crown of Castile and Leon."

The other foundation for Spain's imperial claim to Pacific America stemmed from the concept of prior discovery, the notion that a land belonged to the nation whose agent first laid eyes on it or sailed past it, or some other ephemeral legalistic claim. In this instance, Spanish historical precedent dated back to Vasco Núñez de Balboa, who in 1513, after crossing the Isthmus of Panama, boldly strode into the surf, allowed his wandering gaze to search the horizon south, west and north, and promptly claimed it all for Spain, as far as he could see. Giving free rein to the imperial impulse, Balboa believed that his claim extended to the shores of all the lands that the waves should eventually touch—despite having no idea how far those waves might reach or the extent of the undiscovered lands touched by those waves.

Spain's claims to sovereignty over Pacific America, anachronistic even by late-eighteenth-century standards (the Treaty of Madrid in 1750 abolished the Treaty of Tordesillas's line of demarcation), were nevertheless secure so long as British interest, or Russian or American interest, remained sporadic and fleeting. The other British voyages that theoretically trespassed on Spanish domain—those of Drake, Cavendish, Anson and Byron—were piratical and infrequent rather than commercial and imperial, and posed no threat to Spanish sovereignty. This fragile and conveniently ignored situation changed with the sea otter fur trade in the wake of Cook's third voyage. Not only did the trade hold the promise of being lucrative, but it would also provide another market for the manufactured products of Britain's burgeoning Industrial Revolution. Britain's view of the range of activities that should be possible for its merchant adventurers was naturally different from that of imperial Spain, with its strictly regimented, government-affiliated notion of trade and travel and its archaic historical precedents for sovereignty.

British politicians, merchants and thinkers, following the increasingly influential arguments of the economist Adam Smith, espoused the concept of effective occupation and of the *mare liberum*—the open sea and free trade. Ships should be able to sail wherever they wanted, and blanket claims to sovereignty based on ancient papal proclamations, pronouncements by the head of a foreign church or Balboa's grandiose gesture were baseless and fanciful distractions from the reality of effective occupation. If British ships sailed the open seas and happened to come to a region uninhabited by other Europeans, as they did in Pacific North America, and then established settlements and commercial bases, as they also did here, according to Meares, then those outposts, harbours and coasts were subject to British dominion, or were at least open to free trade, unhindered and unmolested by the agents of other nations. Thus, if the people of Friendly Cove and elsewhere along the coast wanted to trade with British merchants, then Spain had no legal right to interfere. By extension, although unstated, the same argument applied to all regions of the globe, including the South Atlantic, where Spain also sought to restrict trade and travel along the coast of South America.

Neither Spain nor Britain seemed particularly concerned about the fact that thousands of people already lived along the so-called lonely and desolate coast—people who spoke neither Spanish nor English, except as a trade jargon, and who certainly had no interest in surrendering their independence to the smothering embrace of a foreign empire. Although the question of native sovereignty was raised briefly by the British statesman Edmund Burke in parliament, it was drowned out in the roar of patriotic rhetoric, and the issue dropped from view. The ideological battle was quickly reduced to a contest of pride and conflicting world views between the two pre-eminent maritime powers of the era. The struggle over Nootka, over Pacific America, represented two competing paths for the future of the world: one in which free trade and the freedom of the seas was paramount and another in which a much more conservative structure was championed—where the seas were to be regulated as imperial domain, where trade and travel were to be undertaken as a privilege, at the whim of or as a favour granted by the state, and where sovereignty was based on historical precedent. What hung in the balance was not the ownership of a collection of huts of dubious value on a pebbled shore on the far side of the world but the question of which world view, which civilization, would become ascendant.

SENSING A GOOD opportunity to gain public sympathy, Meares pressed a hastily written account into the eager hands of members of the House of Commons, desperate for news of these distant events. As a lieutenant in the Royal Navy, he was respected and believed; the extent of his gross exaggerations and his inflated claims regarding the size and value of his land and factory were not immediately apparent, and he avoided any mention of the fact that several of the captured ships were technically sailing under Portuguese flags. With theatrical flair and little regard for truth, Meares told a story of innocent British merchants and traders conducting their lawful business on the open seas, along uncharted coasts far from Spanish settlements, but who were unjustly assaulted by a violent Spanish naval commander. In Meares's telling, his ships and onshore premises, legally purchased from the natives prior to any Spanish arrival, were plundered and stolen by Spanish pirates who used them for their own gain. Meanwhile, British sailors and officers—British citizens—languished and died in a miserable Mexican prison. Meares claimed that the total losses to the Etches conglomerate consisted not just of the actual property seized by Martínez. More importantly, the losses included "great and certain prospects." There had been gross insults to the British flag, and poor Colnett's insanity was undoubtedly due to his brutal treatment at the hands of the Spanish. Throughout the spring of 1790, British agents reported an increase in Spanish fortifications and naval mobilization. As Bern Anderson has noted in *Surveyor of the Sea,* "these measures were ominous signs that Spain did not intend to yield and was preparing to fight for her position."

Not surprisingly, given Meares's account, Martínez's seizure of British ships and property incited a patriotic outcry in England. After Captain Cook's glorious exploration of the Pacific, they asked, how could the Spanish dictate where British ships would sail and trade? The Royal Navy prepared for war amid a public barrage of anti-Spanish rhetoric from an eager and supportive public. Meares's account, known as the *Memorial,* provided the juicy and dramatic ammunition the government of Prime Minister William Pitt needed to demand from Spain an "immediate and adequate satisfaction for the outrages committed by Martínez" and "full satisfaction to the nation for its insulted honour." It also provided the legal foundation to support Britain's claims by furnishing an example of "effective occupation" of the region that predated any Spanish occupation.

On April 30, 1790, the British cabinet ordered the mobilization of the fleet, and the treasury allocated £1 million for naval defence and the manning of the Royal Navy. On the night of May 4, there was a general impressment of sailors in all British ports. Even the crew and officers of the *Discovery* were ordered to join the press recruitment. Joseph Whidbey, Vancouver's long-time companion and ship's master, reported that at "AM 3 went with the Pool & began to Impress Men. 8 the pool returned—served grog (there being no Beer) to the Ships Company & imprest Men." The Royal Navy needed thousands of new able-bodied men to man the ships during what became known as the Spanish Armament. The Pitt administration was determined to crush any lingering Spanish claims to sovereignty over any region of Pacific America other than the territory it already occupied. Meanwhile, Spain itself prepared to defend the Pacific Northwest from the incursions of foreign interlopers.

The mobilization of the Royal Navy proceeded rapidly and smoothly and was truly impressive from a logistical point of view. Dozens of mighty ships-of-the-line and frigates were called into immediate action, and all the men required to crew them were somehow found. The number of mariners in the Royal Navy grew from just over 17,000 on salary in April to over 55,000 by September. Caught up in the chaos and turbulence of an impending war, Vancouver's orders were changed again. First his voyage of exploration had been replaced by a more muscular enterprise involving nautical charting, blended with a defence of British commercial interests in Pacific America; now he was to help unload the *Discovery*'s stores and provisions and then join the fleet as a third lieutenant on the mighty seventy-four-gun ship-of-the-line *Courageous*. Vancouver's patron, Sir Alan Gardner, left the Admiralty Board to take command of the ship, and Vancouver joined the ship's company in late May.

Responding to the overweening belligerence of Britain, Spain turned to France as her natural ally: they had been united for twenty-nine years under the Family Alliance of the Royal House of Bourbon. But France, in the early throes of a turbulent revolution that pitted reformers against the hereditary aristocracy, was unable to offer aid. Throughout the summer of 1790, the National Assembly debated whether the responsibility to declare war rested with the Assembly or with King Louis XVI. Revolutionary sentiment turned in favour of the Assembly, which then delayed for over a month and ultimately abandoned Spain as an aristocratic power unworthy of support. Meanwhile, the Dutch Republic sent ships to support Britain, and Prussia also pledged its support. Britain's superior naval power and secure allies had become a force that Spain could not defeat.

For months Britain and Spain played a game of brinkmanship— threatening, demanding concessions and theatrically manoeuvring their navies—as they argued for a compromise. In mid-October the British ambassador in Madrid informed the Spanish court that Spain had ten days to accept British demands, or the two nations would officially be at war. Spain could not afford a full-scale war, particularly against the might of British sea power. Although Britain did not want war either, it had much to gain from a symbolic defeat of Spain. Some

historians have suggested that Pitt and his ministers may have suspected that a war with revolutionary France was inevitable and were
"riding the Nootka wave" as an excuse to test and strengthen the Royal
Navy or to regain the international prestige Britain had lost after the
American Revolution. The historian Alan Frost, in "Nootka Sound
and the Beginnings of Britain's Imperialism of Free Trade," writes
that forcing a showdown over Nootka Sound was the perfect excuse to
deflate Spanish pretensions of sovereignty in the Pacific while British
national temperament was on side and that the tactic was part of a
deliberate long-term strategy by the Pitt administration. Vancouver's
unsurprisingly patriotic comment on the armament was that "the
uncommon celerity, and unparalleled despatch which attended the
equipment of one of the noblest fleets that Great Britain ever saw, had
probably its due influence upon the court of Madrid." The strategy had
the desired effect. By the end of October both nations had signed the
Anglo-Spanish Convention, also known as the Nootka Sound Convention, in Madrid.

The Nootka Sound Convention strongly favoured British demands.
It permitted the two nations to freely trade and explore "north of parts
of the Coast already occupied by Spain" (that is, north of northern
California), and guaranteed that any future settlements in this region
would be free ports. Although the United States was not a signatory,
the convention held significance for American merchants as well:
through a combination of geography, mercantile instinct and freedom
from restrictive trade monopolies, the majority of ships sailing the
North Pacific coast by the late 1790s hailed from Boston and New York,
not London. Newly freed from British rule in 1783, but denied access
to British markets, the United States relied on the sea otter trade as a
valuable source of income.

Meares and Etches were given a huge payout—less than what they
had asked for, but far more than their ramshackle establishment was
worth. Britain had succeeded in using its mighty naval power and
willingness to intimidate into a legal and moral victory over Spanish
sovereignty and the entire concept of the *mare clausum*—the belief
in the closed and heavily regulated global trade and travel that was
the Spanish Empire's preferred structure for the Pacific rim—and,

by extension, any similar claims by any other less powerful nations. It had pried open a crack in the gateway and moved one step closer to the global acceptance of the concept of the *mare liberum*—the free seas and the free trade that was associated with them. After the Nootka Sound Convention, the tide of the Spanish Empire was clearly ebbing, while that of the British Empire was on the rise.

Although the convention ensured that neither Britain nor Spain could claim sovereignty over all of Pacific America, one key point left undefined was the northern limit of Spanish sovereignty along the coast, partly because no accurate map existed of the region for the negotiators to use. The Spanish suggested Nootka Sound, while the British implied that 40 degrees north latitude (northern California) would be appropriate. Despite the terms of the convention that limited claims of exclusive sovereignty, Spanish naval exploration along the coast in the early 1790s increased, with expanded and strengthened fortifications at Friendly Cove, a stronghold now famous throughout Europe that Spain did not intend to relinquish. The British, however, still hoped to discover a northwest passage leading east into a great inland sea, a waterway that would be of inestimable value to global trade or that would at least benefit Britain's North American fur trade monopoly, the Hudson's Bay Company.

SIX

Discovery
and *Chatham*

———◈———

APORTRAIT FROM LATER in life shows Archibald Menzies with a stern, perhaps even disdainful, expression. His angular face, strong profile, neatly trimmed hair and sober formal clothing show him as a man of distinction and responsibility, a defender of the natural social order. Staid and ponderous, he was a respected medical doctor and briefly the president of the Linnean Society. In his youth, however, he had been a footloose, adventurous naturalist and surgeon in the Royal Navy. He had twice circumnavigated the world, had seen strange things and people on distant shores and had participated in naval battles of incredible violence, sewing up ragged gashes and amputating mangled limbs while cannons roared on the decks above him and men screamed in pain. But war was not his forte. His affinity for the natural world had led him on a different path, as a collector of plants on distant shores. For decades, he sailed the world locating new species and nurturing and studying them for his patrons, powerful aristocrats. Trusted, dependable and brave, he could also be prickly, stubborn and unrealistic in his expectations. He was never an easy-going companion.

Archibald Menzies was born into a family of middle-class respectability, in Perthshire, in the highlands of Scotland, on March 15, 1754. His father was a gardener and forester to the laird, who was a distant relative. As a youth Menzies was sent to the Royal Botanical Gardens in Edinburgh to study botany and medicine. These sciences were closely linked in the eighteenth century as botanical discoveries led to new and better drugs and improved agricultural practices. In 1781, Menzies passed his examinations for surgeon and apothecary, and after a brief stint as an assistant surgeon in Wales, where he collected plants on Snowdonia, he joined the Royal Navy as a surgeon. At the time this position in the Royal Navy was often intermingled with that of naturalist, and Menzies was eager to visit little-explored shores in search of new plants. After serving in the Caribbean on the ship *Nunsuch*, where he fought in the famous Battle of the Saints in 1782, Menzies was assigned to the *Assistance*, based in Halifax. From this region he collected many specimens; times were slow after the American War of Independence, and Menzies's commander allowed him a great deal of leeway in pursuing the activities of a naturalist.

At the suggestion of Dr. John Hope, his old botany professor in Edinburgh, Menzies began to send letters containing plants, seeds and precise botanical drawings to Sir Joseph Banks at the Royal Botanical Gardens at Kew. It was the beginning of a long and contorted relationship between Menzies and the famous and whimsical Banks. Banks would be a powerful patron, and Menzies strove to strengthen his connection to the famous, aristocratic and extremely wealthy botanist. After being thwarted in his attempts to make Cook's second voyage conform to his own objectives, Banks had continued his ascent in Britain's stratified society. He was intimate with such luminaries as Lord Sandwich and Philip Stephens, powerful lords of the Admiralty; William Wyndham, Lord Grenville, the foreign secretary, and even King George III. Elected to the Royal Society at the tender age of twenty-three, Banks continued to pursue his interest in and patronage of the natural sciences in general and botany in particular. A correspondent of scientific luminaries in Europe and America, he was often consulted about British overseas projects and was the king's adviser on the organization of the Royal Gardens at Kew. He had begun sending plant collectors to remote regions of the earth to bring him specimens for the royal gardens.

When Menzies's tour of duty in Halifax ended, he returned to London and wrote to Banks inquiring about the possibility of joining another voyage about which he had heard rumours. "I am informed that there is a Ship, a private adventurer now fitting out at Deptford to go round the World—should I be so happy as to be appointed surgeon of her," he hinted, "it will at least gratify one of my greatest earthly ambitions & afford one of the best opportunities of collecting Seeds & other objects of Natural History for you & the rest of my friends." Banks, who was aware of the voyage, applied his influence with the Admiralty to get Menzies a leave of absence from the navy so that he could join the private venture as a surgeon. During the next three years, Menzies toured the world with James Colnett, captain of the *Prince of Wales,* on a fur-trading adventure to distant Pacific America as part of the Etches enterprise, which later joined with Meares.

After landing at the part of the western coast that would become known as Vancouver Island, he spent considerable time at Friendly Cove in Nootka Sound wandering in the forests, aided in his botanical discoveries by the wife of Chief Maquinna's younger brother. In this traditional society, women were the most knowledgeable collectors and gatherers, with impressive knowledge of the properties of plants, roots and seeds. Menzies also spent two winters in the Sandwich Islands (Hawaii) as well as touring as far north as the Queen Charlotte Islands (Haida Gwaii). When he returned to London in July 1789 he went to work for Banks in the aristocrat's library, organizing his collections and classifying them. He was elected a fellow of the Linnean Society, and when he heard a rumour of the scientific voyage then being organized under the command of Henry Roberts, he eagerly sought the position of naturalist. With Banks's support and influence he secured the appointment in the fall of 1789, but the Nootka Sound Crisis and the near-war with Spain postponed the voyage.

Although he had remained on salary as a botanist and naturalist for Roberts's expedition throughout the Nootka Sound Crisis, Menzies was in a quandary when the conflict was resolved and the plan for the original voyage was changed. Should he wait for Roberts to be appointed captain of another voyage in a different ship, or should he try to join the *Discovery* under the new commander, George Vancouver? The *Discovery* had no formal position for a naturalist. "As a state of tedious suspense was more intolerable to me, than the hardships of a long Voyage... I requested leave of the Treasury to go out as a Surgeon of the *Discovery,* promising at the same time that my vacant hours from my professional charge, should be chiefly employed... in making such collections and observations as might elucidate the natural history of the Voyage." Rather than being bored while awaiting the possibility of a better posting, Menzies wanted to get going. Now thirty-six years old, he was not interested in settling down or in pursuing a mundane career. He was particularly anxious to return to the misty shores of Pacific America. Banks quickly began drafting a set of instructions to govern Menzies's actions and responsibilities during the voyage.

For unknown reasons Vancouver, who was responsible for choosing most of his officers, objected to Menzies's appointment. "The Commander of the Expedition made some objections," Menzies wrote, "what they were I never heard." Vancouver's objections had nothing to do with Menzies personally—indeed, his credentials for such a voyage could hardly be matched—but had more to do with the fact that he felt Menzies was being pushed on him against custom by Banks. In the end Vancouver appointed his own surgeon, Alexander Cranstoun; and Banks then had Menzies appointed as official botanist, at a higher salary. Menzies's official instructions annoyed Vancouver. Drafted and signed by Banks rather than the Admiralty, they essentially removed Menzies from Vancouver's authority while at the same time requiring Vancouver to bow to Menzies's demands on several points that were to become irritants during the voyage. The historian W. Kaye Lamb has observed that Banks's notes for Menzies's position, and in his official orders, state that his professional journal would belong to "his employers," that is to say, to Banks and the secretary of state rather than to the Admiralty—a seemingly minor distinction that was to have major repercussions.

Menzies's field of study was to be vast and comprehensive: "an investigation of the whole of the Natural History of the Countries you are to visit as well as an enquiry into the present State & comparative degree of civilization of the inhabitants you will meet with." He was to report on the climate, soil, edible and non-edible produce and vegetation and the location of coal deposits and other useful or valuable minerals. He was to collate zoological information on the many unusual animals and birds and procure specimens of new and inter-esting plants for Kew Gardens. Finally, he should be able to suggest locations for settlement, from an agricultural point of view, and note good locations for hunting seals and whales. It was a lofty objective for a single man stationed on a tiny ship with no safe ports at which to land, and working out of a makeshift herbarium on the quarterdeck. Menzies's orders called on Vancouver as captain to aid him in these tasks, not merely to tolerate them. Vancouver was to provide Men-zies with a boat and crew upon request for use in botanical collecting excursions, to supply Menzies with trade goods to ease his relations with the native peoples, to increase his ration of fresh water so as to ensure the robust growth of the plants in the herbarium garden frame and to issue commands to the crew to keep all dogs and other animals at bay.

The garden frame, an eight-foot by twelve-foot wooden frame with a flat glass roof, was to be constructed on the quarterdeck of the small ship, normally reserved for the captain. It was to be filled with flower pots and other gardening paraphernalia to keep the botanical specimens alive until they were brought to Britain years later. Not only did Vancouver suspect that the garden frame would be a nui-sance and hindrance—using scarce deck space that would be needed for the nautical survey equipment while cluttering his free strolling space—but the reverence with which the plant frame was discussed seemed to overshadow his own requirements for deck space to carry out his orders from the Admiralty—the original and far more impor-tant purpose of the voyage. The garden frame, he knew, was also the product of Banks's meddling; no other Royal Navy ships were so bur-dened, and Cook certainly would not have submitted to such an indig-nity (at least on his second and third voyages). "This frame was built from a particular plan of Sir Joseph Banks," gushed Menzies, "who in his great attention to this & every other accommodation showd such a particular zeal for the success of my department as deserves my most grateful acknowledgment." Finally, to add insult to injury, Menzies's orders contained a section specifying how Vancouver "should regulate his conduct to Mr. Menzies."

Near the end of January, Menzies visited the *Discovery* while its crew stored the last supplies and completed other preparations for the voyage. In the small boat that carried him out to the ship he brought a distinctive-looking young visitor: Towereroo, a sixteen-year-old native of Molokai, one of the Sandwich Islands. The lad had begged to be brought to Britain on a ship several years earlier, had sailed from China on the *Prince of Wales* (commanded by Colnett, with Menzies as surgeon) and had been a distinguished visitor in London. After being inoculated for smallpox, he attended school, taking language and drawing lessons. Now, although several powerful men of the city had taken an interest in Towereroo's welfare, he desired to return home. His patrons hoped his knowledge of English and his sailing skills would help British traders and the Hawaiians to develop better relations. Menzies brought Towereroo aboard at Banks's request. Banks, who wanted the lad safely returned to his home, charged Vancouver with the task. It was yet another annoying non-naval task imposed on Vancouver by Banks, with Menzies as proxy.

The developing quarrel between Menzies and Vancouver, two men of similar social standing and age who had a shared love of the adventure of sailing to distant shores, stemmed from Vancouver's distaste for Banks's meddling in the organizing and outfitting of what he believed was his voyage to command. No doubt it brought back memories for Vancouver of a similar altercation more than two decades earlier, in 1772, when he was a fourteen-year-old boy boarding the *Resolution* for the first time. Cook had just succeeded, after a prolonged struggle with a much younger Banks, in denying the lord the outrageous modifications to the ship that he had demanded to accommodate the unruly host of servants, savants and natural historians he had planned on taking with him on Cook's second voyage of discovery. When Cook's pilot refused to take the ship to sea with all the top-heavy modifications, Cook forcefully complained to his superiors in the Admiralty and had the ship returned to its original structure. In a huff, Banks had quit the expedition. The young Vancouver had witnessed Cook's triumph over the overweening demands of the rich and arrogant Banks and had no doubt shared the pleasure of the crew at this humiliation of the high and mighty.

Vancouver's first knowledge of Banks was of a spoiled aristocrat whose pushy manners "allowed him to interfere in matters which were the proper province of trained seamen." Thus, when he in his turn found himself in charge of an important voyage of science and exploration on distant shores, he felt Banks was again stepping on turf that was the province of seamen, not armchair voyagers. But here Vancouver made a serious error in judgment. In the intervening decades Banks had emerged as a powerful figure, whose influence extended into government, the aristocracy and scientific circles. He meddled where his fancy led him, and he was not accustomed to being challenged. Vancouver was not a celebrated mariner like Cook in 1772; he was a newly promoted lieutenant of middle-class upbringing and middle-class connections and family affiliations.

Vancouver's antipathy to Banks and Menzies bred an unorthodox relationship between them. During the voyage, Menzies always complained directly to Banks instead of following the normal pattern of conflict resolution on the ship. Secretly, and behind Vancouver's back, every little disagreement was amplified, taken out of context and transmitted to Banks in letters mailed along with Menzies's seeds and botanical descriptions. And on the far side of the world, in a luxurious study in London, the letters were collected in an ever-growing anti-Vancouver file. Banks was not used to being thwarted, particularly by his social inferiors. "How Captain Vancouver will behave towards you is more than I can guess," he wrote to Menzies, "unless I can judge by his conduct towards me—which was not such as I am used to receive from persons in his situation... As it will be highly imprudent of him to throw any obstacle in the way of your duty, I trust he will have too much good sense to obstruct it."

But Vancouver had his own duties—a seemingly endless series of tasks, meetings and decisions to finalize his orders and get both ships ready for the voyage. He had also suffered an attack of indeterminate illness while in London in February.

DURING THE SPANISH armament, George Vancouver had been posted as third lieutenant on the *Courageous* under the command of his erstwhile patron, Sir Alan Gardner. During the tense but uneventful months between the spring and fall of 1790, his ship had been engaged in manoeuvres in the English Channel and along the continental coast. Vancouver had proved to be an excellent lieutenant, and by September Gardner had promoted him to first lieutenant. When Britain and Spain agreed to the Nootka Sound Convention at the end of October and the ships of the Royal Navy demobilized, Vancouver was in a good position. Gardner, whom Vancouver referred to as "my highly esteemed friend," returned to his position at the Admiralty Board and brought him to the attention of other decision makers. Vancouver was ordered to attend a meeting of the Admiralty Board in November 1790, and he was confirmed in his command of the *Discovery* in December.

Vancouver's new assignment was similar in many ways to the aborted earlier voyage, where he was to be second in command under his colleague Roberts. He was promoted from senior lieutenant to captain and was to be Britain's proxy agent of empire in Pacific America. So far in his life and career, he had played an active role in historic events but never a leading or decisive role. All would change with this promotion. He was to be tasked with achieving objectives vital to Britain's imperial ambitions. Vancouver was understandably very pleased with his new circumstances. "The outline of this intended expedition was communicated to me," he wrote, "and I had the honour of being appointed to the command of it." He was thirty-four years old. A command of this nature was not only unusual for someone of Vancouver's social background but was also to Vancouver somewhat of a dream job—to follow to Pacific America in his mentor's wake while engaged in a multi-faceted expedition of national importance: reclaim British territory and restore British honour at Nootka Sound while pursuing more esoteric but fashionable scientific and geographical objectives. "At this juncture," he wrote, nearly concealing his excitement, as he did in all his official correspondence, "it appeared to be of importance, that all possible exertion should be made in its equipment."

The final version of Vancouver's orders for the voyage was much debated and changed during the early months of 1791 and did not arrive in final draft for him until March 8. He was to be both diplomatic representative of Great Britain and scientific explorer and surveyor. The first-mentioned general objective was to "acquire a more complete knowledge, than has yet been obtained, of the north-west coast of America." The first specific requirement of his expedition was to discover the location of any significant waterways that could lead east into the interior of the continent to collect "accurate information with respect to the nature and extent of any water communication which may tend, in any considerable degree, to facilitate intercourse, for the purposes of commerce, between the north-west coast, and the country upon the opposite side of the continent, which are inhabited or occupied by His Majesty's subjects." He was also to determine the location of any and all European communities or settlements along the coast "and the time when such settlement was first made."

Among his long list of responsibilities was the completion of a nautical survey of the coastline from about 30 degrees, around Baja California, to 60 degrees, around Cook Inlet in present-day Alaska. Vancouver was specially advised to search for an inlet around "Cook's River" in Alaska, and "If you should fail of discovering any such inlet, as is above mentioned, to the southward of Cook's river, there is the greatest probability that it will be found that the said river rises in some of the lakes already known to the Canadian traders, and to the servants of the Hudson's Bay Company... but the discovery of any similar communication more to the southward (should any such exist) would be much more advantageous for the purposes of commerce, and should, therefore, be preferably attended to." Canadian fur trader Peter Pond had suggested that a great river he had seen leaving from the western end of Great Slave Lake was Cook's River. Pond sketched a chart that showed Great Slave Lake as a giant inland sea extending west nearly as far as the Pacific coast. In December 1790, however, word had travelled back to London that Alexander Mackenzie had followed Pond's huge river to its outlet in the Arctic Ocean, not the Pacific Ocean. Vancouver's advisers should have known this information, but perhaps they were unconvinced or didn't want to give Vancouver any reason for failing to explore Cook's River. Vancouver was also instructed to search between 48 and 49 degrees for the supposed Strait of Anian, where a passageway might lead eastward and connect with lakes in the interior of the continent. How these goals were to be accomplished was left up to him, although he was advised to ignore all rivers unless they were navigable for seagoing ships. And, while spending his winter months in Hawaii, Vancouver was to employ himself "very diligently in the examination and survey of the said islands."

A point that was emphasized in Vancouver's orders was that he should "avoid, with the utmost caution, the giving any ground of jealousy or complaint to the subjects of His Catholic Majesty." He should be friendly and offer assistance to any Spanish ships and captains he encountered and offer to share geographical information with them. In his dealing with native peoples he was "to endeavour, by a judicious distribution of the presents, (which have been put on board the sloop and tender under your command, by order of Lord Grenville) and by all other means, to conciliate their friendship and confidence." All this work was to be completed by the end of 1793 "if carried on with a view to the objects before stated, without too minute and particular an examination of the detail of the different parts of the coast laid down by it." En route home via Cape Horn, Vancouver, if "practicable," might also consider surveying the western coast of South America as well, searching for the southernmost Spanish settlement there. The statement in the orders to conduct his survey "without too minute and particular an examination of the detail" was an ill-defined and vague statement—to what level of detail should he conduct the survey? For a perfectionist like Vancouver, leaving this decision to his judgment could have been either a warning or an invitation.

The final objective the Admiralty laid out for Vancouver's expedition was to reclaim the property of Meares's trading outpost and the British lands at Friendly Cove and "relieve" any British subjects still under the power of the Spanish crown, particularly any of the Chinese labourers Meares had brought to Nootka. Although this final task was ostensibly the main and most immediate objective of the voyage and ought to have been clear and obvious, the information provided to Vancouver was vague and misleading. British officials questioned Meares under oath for several days in February, and from this questioning the specific details of his and Etches's property were determined. Meares claimed that he had given "considerable presents" to Maquinna for his property, which was about an acre in size and included a large house, surrounded by an earthwork ditch and sturdy fence, that could shelter about thirty-five people. He also claimed that he had negotiated with another powerful leader, Chief Wickaninnish, for the right to build a similar factory farther south at Clayoquot

Sound. Meares's description of these buildings was unclear—not surprising, because he was essentially extrapolating and fabricating the extent of his establishment for personal benefit. Meares was playing a dangerous game, essentially attempting to defraud both his own and the Spanish governments. He was deliberately vague in his descriptions so that he would not later be caught in an untruth, and counted on the great distance between Friendly Cove and London to keep the truth from becoming known. In the end, his credentials as a lieutenant in the Royal Navy and his association with the politically connected Etches ensured that he received his "compensation" from the Spanish government and that Vancouver would have to await further details about the "particular specifications" of the land and structures that he was to formally receive back from Spain.

The first several months of 1791 saw Vancouver extremely busy supervising workers as they outfitted his ships, tested the rigging, masts, spars and sails, and stowed vast casks of food, crates of equipment and other provisions, including tons of trade goods and gifts for the native peoples he might meet. The trade goods, mostly decided upon by Banks and Menzies, included several styles and sizes of axes and many other woodworking tools, such as hammers and chisels, as well as shovels, knives and pickaxes; kettles, pots and pans; cutlery, scissors, needles, cloth, beads and other trinkets; and copper and brass plating and iron bars. Also included was a variety of fireworks, to amuse and awe the natives.

Vancouver also examined both ships, searching for latent deficiencies or problems in order to solve them while it was still possible to do so, in the naval yards before they departed. He was pleased with the lack of bureaucracy and obfuscation that commanders usually experienced in trying to secure provisions, equipment and supplies. "The Board of Admiralty," he wrote, "greatly attentive to our personal comforts, gave directions that the *Discovery* and *Chatham* should each be supplied with all such articles as might be considered in any way likely to become necessary, during the execution of the long and arduous service in which we were about to engage. Our stores, from the naval arsenals, were ordered to be selected of the very best sorts, and to be made with materials of the best quality."

In his official account of the voyage he listed much of what he ordered on board—items such as "a large proportion of sour-krout, portable soup, the essence of malt and spruce, malt hops, dried yeast, flour, and seed mustard: which may all be considered as articles of food. Those of a medical nature, with which we were amply supplied, were Dr. James's powders, vitriolic elixir, rob of lemons and oranges in such quantities and proportions as the surgeon thought requisite, together with an augmentation to the usual allowance, amounting to a hundred weight, of the best Peruvian bark." The unusually large quantities of Peruvian bark that Vancouver was anxious to secure may have been related to his own health—it was the bark of the cinchona tree, used to make quinine, a malaria cure. The debilitating sickness that struck Vancouver in February, that laid him low for weeks, was probably a recurrent bout of malaria contracted in the West Indies— the first in a series of disturbing illnesses throughout the voyage. He still hadn't fully recovered by early March, and only near the end of the month did he inform his superiors that he was "wonderfully improved."

The *Discovery*, at 330 tons, was slightly smaller than the ships used on Cook's voyages. It was about one hundred feet long and held a crew of a hundred, which included three lieutenants and six midshipmen; fourteen marines and a marine corporal and lieutenant; Menzies, the botanist; skilled tradesmen, which included a carpenter, gunner, sail maker, armourer, clerk, surgeon, quartermaster and cook; and thirty-eight able seamen. It was a lightly armed ship, with weaponry of ten four-pounders (small cannons) and ten swivel guns. The hull was double-planked and sheathed in copper plating to protect it from the teredo worm, which devoured wood in hot climates. Vancouver recorded that the vessel looked somewhat "unsightly" because of the "construction of her upper works, for the sake of adding to the comfort of the accommodations." But the ship sailed well, and the comfortable quarters for the officers, though ugly, proved useful on such a long voyage to distant regions. The *Chatham*, however, was a different story. It was much smaller at 131 tons and only fifty-three feet long. It contained four three-pounders and six swivel guns. Although the hull was copper-sheathed, it was only single-planked. The *Chatham*

was a sluggish and unstable vessel that experienced difficulties sailing
from London to Falmouth and had to be re-ballasted before her official departure. Her slow sailing speed was to be a constant irritation
on the voyage. The forty-five men aboard included the commander,
a lieutenant and four midshipmen, in addition to a complement of
skilled workers and one large Newfoundland dog.

The Admiralty allowed Vancouver the "honour," according to tradition, of selecting at least a portion of his officers and crew. Although
he was overruled in a few cases, and several men, including Menzies, were foisted upon him, mostly he made discriminating appoint-
ments. Not surprisingly, when selecting his officers for the *Discovery*,
Vancouver looked to his past years in the Caribbean on the *Europa*.
Joseph Whidbey was to be the ship's master, as he had worked with
Vancouver for years in a similar capacity. They had an excellent working relationship, and Whidbey's experience would no doubt prove
invaluable. The others formed a young trio. The twenty-year-old
Zachary Mudge, already with a decade at sea and service as a lieutenant during the Nootka Sound Crisis, was the first lieutenant, and the
not much older Peter Puget and Joseph Baker were second and third
lieutenants. Puget had completed an eighteen-month voyage to the
East Indies after leaving the *Europa* and was serving on the *Discovery* as master's mate during the Nootka Sound Crisis. He had only just
passed his exam for lieutenant in November 1790; Baker had passed
for lieutenant on December 18. The voyage not only represented a promotion for these young men, but it would also be a test of their abilities and potential. Although Vancouver was pleased with the number
of officers on his small ships, he was undoubtedly concerned about
their youth and relative inexperience.

Vancouver was also fortunate to have quality midshipmen, such as
nineteen-year-old Spelman Swaine, born in King's Lynn like his commander and experienced enough that Vancouver soon promoted him
to be master of the *Chatham*, and twenty-year-old Thomas Manby,
the senior midshipman. Descended from Norfolk gentry, Manby was
boastful and brave and not always in harmony with his commander.
Manby wrote a colourful narrative of the voyage from his perspective
as a young aristocrat seeing the world for the first time. Manby was

far more interested in beautiful women and unusual social customs than in diplomacy and the tedious minutiae of inshore survey work. His account is a lighthearted pleasure to read, compared with Vancouver's ponderous official account, weighted down with its view to posterity.

Selecting the remainder of his officers was out of Vancouver's direct control, since he had no prior relationship with any of them or their patrons. Nevertheless Vancouver considered them to be "men of known character, possessing good abilities, and excellent dispositions." Twenty-eight-year-old lieutenant William Broughton was chosen as the commander of the *Chatham*. Broughton had fought and been taken prisoner in 1776 during the American War of Independence and had served during the Nootka Sound Crisis. The recently promoted young Lieutenant James Hanson was second under Broughton, and James Johnson was appointed master. Like Whidbey, Johnson was an older steady seaman. Serving in the Royal Navy since 1778, he had toured with numerous ships from the West Indies to Halifax before joining James Colnett on the *Prince of Wales* on his commercial voyage to Pacific America, where he met Archibald Menzies. Johnson commanded the ship for a portion of the return voyage and rejoined the Royal Navy during the Spanish Armament. He was appointed to *Chatham* by John Pitt, Earl of Chatham, First Lord of the Admiralty, and Philip Stephens, secretary of the Admiralty. No doubt his past familiarity with the coast and the sea otter trade recommended him, but so must have his reputation as a seaman and his seniority among such a young cadre of officers. Lord Chatham made a specific request to Vancouver to promote Johnson at the first opportunity.

In mid-March 1791, with the crew and officers settled and the final preparations under way, Vancouver was paid a visit at Falmouth that he would live to rue. Thomas Pitt, the first Lord Camelford, a cousin to Prime Minister William Pitt and Lord Chatham, the First Lord of the Admiralty, brought on board his sixteen-year-old son Thomas Pitt, a tall, stylish youth with bushy sideburns, deep-set eyes and a prominent chin. Despite his youth, the junior Thomas Pitt had been in the Royal Navy for several years earning a reputation for fearlessness and gallantry. When his ship, the *Guardian*, hit an iceberg off South Africa,

Pitt was one of the few who refused to abandon ship, eventually pilot-
ing the crippled vessel into Table Bay. In a period portrait, Pitt looks
faintly ridiculous, decked out in a fine beaver top hat, a long coat and
a frilly poof of patterned neck scarf. Nothing in this portrait hints at
danger or volatility. The young Pitt was, however, also wild tempered,
arrogant and acutely aware of his exalted status, and highly sensitive
to any perceived slight to his rank. In a slim biography of Pitt printed
after his untimely death, the anonymous author hints at the true
personality lurking beneath the innocuous attire: "His eccentricities
exposed him to repeated disadvantages, without any evil intentions,
though [because of] the natural impetuosity of his temper, joined to
his very high sentiments of honour, he involved himself in a variety of
disputes... Unfortunately such was the violence of his temper, that on
many occasions he totally forgot what was due to his rank, and in the
moments of passion had recourse to the most violent measures."

The elder Camelford urged Vancouver to take his son on as a midshipman. Although no official midshipman berths remained, Vancouver bowed to the pressure to receive the youth as an able seaman.
Pitt's aristocratic status, his government connections and his family's
friendship with Banks all added up to a force Vancouver dared not
oppose. The young Pitt was not the first midshipman he had been
compelled to accept. Vancouver had also taken on Charles Stuart, the
sixteen-year-old son of the Earl of Bute, among others. In fact, nearly
every midshipman on both ships was the relative or protege of some
lord, admiral or politician. The historian Nigel Rigby, in *Pioneers of
the Pacific*, observes that "the proportion of well-connected midshipmen on this humble exploration ship was unusually high." Vancouver was faced with the same problem Cook had encountered: how to
diplomatically disengage or put off requests from powerful figures,
a challenge that Cook was able to manage more diplomatically than
Vancouver. The fact that so many powerful families sought out places
for their young sons also reflected the growing status of exploration
voyages in the wake of Cook and the dearth of other quality positions
in the Royal Navy during peacetime.

For the most part, Vancouver was pleased with his officers. The
sailors, however, were a mixed bunch, including some rough hands

who seemed bent on taking advantage of every opportunity to violate orders and hierarchy. Keeping order and preserving harmony was a prime role of the captain on a small ship crammed with men living in close quarters, under dangerous conditions and for a voyage lasting years. Vancouver's ships, although small in size and number of crew compared with the greatest warships of the day, were buffeted by crosscurrents of competing personalities, issues and interests. It was a responsibility Vancouver had never faced before, acting as a diplomatic intermediary between parties of various ranks without losing control. It was a skill that could not be taught as part of standard naval education, nor was it fully gained from experience; rather, it required a blend of observation and natural disposition. James Cook was a master at this type of leadership, at taking charge without ruffling feathers or prickling pride. Oddly, Menzies, who had Banks overrule Vancouver's objections to his own appointment, wrote in his journal of his belief in the tradition of a captain choosing his own officers and crew. He claimed that it was "an indulgence that ought always to be allowed on any similar occasion, as the success of an Expedition of this nature may greatly depend on the harmony & good understanding which is more likely to subsist among those of the Commander's choosing."

Before the ships had departed, Menzies complained to Banks that Vancouver was not being attentive to the proper construction of the plant frame on the quarterdeck, that Vancouver was neglecting this responsibility in favour of his other duties as commander. Perhaps, he suggested, Vancouver was even passively attempting to obstruct Menzies's efforts to fulfill Banks's wishes. As a result, and not surprisingly, Banks, in his subsequent correspondence with Menzies, instructed him to keep an accurate journal noting the instances in which Vancouver obstructed him. If Vancouver did attempt to obstruct Menzies in his duties, Banks wrote, "the instances whatever they are will of course appear as they happened in your Journal which as it will be a justification of you [it] will afford ground for impeaching the propriety of his conduct which for your sake I shall not Fail to make use of."

A cloud of anxiety was already shadowing a key relationship on the voyage. Under the threat of war with France, arising from the deepening French Revolution, the *Discovery* and *Chatham* were finally ready for their monumental voyage, after a year of delay and months of preparations. They weighed anchor and cruised into the Atlantic Ocean on April 1, 1791. It was, as members of the crew later ruefully recalled, April Fool's Day.

PART III

AGENT *of* EMPIRE

SEVEN

The Far
Side of the World

◄━ ◈ ━►

AS THE *Discovery* and *Chatham* pulled away from land, Vancouver paced the quarterdeck of the *Discovery*. Feeling the slow rise of the ship as it surged into the swells of the open ocean, he might have reflected on his prospects for the future. All must have seemed bright, for the moment: finally he was a captain in command of an important scientific and diplomatic voyage, following the lead of the master mariner Cook. Yet a cloud of uncertainty and apprehension may have clouded his musing on the future. How would he hold up as a commander on such a long and arduous voyage? How would his actions be perceived by the public, by his superior officers? Was he up to the complicated and intricate task that his country required of him? "The remote and barbarous regions which were now destined for some years to be our transitory places of abode," he wrote later in his cabin, "were not likely to afford us any means of communicating with our native soil, our families, our friends or favorites, whom we were now leaving far behind."

Other men on the ships voiced similar sentiments. The political situation in France had worsened, and Vancouver remembered leaving home under similar circumstances as a youth on Cook's third voyage, on the eve of the American Revolution. "These were," he remembered, "circumstances similar to those under which, in August 1776, I had sailed from England in the *Discovery*, commanded by Captain Clerke, on a voyage which in its object nearly resembled the expedition we were now about to undertake." In the tedious prose then coming into fashion—a style commonly favoured by the tongue-tied Arctic explorers of the Victorian era half a century later—Vancouver commented that "it was the source of inexpressible solicitude, and our feeling on the occasion may be better conceived than described." In short, he and his crew were feeling uncertain, insecure and apprehensive about their multi-year voyage to *terra incognita*. And well they should have been.

Although the *Discovery* sailed splendidly—the only annoyance being Menzies's cursed "plant cabbin"—the fact that the *Chatham* had serious problems soon became apparent. Vancouver wrote to the Admiralty complaining that "the *Chatham* was so exceedingly crank as to entirely prevent her carrying the common necessary sail, which in course infinitely retarded our progress; and in which state, it was self evident fact, she never would have been able to encounter the South East trade." He altered his plans to stop in Madeira and instead put into Santa Cruz, Tenerife, in the Canary Islands, which was much closer. The distance from Britain still took almost a month to sail. After they weighed anchor, Vancouver, Whidbey and Menzies went to meet the Spanish governor, Antonio Gutierrez, while the crew loaded the *Chatham* with twenty-three tons of additional ballast to correct her awkward sailing. The following day Menzies asked permission from Vancouver to go botanizing and took Towereroo with him to scour the landscape for unusual plants. Vancouver and Whidbey, meanwhile, went on an excursion to the nearby city of Laguna. The next day, Vancouver ordered a general ships' holiday, which according to his official report went smoothly and passed with nothing worth mentioning.

Puget, Menzies and others, however, noted an incident of great interest in their journals. Menzies relayed the particulars in a personal letter to Banks, who then passed it on to others. What Vancouver failed to mention in his official dispatch, although it became well known afterward—causing no small amount of embarrassment to him at being caught out in a deception—was a drunken brawl between members of the ships' companies and a Spanish shore patrol. While drunken sailors from the *Chatham* clustered on the wharf, waiting to return to their ship, an unnamed midshipman from the *Discovery*, probably the arrogant and belligerent Thomas Pitt, who was in charge of the *Discovery*'s shore party, began insulting and provoking the *Chatham*'s crew. The fracas degenerated into a brawl between the two ships' companies. A Spanish guard rushed to the scene to stop the riot, but he "inflamed the Sailors still more (for they have an unalterable hatred for a Spaniard)." When the British sailors wrenched his gun from his hands, the Spaniard screamed for reinforcements.

Vancouver and Whidbey, just finishing their coffee after dinner, leaped up from their table in town and rushed to the waterside to stop the fight. Neither was in uniform, and no one heeded their cries. A Spanish soldier slammed the butt end of a musket into Vancouver's gut and sent him flying off the wharf and into the water, where he sputtered and swam until retrieved by a longboat. Whidbey dodged the thrust of a Spanish bayonet, which speared a stone wall behind him and snapped. Lieutenant Baker, the only officer in uniform, was attacked and beaten over the head, and numerous other sailors were wounded. Midshipman Pitt and a few others quickly jumped into the water to save themselves and were picked up by the longboat that retrieved Vancouver. Although Vancouver wrote a letter of protest to the Spanish governor, Gutierrez responded that the British were to blame and claimed that if Vancouver had been in uniform, he could have controlled his crew and would certainly have been respected by the Spanish guard.

Word of the riot spread to London, where it appeared in the newspapers in a brief paragraph, probably supplied by Banks and based on Menzies's letter (which was sent to London at the same time as Vancouver's dispatch). Vancouver's patron, Sir Alan Gardner, reading nothing of the incident in Vancouver's report, assured his sister that her son, his nephew Robert Barrie, a midshipman on the *Discovery*, was in no danger. "The Paragraph in the papers... is without foundation," he told her, "as a letter has been received from Captain Vancouver dated the 5th of May... which does not mention a syllable of the matter, and if any dispute had happened between his people and the Spanish Inhabitants I am confident he would have given the Admiralty an account of it."

Gardner soon realized, however, that Vancouver was concealing the affair—a foolish and immature attempt by Vancouver to try and cover it up. He was still nervous in command and wanted to appear perfect to his superiors. He could not tolerate appearing undignified and not in control of his crew, and he must have felt that his crew had taken advantage of his leniency and betrayed him, because he seldom allowed such freedom again. Gardner was embarrassed and annoyed. Although Vancouver did not know it then, his reputation was beginning to be tarnished; people were starting to doubt his opinions and reports.

A few days later the two ships again sailed off into the Atlantic, heading southwest to within a few hundred miles of the coast of Brazil before changing course and recrossing the Atlantic towards South Africa. In the Age of Sail, pursuing a direct line to a destination was not normally possible, as ships were entirely dependent upon the whimsy of the wind for their power. The *Chatham* was still slow, despite the extra ballast, again frustrating Vancouver, who was anxious to move. On one occasion he displayed the temper for which he became so famously, or infamously, known. In a fury, he shortened sail on the *Discovery* and called for Broughton to row to meet him in the ship's boat. Then on the deck he bellowed at the young officer for not following his signals to increase speed.

This first outburst of Vancouver's "passion" was certainly not the last. It coincided with his growing medical problems. Shortly after leaving Tenerife, in May 1791, Vancouver had a serious relapse of his mysterious ailment. He was exhausted, impatient and frustrated with his dwindling strength. Menzies wrote to Banks about the incident, and Banks recorded that Menzies "Sav'd Vancouvers Life by putting him upon a nutritive diet when he thought himself within a few days of his dissolution by having adhered to a shore one."

By June 28, Vancouver had become so impatient and annoyed with the *Chatham*'s slow sailing that he communicated to Broughton that the ships should separate and meet up at the Cape of Good Hope. The slow progress made Vancouver nervous in his first command and inclined to rigidly follow procedures and directives, including those that had little to do with navigation. One of the policies always followed on Cook's ships was to cleanse the ship to prevent disease.

Accordingly Vancouver gave orders to the crew to swab out the store-rooms with vinegar and to light pots of gunpowder and vinegar to smoke the decks of the ship. The fires were to burn constantly for days, "to keep up a circulation of fresh air." The accepted theory of the age placed the blame for most diseases on malignant vapours and bad air. Vancouver followed the book, smoking the decks without moving the sick mariners. Though intended with the greatest concern for the health and well-being of his crew, Vancouver's excessive cleansing soon resulted in a disagreement with Menzies. Banks, who received word of the dispute from Menzies, wrote that Menzies "remonstrated severely against V's Practices particularly against the inhumanity of Smoking between decks while men in Fevers were laying there in their Hammocks & at last Prevailed."

When the *Discovery* entered the harbour at the cape on July 9, Vancouver was both vexed and pleased that the *Chatham* was safely at anchor. Broughton claimed she was a slow ship, but she had beaten the *Discovery* by a day. Menzies somewhat snidely wrote in his journal that it verified "the scriptural proverb that 'the race is not always to the swift.'" The *Chatham*'s early arrival was the start of a peculiar tradition that whenever the two ships sailed together the *Chatham* was slow, but whenever they separated the *Chatham* seemed to speed up and reach the rendezvous ahead of the *Discovery*. (Although there is no evidence to support the supposition that Broughton was acting the trickster in this phenomenon, the possibility is difficult to dismiss.)

The officers were billeted at Cape Town and received, in midshipman Manby's words, "a handsome reception" because of the Dutch veneration for navigators and Vancouver's past voyages with Cook. But although the gesture was gratifying and the lodgings comfortable, Vancouver nervously checked off the days, and then the weeks, as complications and delays prolonged their visit. Supplies had to be carted to the ships from a great distance over rutted roads, and both ships needed extensive repairs. Vancouver cursed the poor quality of the equipment he had been supplied with: they were barely into their years-long voyage, and already things were falling apart, including several new cables, causing the loss of an irreplaceable anchor. Shoddy equipment was to plague the voyage for years, causing Vancouver to later remark with rare sarcasm after the loss of a second anchor: "Such were the anchors with which were supplied for executing this tedious, arduous, and hazardous service... A loss of confidence in the stability of these our last resources, must always be attended with the most painful reflections that can occur in a maritime Life." Menzies, however, free from logistical responsibilities, was delighted to have the time to go botanizing ashore. "I am so charmed," he remarked, "by the romantic appearance of the mountains which now surround me that I promise myself some pleasant excursions."

Not until five weeks later, in mid-August, were the ships cruising again, this time towards the western coast of New Holland (Australia). Although it had not specifically been mentioned in his instructions, Vancouver wanted to explore this little-known coast "which in the present age appears a real blot in geography, particularly when we reflect on the many vessels that in this improved age of navigation have passed the meridians." But more prosaic concerns drew his attention from reverie and dreaming. Just after leaving the Cape of Good Hope, Vancouver's crew had started to suffer from severe dysentery, likely from contaminated vegetables, fruits or water. The sickness spread rapidly through the crew, affecting the surgeon, Cranstoun, and dozens of others. It left them ill for weeks and transformed life below the decks, barely habitable in the best of conditions, into a nightmare. One sailor eventually died, and Cranstoun never fully recovered. Vancouver asked Menzies to take over the surgeon's role temporarily in addition to continuing with his botanist responsibilities. The peripatetic pair had a strange relationship. Even while Menzies was becoming Vancouver's personal physician and a trusted and responsible officer, the two men quarrelled over the plant frame and Menzies's duties, among other things. And Menzies continued to send his dispatches, mainly critical, directly to Banks.

After a month and a half at sea under dreadful conditions, the two ships reached the jagged coast of southwestern Australia on September 26. "The shores," Vancouver wrote, "consisted either of steep naked rocks, or a milk-white barren sand, beyond which dreary boundary the surface of the ground seemed covered by a deadly green herbage." Here he began his great naming enterprise. He named the first uncharted promontory he saw Cape Chatham, after the current political head of the Royal Navy, then sailed into a beautiful clear inlet and named it King George the Third's Sound (now King George Sound) after the king. Spying a majestic mountain near the modern Australian town of Albany, he promptly named it Mount Gardner after his patron in the navy. During the next several years he would officially name more than two hundred geographical features—islands, inlets, waterways and mountains—many of whose names are still in use today. As they cruised south and east along the coast, Vancouver and Whidbey fixed the longitude positions of major headlands, scouted safe harbours and corrected the inaccurate details of existing charts. Menzies spent many days ashore, scurrying over the coastal terrain, exploring abandoned villages and collecting plant specimens. He met no people, but he liked the terrain. The "soil is light and good," he reported; "the country appears chiefly covered with wood diversified with pleasant pasturage and gently rolling hills of a very moderate height well watered in places by small rivulets. Whatever grows at the Cape would I am certain flourish here in greater perfection—in short it is a delightful country."

The weeks along this stretch of Australia were a pleasure for all. None of the surviving journals or letters from the voyage record any outbursts of anger or irritability on Vancouver's part, and Menzies makes no mention of Vancouver's recurrent health problems. Indeed Vancouver seemed to be enjoying himself, naming prominent landmarks, assessing the terrain and its potential, correcting the mistakes of earlier navigators (in a most humble and self-deprecating manner, apologizing for having to do it). On one occasion he and his shore party feasted on "oysters of a most delicious flavour, on which we sumptuously regaled; and loading, in about half an hour, the boats for our friends on board, we commemorated the discovery by calling it Oyster Harbour." The two ships explored over three hundred miles of coast until mid-October, when Vancouver called an end to his "favorite project of further examining the coast of this unknown though interesting country...with great reluctance." Contrary winds and lack of time prevented him from sailing further into the Great Australian Bight or exploring Van Diemen's Land (Tasmania). Despite Britain's recent strenuous arguments with Spain concerning land claims not having any validity in international law, Vancouver stopped to take formal possession of the entire coast in his king's name. The *Chatham* and *Discovery* then passed south of Tasmania, crossed the Tasman Sea, cruised back into the open Pacific and dropped anchors in Dusky Sound, New Zealand, on November 2.

Dusky Sound was a sheltered cluster of deep inlets that wound through mountainous, heavily forested terrain. Menzies, whose journal is far more lyrical and descriptive than Vancouver's official report, wrote of "the calm serenity of the evening and the wild hideous noises of the surf dashing incessantly against the rock and the cavernous shores." He also observed excitedly "a vast variety of Ferns and Mosses I had never before seen." The ships needed to replenish their stores of wood, water and fresh provisions and, most importantly, to brew spruce beer as an antiscorbutic. Spruce beer was essentially fermented molasses and spruce needles. Cook had brewed the lifesaving beverage in this very spot with Vancouver aboard seventeen years before. The men were overjoyed to discover fish in "plenty beyond description" and gorged themselves. Twenty-two of them were still suffering the lingering effects of dysentery.

Vancouver had a personal objective to meet in Dusky Sound. Cook had surveyed most of the sound with his usual minute accuracy, but he had left a small portion unexplored. Vancouver was anxious to complete Cook's unfinished work, and after probing the farthest depths of the sound he proudly replaced Cook's whimsical description of the unknown region "No Body knows what" with his own playful "Some Body knows what." Lounging on the beach after completing the surveying work, the small shore party discussed old times, and Vancouver regaled them with tales of his adventures. They then, according to Menzies, "drank a cheerful glass to the memory of Captain Cook."

Refreshed and in good cheer, the *Discovery* and *Chatham* hoisted sails and headed northeast into the Pacific, to rendezvous at Tahiti. The night they departed, November 22, dark clouds gathered ominously, the pressure dropped and a terrifying storm rolled across the ocean towards the tiny ships. It came upon them quickly and soon "reached such violence that every wave was breaking over *Discovery*'s deck." The ships could not be steered or controlled, as they pitched about like toys in a tub. "In this critical moment," wrote midshipman Manby, "I was sent below and to my astonishment found seven feet of water in the hold." The ship had sprung a leak. The total depth of the hold was only just over twelve feet, so having more than half of it filled with water required immediate attention. Vancouver ordered the men to begin pumping in order to keep the ship afloat, but the water in the hold stubbornly remained. As the crew were tiring and starting to despair, someone discovered that the flooding was caused not by a leaking hull but by clogged pumps. They cleaned the pumps and soon the water in the hold began to recede, but the helm was still sluggish. When dawn arrived, the lookout was stunned to see that during the night the ship had drifted into a mass of uncharted reefs and small jagged islands. "Had darkness continued two hours longer," a frightened Manby recorded, "the Ship must have been inevitably dashed to pieces." Vancouver named the group The Snares, "as being very likely to draw the unguarded mariner into alarming difficulties." They retain that name today.

During the storm the two ships drifted apart, so they proceeded separately to their rendezvous at Matavai Bay, Tahiti. Broughton steered the *Chatham* on a northerly course and came upon another island that did not appear on Cook's charts. He led a small party ashore in an attempt to communicate with the inhabitants, who appeared standoffish and reticent—not good signs when two strange peoples meet for the first time. Their relations were initially peaceful, but as several mariners ventured unarmed among the people, some incident, no one knows what, set off an angry argument. Broughton's men were attacked and fired shots in return, killing one man before they rushed back to their boats and rowed out to the *Chatham*. Before departing, however, Broughton took formal possession of the island and astutely named it Chatham Island—the second landmark named after Lord Chatham on this voyage, and not the last. He then cruised on to Tahiti without incident, displaying his own considerable navigation skills. The *Chatham*, which her crew derisively nicknamed the "dung barge," arrived on December 27. To everyone's dismay, no *Discovery* awaited them.

The *Discovery* had sailed northeast and sighted land on December 22. Vancouver noted that "the land being at a considerable distance from the tracks of former navigators" was probably not known and decided to investigate. He described Rapa Island, a few hundred miles south of Tahiti, as having "high craggy mountains, forming in several places most romantic pinnacles with perpendicular cliffs reaching from their summits to the sun." At the *Discovery*'s arrival dozens of canoes launched from the beach, and soon the ship was surrounded by hundreds of curious islanders. Once they felt that the newcomers intended them no direct harm, the islanders clambered up the ropes onto the *Discovery*'s deck. For most of the crew, this encounter was their first with non-Europeans. It proved an enlightening experience. The islanders were amused by the large Newfoundland dog, which when commanded to "fetch, and carry a Pocket Hendkerchief, their gestures and Acclamations, were unbounded."

Most astonishing to Vancouver's crew was the islanders' "dexterity in thieving." Lieutenant Mudge phrased it best: "Thieving every thing that could be got at, or rather taking as a matter of Course whatever caught their attention, not having the smallest Idea of the Fraud." Anything made of iron was of immediate interest to the islanders, causing them to gather around curiously, gesturing and trying to grab the object and escape the ship. Most amusing to the crew were the islanders' repeated attempts to pilfer very heavy items. On several occasions they tried to grab anchors, cannons or the anvil and became annoyed when they could not lift them. After a few hours of visiting, Vancouver ordered the *Discovery* back to sea and cruised to Tahiti, arriving in Matavai Bay on December 30, 1791.

Having been to Tahiti three times before—in 1773, 1774 and 1777—Vancouver knew well the island's charms. Not only were the people friendly, but it was an ideal location for repairing damaged ships and recuperating after a long voyage at sea. As word of the European ships' arrival spread, a chaotic flotilla of canoes rushed from the beaches to surround the *Discovery*. Always mindful of his crew's health, Vancouver immediately procured the makings of a feast, according to Peter Puget, of "Fresh Pork to the ships Company with Bread fruit Cocoa Nuts & Plantains, which we continued to do

During our stay & afterwards at Sea while it lasted." Other fresh foods for the sailors, who by now were undoubtedly weary of the salted monotonous fare, included chicken, pork, coconut and yams. Vancouver placed Puget in charge of establishing a small shore community of three large tents, an astronomical observatory and a large workshop. Whidbey, Vancouver's favourite (and only confidante), and Broughton, the second in command, accompanied their captain to meet the boy-king Otoo and pay their respects.

Vancouver searched the islanders' faces, looking for any of the people he had met in past years. One of the few who remembered him was Pomurrey, formerly King Otoo, who had abdicated the throne for his son. The old man regally approached the *Discovery* in a giant double war-canoe surrounded by a retinue of smaller canoes and was carefully brought aboard the *Discovery* in a hoist for a prolonged stay. Vancouver recorded: "He frequently observed I had grown very much, and looked old since we parted." At age thirty-five, Vancouver already appeared prematurely aged from the weight of his responsibilities and the ravages of his illness. Nevertheless, the former king was pleased to meet Vancouver again and promised his support in repairing and provisioning Vancouver's ships. Vancouver established diplomatic relations with all the other major chiefs as well. Bern Anderson, in his book *Surveyor of the Sea*, noted that the captain had "an uncanny faculty for sifting out the various ranks and relative importance of the native chiefs, and of treating each with the deference due to his rank and position." If only Vancouver had had a similar facility for understanding the needs of his own crew.

Matavai Bay was famous for more than just the hospitality of its people. Vancouver, and indeed all his officers and crew, could not help but be reminded of the shocking tale of another Royal Navy voyage, a story that had made the rounds in London just before the *Discovery* and *Chatham* had set sail. Two years earlier, one of Vancouver's fellow officers from Cook's third voyage, William Bligh, had anchored in Matavai in his ship, the *Bounty*. This voyage too had been conceived by Banks, to take sprouting breadfruit plants from Tahiti and ship them to the Caribbean, where they would, it was hoped, take root and provide nutritious and cheap food for slaves on the sugar plantations.

The task took longer than anticipated—Bligh had allowed his crew and officers extensive shore leave, and they refused to depart. They would not leave behind the women and the lifestyle they had grown attached to—not for a return to the brutality, meagre pay, danger and drudgery of the navy. The conflict between Bligh and some of his officers escalated into the famous "Mutiny on the Bounty." The story was fresh in Vancouver's mind as his ship pulled into Matavai Bay and as his men cheered and waved at the scantily clad women who held up coconuts and fruits in their canoes. He would need to be extra vigilant and restrict his crew's freedom to avoid a similar fate for his own expedition. So he made two unpopular decisions, which were to cost him dearly both personally and professionally, in prestige and in the respect of his men. First he issued orders denying his men shore leave.

For hardened sailors who had spent months at sea, who were more than a year's journey from home and with years of further voyage ahead of them, facing terrifying storms, possible shipwreck and disease, to be denied what a good number of these men in their short, harsh life lived for—momentary freedom from the shackles that bound them to the ship, a celebration in the tropical paradise of Tahiti surrounded by friendly and willing women—was a cruel blow. Undoubtedly Vancouver looked to the health of his crew in a physical sense, but somehow he overlooked or seemed not to comprehend their psychological needs. He provided them with fresh food and ensured they would have their regular allotment of spirits or spruce beer, but he would not allow them off the crowded wooden vessel to stroll the beaches and lounge in the shade of the leafy trees, to drink water fresh from a brook and to dally with women in privacy. Only the men on work duty at Puget's encampment would be permitted to escape the ship. Technically the needs of the men were being met— even exceeded, by navy standards—and Vancouver felt he was doing them a favour. But it rankled them that they were not given their temporary freedom and soured the visit to Tahiti.

Vancouver did, however, allow women aboard the ships at certain times. Midshipman Manby relates that "Love kisses, and delight were the recompense each tar experienced for traversing many thousand miles... our joys are not to be described at our quick transition from

the raging Elements we had long encountered." But the men nevertheless remained locked up on the ships, staring morosely at the luxuriant foliage and golden beaches, seeing the "beautiful Brunettes" with
"sparkling Eyes," powerless to respond to the women's "Reproachful
glances" as they paddled around the ships and beckoned the sailors
to the shore. The atmosphere on the ships was sultry and humid, particularly between decks, where fetid airs lingered and a breeze seldom
stirred. The ships rolled uncomfortably on the waves, with paradise
so tantalizingly close. The situation must have driven the men mad,
especially when Tahitian dignitaries came aboard daily and officers
were allowed shore leave daily. Another midshipman, Edward Bell,
asked the question that must have been on the mind of all the crew
and young gentlemen: "Why should poor sailors... be debarr'd those
recreations which they see every Officer on board enjoy?"

Taking his cue from Cook, Vancouver also ordered no trading
between crew and islanders until the ships' needs had been met. Trading would be strictly controlled by the captain. The reasoning behind
this was sound: the needs of the ships were paramount to the survival
of everyone and the success of the mission. Unregulated trading and
independent bartering would lead to an escalation in prices for the
supplies and provisions needed to continue the voyage. Vancouver
had experience with the drunken and violent antics of his sailors on
shore leave, as well as with the all-too-likely possibility of deadly conflict that would sour relations with his hosts and endanger the ships
if they were prevented from reprovisioning and resting. At least one
individual found Vancouver's edicts too much to bear.

Vancouver had issued orders strictly prohibiting any crew or officer
from allowing any metal objects or tools to be stolen from the ships—
the temptation for the Tahitians to steal metal was too great, and
metal was in short supply and vital for the success of the voyage. Midshipman Pitt evidently felt himself above such orders. When a beautiful Tahitian woman paddled near the ship in her canoe, he leaned
over and attempted to offer her an iron cooking utensil belonging to
the ship in exchange for sexual favours. Word soon reached Vancouver in his cabin, and he flew into a rage—Pitt had directly violated
two of his orders: not to trade and not to thieve the ship's property.

Pitt's insolence, borderline insubordination and quarrelsome nature had been irritating Vancouver for months, perhaps since the incident at Tenerife. When he heard of Pitt's latest disobedience, Vancouver snapped and ordered the young man seized and brought into the great cabin. There, according to Banks, who collected reports of the incident afterward, "in the Presence of all the midshipmen who were summoned on the occasion" Vancouver ordered Pitt to be flogged.

Certainly Pitt's act constituted insubordination, and Vancouver knew from his years in the Royal Navy and the recent example of Bligh that small acts of defiance, if not checked, became the kernels of mutiny. If he did not stop Pitt immediately and definitively, he risked losing his authority. Royal Navy ships in the late eighteenth century were definitely not floating republics guided by a code of human rights. They were harsh and violent dictatorships, where the lash and other cruel punishments were used to keep men in line and to compel them to perform dangerous or unsavoury tasks. Pitt was foolish enough not to realize that his actions placed Vancouver in a serious dilemma: his insubordination could not be ignored or passed off as a youthful prank; it was a serious offence in principle, even though the material involved was insignificant and the objective of securing a female companion was innocuous. An example had to be made of Pitt, and Vancouver, true to form, followed the book. A leader of Cook's charisma might have come up with an alternative solution or anticipated the problem and might either have changed his orders to reflect reality or have devised a less humiliating punishment. Vancouver ordered the lash.

A restrained Pitt was dragged into the great cabin, and the room was filled with the ranks of the other officers and midshipmen who were ordered to bear witness to the deed. Lieutenant Mudge, who had been charged by Pitt's father to keep an eye on him, offered to reduce the punishment if Pitt admitted guilt. Pitt refused, evidently believing that he had done nothing wrong. He was tied over a cannon, and a sailor wielded the dreaded cat-o'-nine-tails, leaving red, angry welts across Pitt's back. We do not know if Pitt screamed—probably not, given his nature—but the lash was not only a physical punishment. It was equally an exercise in public humiliation. The others in the room fell silent, uncomfortable in their complicity and bewildered by the turn of events. Could Vancouver not have found another solution than to flog a relative of the prime minister? But shipboard their social roles were reversed: Vancouver was king, and Pitt was second-class. Vancouver was grim and determined that henceforth his orders would be obeyed. He was the captain, and in the Royal Navy his word was law.

It was the way ships had been ruled for centuries. It was the way Vancouver had been reared, from his time as a young midshipman with Cook and particularly during his decade at war in the Caribbean. And it was the way other ships in the Royal Navy were ruled at that very moment, thousands of miles distant, all around the globe. He may not have liked it—he may even have anticipated the problems he would be creating for himself—but Vancouver knew that technically he was within his rights. Perhaps it was even his duty not to show favouritism to the high-born, to teach a lesson to a spoiled princeling who secretly sneered at Vancouver for his middle-class birth and upbringing, who showed disrespect for the Royal Navy. Although Vancouver did not lust for the power he held over others, he was prepared to exercise the authority of his office.

THE TAHITIANS' PETTY thieving of the ships' stores and equipment continued throughout the stay in Matavai Bay. Vancouver reported that several culprits were caught in the act and turned over to their chiefs for punishment, which usually involved having their heads shaved in public. As the ships were getting ready to depart, near the end of January 1792, after about a month's sojourn, Vancouver's leadership and authority were tested again. The first incident involved a stolen axe and some stolen linen. The axe could be easily replaced, but its theft hurt Vancouver's feelings because it was taken by Chief Moeroo, whom the captain had trusted to borrow the item. The axe was returned only when Vancouver threatened to burn Moeroo's house down and made preparations to do so.

The theft of the linen shirts was more a serious matter, particularly for Lieutenant Broughton, who lost more than a dozen, because they could not be replaced on the voyage. Vancouver flew into a rage and issued what Menzies called "thundering threats" to local peoples. He placed a choke halter around a servant's neck, roughly hauled him to the ground and threatened to kill him unless the shirts were returned. He madly swore that if they "were not brought back very soon, he would desolate the whole district & destroy all their Canoes." The people fled, and only after some negotiations were relations restored between Vancouver and his Tahitian friend Pomurrey. Ironically, although neither Vancouver nor his officers imagined themselves as thieves, they routinely collected water and vegetation, hunted game and cut wood without payment to local peoples. But as George Godwin wrote with great understatement in his 1930 biography, *Vancouver: A Life*, "if these simple islanders took rather too casual a view of theft, it might appear that Vancouver erred in the other direction."

Vancouver's final vexatious problem was the desertion of Towereroo, who had spent a lot of time ashore botanizing with Menzies. The young man had fallen in love with the daughter of Poeno, the chief of Matavai. First Towereroo gave the beautiful maiden all of his possessions, and then in the middle of night he slipped over the rail of the *Discovery* and swam the mile or so to shore and disappeared into the forest. Vancouver told Pomurrey that until Towereroo was returned, he would not distribute any of his parting gifts or give the promised fireworks display. Only after hearing this news was the sheepish young man eventually returned, without his clothes or other possessions, but with several canoe-loads of gifts from the local chiefs. Broughton persuaded a testy Vancouver to distribute the parting gifts—numerous trinkets and minor metal items—but he could not convince Vancouver to authorize the fireworks display. The shirts were never recovered.

Vancouver punished Towereroo by turning him out of the gunner's mess to fend for himself among the general crew, an act that further decreased his authority among his men. Menzies was repulsed by Vancouver's obstinacy in demanding Towereroo's return and then punishing him. Technically Towereroo's flight could be viewed as desertion, but Menzies felt it made Vancouver look like a fool to his crew, endangered his precious relationship with the Tahitians and showed no empathy for the fate of the displaced Hawaiian. The complete disregard for the young man's welfare was certainly against the spirit of his official orders to return him to his home, if not the letter. Most of Vancouver's crew and officers, probably all of them, silently agreed with Menzies's sentiment and wished that Towereroo could have remained on Tahiti with the woman he had fallen for, where they felt he had the best chance for happiness. But Vancouver always adhered to the letter of his instructions, fearing that leniency would bring him censure or reprimand.

As the *Discovery* and *Chatham* left Tahiti on January 24, headed north across the Pacific to the Hawaiian Islands and then east to America, it was apparent that whatever camaraderie and harmony had existed among the ships' company at the start of the voyage had vanished. The *Discovery* was not a happy ship, and neither was the *Chatham*. Relations between the sailors and the officers were strained; particularly problematic was the pervasive animosity between factions of the officers. The persistent violent punishment of a few bad men had spread disharmony and fear throughout the crew, creating a gloomy and tense atmosphere. Vancouver had made several terrible blunders at Tahiti, blunders resulting from his lack of experience and confidence. He so feared making a mistake for which he could be chastised that he stuck to poor decisions that had been made before the ships had departed Britain. He refused to make decisions that veered from the orders prepared by his naval superiors.

Unlike his first commander, James Cook, who excelled in the fluid decision making that was needed on a voyage lasting years and encouraged a social and professional network that sustained traditions and relationships, Vancouver was unable to meet the management challenges brought on by new and ever-changing situations. He preserved the command structure that served the Royal Navy so well on warships that operated in home waters, where protocol was established and bolstered by the presence of other commanders and ships took short-term orders from higher authority, an authority that was always visible, a tangible reminder of the hierarchy. In home waters, the duration of voyages was shorter between ports, and shore leave for the crew and officers a frequent occurrence. Vancouver was out of his depth, so to speak, when stripped of the web of relationships and customs that smoothed the operation of the Royal Navy. Afloat on distant oceans on the far side of the world, he faced problems and questions for which there was no established and expected answer; and the solutions to these problems did not come to him naturally, as they did to Cook. Vancouver could manage his ships and structure the incredible logistical difficulties of his expedition. He was a magnificently skilled scientific observer and a meticulous and talented marine surveyor. He even possessed an innate talent for diplomatic protocol with native peoples. But he did not know how to keep his crew engaged and motivated on this tremendously long and stressful voyage. He was unable to punish or placate the troublemakers without poisoning the morale of the rest of the men, and he did not know how to assess the relative severity of transgressions and mete out appropriate punishment so that justice would appear to be served. In trying to retain the order and authority that he occasionally felt was slipping through his fingers, Vancouver grew more autocratic and harsh.

Punishment on the *Discovery*, and to a lesser extent on the *Chatham*, sometimes exceeded the standard for the time. Life in the Royal Navy was a harsh life, but Vancouver's voyage stands out even for his era. Cook used to keep lashes to a dozen, or in extreme cases to two dozen. Vancouver ordered a dozen lashes frequently, two dozen regularly and upwards of three or four dozen lashes occasionally. A small cadre of repeat offenders brought the average up. Drunkenness, fighting and theft (usually of liquor in the ship's hold) were the most common offences and occurred with increasing regularity as the voyage progressed. Confined for months on end, as they were in the fetid forecastle, squeezed together and denied shore leave, reliving the same quarrels and disagreements with the same people daily, never out of sight of each other—is it any wonder that the men began to fight or look for relief through the ships' liquor stores? Vancouver was a stickler for regulations, and in many cases he merely ordered the standard punishment prescribed by the navy but without the benefit of the doubt or taking into account the type of voyage he was on.

Pitt's flogging in the cabin at Tahiti was a turning point for the voyage. Pitt never forgave Vancouver, and far from improving Pitt's behaviour, the flogging had the opposite effect: he grumbled about the captain, trod the border of insubordination, fomented dissent among the midshipmen and tore the social fabric of the ship asunder. His resentment and sense of having been wronged festered and created factions and undercurrents of challenge that Vancouver could not have failed to notice. Vancouver's response was to fall back on discipline and on the knowledge that at least, going by the book, he was in the right. Vancouver could not really have ignored Pitt's blatant flouting of his direct orders, and it is not entirely clear even with centuries of hindsight what he could have done to defuse the situation. He had a true dilemma on his hands. Someone of his social standing could not have come up with any perfect solution to deal with Pitt.

As the captain's fear of mutiny increased—and being in Matavai Bay must certainly have been an ever-present reminder of the possibility—so did the use of the lash to keep order. And Vancouver's relationships with certain of his young officers suffered. Midshipman Charles Stuart, according to the testimony of Joseph Banks, who wrote about it after the voyage, "soon fell into a Quarell with the Capt & never would or did make it up he always refused to dine with him & once only when they got tipsy together on the Kings birthday was at all familiar with him. He then took a Razer from his waist-coat pocket & shewing it to V. said if Sir you ever flog me I will not survive the disgrace I have this ready to cut my throat with—Mr. S experienced much inconvenience from the Captain's Revenge from the beginning of the Quarrell." Banks continued: "he was often sent to the mast head as a punishment for trifling or supposed offences & kept there an unreasonable time but his Spirit never gave way he did his duty to the utmost of his Ability & bore the injustice he received patiently."

Even accepting the one-sidedness and possible ulterior motives of Banks at the time of his writing, the account reveals the deteriorating morale and lessening camaraderie among the ships' company. All but one of the midshipmen on the *Discovery* refused to dine with the captain, in a silent struggle against his authority. It was a struggle that they could never win—one that would take a terrible toll on both parties. The historian Nigel Rigby wrote in *Pioneers of the Pacific* that "the issue, to these well-born young men, was one of 'honour' and it was destined to become a recurrent theme on Vancouver's quarterdeck."

The month-long dalliance at Matavai Bay was the beginning of a tide of anti-Vancouver sentiment among the ships' company. If it was a hell for the midshipmen, it was brutally isolating for the captain as well. Vancouver went for months without having companions, with sole responsibility for the voyage and with the constant knowledge that members of his crew disliked and disrespected him, and indeed would delight in reporting any failing or departure from his orders. During his ill-fated third voyage, Cook likewise had begun to crack under the strain of command coupled with his increasing illness. Although Cook's and Vancouver's voyages seem similar at first glance, Vancouver faced a different sort of responsibility: Cook had almost complete latitude to do what he wished on his voyages, with his primary responsibility—apart from his methodical voyaging in pursuit of geographical chimeras—to keep up the health of his crew at sea. Vancouver, in contrast, not only had the health of his crew as a priority but also had orders that were far more specific. Although he was reasonably free to pursue his agenda once away from Britain, Vancouver had to complete a long list of different, and perhaps even incompatible, tasks that were potentially of national importance. He had far less freedom to manoeuvre, less room to recover from mistakes or setbacks and less time to linger in port or to relax at Tahiti or Hawaii. This was not directly his fault, but he bore the brunt of his crews' disaffection. Ruled by his fear of losing control, he kept his men on a tighter leash than was necessary.

Vancouver was backed into a corner: he could not give in, yet he was too proud and insecure in his sense of command to try to heal the rift that had developed between him and his midshipmen and between himself and Menzies. Neither man had the confidence, insight or humility to admit he was wrong, that his actions contributed to the impasse that was corroding the morale of, and possibly endangering the success of, the mission.

Mappe Monde ou Globe Terrestre deux Plans Hemispheres, Jean Covens and Corneille Mortier, 1780. All the eighteenth-century geographical fantasies of Pacific America are clearly evident on this French chart; note the prominent Mer de L'Ouest, the great western sea, and the Strait of Anian leading to Hudson Bay. One of Vancouver's objectives was to prove or disprove the existence of these potentially valuable waterways.

ABOVE Callicum and Maquinna, powerful chiefs from western Vancouver Island. Callicum was shot and killed by one of Martínez's men in 1789 for swearing at Martínez over the Spaniard's trampling of indigenous authority. *(National Archives of Canada)*

TOP RIGHT Death of Cook at Kealakekua Bay on Hawaii, February 14, 1779, at the hands of an angry Hawaiian mob. Young Midshipman Vancouver was instrumental in negotiating the return of portions of Cook's dismembered body. *(National Archives of Canada)*

BOTTOM RIGHT *Spanish Insult to the British Flag at Nootka Sound.* This 1791 engraving aroused a patriotic outcry with its depiction of Don Esteban Martínez's imprisonment of Captain James Colnett and the seizure of British merchant ships. *(National Archives of Canada)*

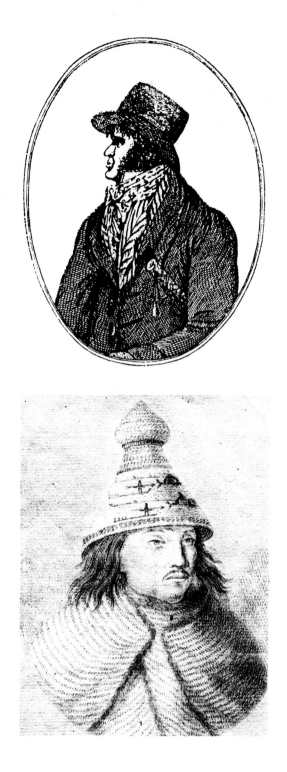

TOP LEFT Thomas Pitt, the "half-mad lord" who despised his captain, Vancouver, challenged him to a duel and used his influence and money to destroy Vancouver's reputation.

BOTTOM LEFT Chief Maquinna of the Mowachaht people of Nootka Sound. For several decades he was the greatest chief in the region, negotiating with Vancouver and Quadra and coordinating the fur trade with merchants from many nations.

ABOVE Lieutenant John Meares, the flamboyant adventurer whose exaggerated claims nearly caused an international war. (*National Archives of Canada*)

ABOVE View of native fishermen and a settlement in Port Dick, near Cook's Inlet, Alaska, from Vancouver's *Voyage of Discovery*.

RIGHT The interior of one of the great cedar longhouses of Nootka Sound, by John Webber, artist on Cook's third voyage, c. 1778. *(National Archives of Canada)*

BELOW A host of native canoes launching from the shore in Cook's Inlet, Alaska, from *Voyage of Discovery*. Cook thought the inlet might be the entrance to a great river or waterway and Vancouver was annoyed to find it blocked. Navigating through the chunks of ice was a "very irksome and tedious task."

RIGHT The *Discovery* on the Rocks in Queen Charlotte Sound, engraving from a sketch by Zachary Mudge, from *Voyage of Discovery*.

M.S. del. J.N.Fitch lith.

Vincent Brooks Day & Son Lith Imp.

L. Reeve & Co London.

REUNION DE LOS CAPITANES BODEGA-QUADRA y VANCOUVER
28 Agosto de 1792
NOOTKA CONVENTION CONFERENCE
Donated by the Government of Spain 1957

TOP LEFT British, American and Spanish ships anchored in Friendly Cove with the Spanish settlement in the background, c. 1790s.

BOTTOM LEFT The Pacific Madrone or western arbutus tree. It was first classified by Archibald Menzies, hence the Latin name, *Arbutus menziesii*.

ABOVE Stained glass window in the church at Friendly Cove depicting the 1792 meeting of Vancouver and Quadra. The window was a gift from the Spanish government in 1957.

BELOW *Exploring an Island in Pacific America*, engraving from a sketch by John Sykes, from *Voyage of Discovery*.

RIGHT *The Caneing on Conduit Street*, etching by James Gillray, October 1, 1796. Gillray painted the terminally ill Vancouver as a cringing, overweight, corrupt coward, shrinking from an onslaught from the imperious Lord Camelford, the erstwhile midshipman Thomas Pitt. The cartoon made Vancouver a laughingstock and had a devastating impact on his career, legacy and health.

CANEING in Conduit Street. — Dedicated to the Flag Officers of the British Navy.

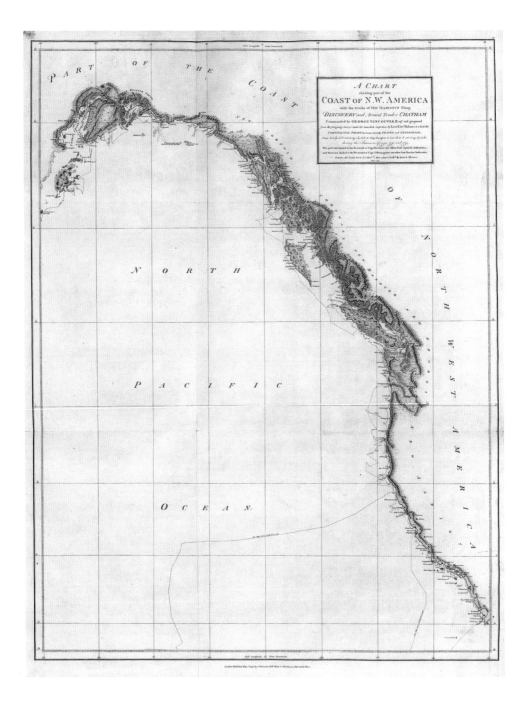

A CHART
shewing part of the
COAST OF N.W. AMERICA
with the tracks of HIS MAJESTY'S Sloop
DISCOVERY and Armed Tender CHATHAM
Commanded by GEORGE VANCOUVER Esq.r and prepared
from the foregoing charges under his immediate inspection by Lieut.t Jos.h Baker; in which the
CONTINENTAL SHORE has been correctly TRACED and DETERMINED.
From Lat.de 52°N and Long.de 232°E to Cape Douglas in Lat.de 60°N and Long.de 207½°E
during the Summers of 1792, 1793 and 1794.
The parts not shaded to the Eastward of Cape Decision are taken from Spanish Authorities,
and those not shaded to the Westward of Cape D'Enragement are taken from Russian Authorities
Drawn the Tylish Cost. Drasher? [illegible] [illegible] by Aaron Arrowsmith.

PART   OF   THE   COAST   OF   NORTH   WEST   AMERICA

NORTH

PACIFIC

OCEAN

London Published May 1798 by J Edwards Pall Mall & G Robinson Pater noster Row.

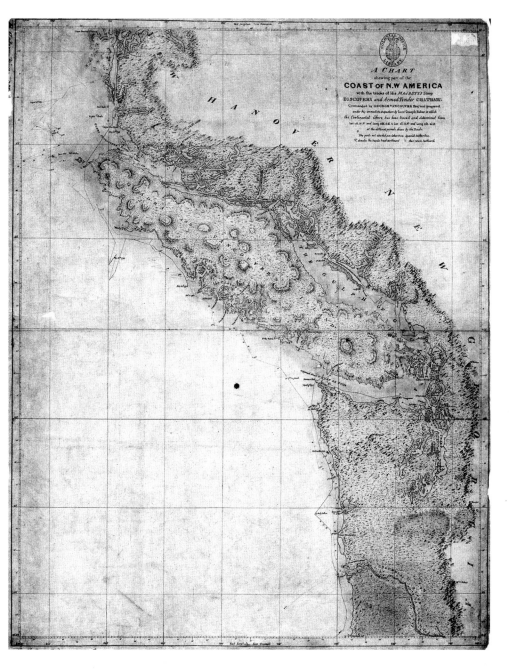

LEFT Vancouver's overview map of the entire coast of Pacific America, from *Voyage of Discovery.*

ABOVE Detail from Vancouver's monumental chart showing the intricate coastal geography of Puget Sound and Vancouver Island. The Columbia River is shown at the bottom.

A

VOYAGE of DISCOVERY

TO THE

NORTH PACIFIC OCEAN,

AND

ROUND THE WORLD;

IN WHICH THE COAST OF NORTH-WEST AMERICA HAS BEEN CAREFULLY
EXAMINED AND ACCURATELY SURVEYED.

Undertaken by HIS MAJESTY's Command,

PRINCIPALLY WITH A VIEW TO ASCERTAIN THE EXISTENCE OF ANY
NAVIGABLE COMMUNICATION BETWEEN THE

North Pacific and North Atlantic Oceans;

AND PERFORMED IN THE YEARS

1790, 1791, 1792, 1793, 1794, and 1795,

IN THE

DISCOVERY SLOOP OF WAR, AND ARMED TENDER CHATHAM,

UNDER THE COMMAND OF

CAPTAIN GEORGE VANCOUVER.

IN THREE VOLUMES.

VOL. I.

LONDON:
PRINTED FOR G. G. AND J. ROBINSON, PATERNOSTER-ROW;
AND J. EDWARDS, PALL-MALL.

1798.

Title page of Vancouver's *Voyage of Discovery to the North Pacific Ocean
and Round the World*, published in 1798, several months after the author's
death at age forty.

EIGHT

The
Greatest Marine Survey
of All Time

———◄◈►———

O MAP A PLACE is to exercise control over it. Creating a map of a region imparts a certain knowledge
of it that is unknown perhaps even to the region's
rulers. It bestows power and implies political jurisdiction. In George
Vancouver's time, maps were coveted documents that contained
national secrets, the key to trade and conquest, to the management
of empires and the control of peoples. In the age of colonial conquest,
increasing global trade and exploration, accurate maps represented
power and wealth. Although many cartographers were curious about
the scientific principles at work in the universe, the workings of the
solar system and the general pursuit of knowledge, much of their work
was funded by rulers with more prosaic intentions—accurate maps
were a tool of imperial domination that paved the way for conquest,
commerce, the building of roads, canals and railways and, ultimately,
settlement. The cartographic work of the eighteenth century was a
powerful tool in the colonial expansion of Europe and the spread of
western civilization.

By the eighteenth century, improvements in scientific instruments
and methods, such as the telescope, logarithmic tables and the mathematical method of triangulation, combined with the reports of hundreds of voyages of discovery and their rudimentary astronomical
observations, led to greatly improved knowledge of the geography of

the world. Yet cartographers' charts were still grossly distorted and frequently contradictory, particularly those for Pacific America. There the discovery of a northwest passage, an imperial dream of Britain since Francis Drake's discoveries in the sixteenth century, was one of the goals of Vancouver's voyage. Although Cook's explorations hinted that this passage might exist only in the realm of fantasy, a detailed and exhaustive survey was required to confirm these suspicions. The rumours had been too frequently contradicted by the shadowy claims of explorers and the unreliable boasting of contemporary traders.

It was with a mixture of relief and apprehension that after more than a year at sea, on April 18, 1792, the *Discovery* and *Chatham* beheld the coast of the land that was the primary focus of their voyage: Pacific America. Near Cape Mendocino on the California coast, north of present-day San Francisco, the ships sailed under a grey sky in the teeth of a violent gale. They pitched in the undulating surf, corkscrewing dangerously near the uncharted shore, which was obscured by sheets of sleet and pelting rain. Monstrous plumes of spray erupted from reefs in the distance, and fog clung to the steeply rising mountains. The scene must have seemed like old times to Vancouver, remembering a similar voyage with Cook along the same coast a decade earlier. Not much else had changed since Cook's voyage, either—despite the annual visits of fur traders, the Pacific Northwest coast remained as wild and unknown to Europeans as it had been in Cook's time; merchants interested in immediate profits had spent little time charting the coast and even less time sharing geographical information with each other. But Vancouver was here to change that state of affairs. After riding out the storm, the sailors awoke to the sun shining over a placid Pacific Ocean. Vancouver eagerly set to his appointed task of exploring and charting the coast of Pacific America.

A hydrographic survey of this wild and largely unknown coast at the end of the eighteenth century involved a seemingly endless series of astronomical observations, compass bearings and depth soundings. In the three weeks before making the expedition's first landfall on the western coast of North America, Vancouver and his crew took eighty-five sets of lunar observations to determine their longitude and establish an accurate starting point for the survey. Both the *Discovery* and the *Chatham* then headed north along the coast. Given the predominantly unbroken coastline from northern California through Oregon and Washington, the early part of the survey was carried out briskly as the ships tracked north several miles offshore, coming closer during the day and standing off at night. Vancouver had little reason to expect a major waterway along this stretch of the continent, especially in view of the mountains that ran parallel to the coast not far inland. He hoped to explore the alleged Strait of Anian before the winter storms began, and his scheduled rendezvous in Friendly Cove brought an end to the summer surveying season. Even so, he kept a detailed record of course and distance. The officers took numerous compass bearings of headlands and other prominent features from successive positions of the ship, which then could be plotted against the ship's course. The information was compiled on charts in large part by Lieutenant Baker, under Vancouver's supervision. The meticulous chart makers filled in the coastline between prominent features by sketching what they saw and estimating distances.

The two ships coasted north for eleven days, until April 29, when Vancouver spied the sails of another ship on the horizon. As they neared the vessel it fired a cannon, a sign that the captain wished to stop and parley. "This was a great novelty," Vancouver wrote, "not having seen any vessel but our consort, during the last eight months. She soon hoisted the American colours, and fired a gun to leeward. At six we spoke to her. She proved to be Mr. Robert Gray, belonging to Boston." The vessel was the *Columbia*, and Gray was the one-eyed Boston pioneer of the American sea otter trade, one of the first American traders along the Pacific Northwest coast. Financially backed by Joseph Barrell and Associates, he had set out from Boston in September 1787, three years after Cook's journals were posthumously published, and had spent three years prowling for pelts before returning to America via China. His was the first recorded American expedition to circumnavigate the globe, and in keeping with the spirit of the new republic the voyage was a commercial venture rather than a government-sponsored mission, as Cook's and Vancouver's voyages were. A year later, in 1791, Gray had set out from Boston on his second trading voyage, and it was then that he met Vancouver on the Oregon coast.

Vancouver and his men had not observed anything unusual on their coastal journey thus far, so when they encountered Gray, they were delighted. Gray was one of the most knowledgeable people sailing the coast at the time and could aid them in their cartographic quest. Gray, however, refused the invitation to join Vancouver on the decks of *Discovery*. Perhaps he was still wary, after the American Revolution, of boarding a British warship. Even though the war was over, he and his men remembered when the ships of the Royal Navy would detain and board American ships to impress any sailors who had been born in Britain. Many of Gray's crew, although American by choice, had been born on the other side of the Atlantic. Vancouver, however, felt it would be undignified to board the *Columbia*, so he sent Lieutenant Puget and Menzies in his stead. Even though he was frequently irritated with Menzies, the captain recognized the Scottish botanist's capacity for clear thinking under pressure and valued him as one of his most responsible men. Gray candidly informed Puget and Menzies that he had found the mouth of a large river south of their present location. He had been searching for the great river on both his voyages in spite of the prevailing belief, after Cook's voyage, that it was a grand myth. Gray had named the river the Columbia, he said, after his ship, and suspected that it would be the perfect spot for a trading post.

Although Vancouver and his officers had indeed observed the mouth of a river, it was obscured by monstrous breakers, and Vancouver had not thought it worth investigating. Gray informed Puget and Menzies that he thought the river was a major one and worth exploring, but Vancouver had no wish to backtrack. Vancouver secretly scoffed at Gray's report—not only did it contradict his own findings earlier in the season (he had dismissed an inlet in the same vicinity as "not worthy of more attention" despite the fact that "the sea had changed from its natural, to river coloured water"), but it also challenged Cook's earlier claims as well as the opinion of another British captain he had conferred with, the fur trader James Meares. "We can now with safety assert," pronounced Meares, "that no such river... exists as laid down in the Spanish charts." Meares and Cook were gentlemen of the Royal Navy; Gray was an untutored Yankee profiteer;

and Vancouver, despite his charitable reputation, was a product of the Royal Navy. Uneducated merchants, particularly ex-colonials, did not rank highly in the navy's social hierarchy. Vancouver, always the gentleman, politely listened to the report of Gray's claims but maintained his own ideas. He had been ordered not to bother with waterways and inlets not navigable to ocean-going ships, so he gave them no more thought, once again following his orders to the letter.

Gray laughed when Puget and Menzies told him that Meares had claimed that Gray had circumnavigated a great island to the east of Nootka Sound. All rubbish, claimed the Yankee skipper. He had cautiously edged into a strait for about fifty miles but found it to be poor territory for sea otters and left. "It is not possible to conceive any one to be more astonished than was Mr. Gray, on his being made acquainted that his authority had been quoted, and the track pointed out that he had been said to have made in the sloop *Washington*. In contradiction to which, he assured the officers that he had penetrated only 50 miles into the straits in question." Gray confirmed that the "supposed Strait of Juan de Fuca" did exist, but where it led no one yet knew. Other traders had entered the waterway, but none had explored it. Reports from the native peoples who lived along the coast suggested that it led to a giant inland sea, which went against Cook's opinions but could certainly not be ignored, given the potential significance of such a body of water. Vancouver, showing his loyalty to Cook, maintained his disbelief until he had actually seen the inlet. Later that very day the *Discovery* and *Chatham* entered the strait, sailing around Cape Flattery and passing a large native village. Vancouver had passed the cape before, in 1778 with Cook, but their ship had been blown away from the coast during a storm, and they had missed seeing the east-leading entrance into what are today known as Puget Sound and the Strait of Georgia.

As Vancouver's ships now cautiously sailed east into the strait, the men stared at the wild and majestic coastline, previously thought to be a myth. According to Lieutenant Manby's somewhat romantic description, "it had more the aspect of enchantment than reality; with silent admiration each discerned the beauties of nature, and naught was heard on board but expressions of delight murmured from many tongues. Imperceptively our Bark skimmed over the glassy surface of the deep, about three Miles an hour, a gentle breeze swelled the lofty Canvass whilst all was calm below." They passed several native villages whose fishermen paid them no attention—sure evidence that the sight of European ships was no longer a novelty. Great multitudes of birds filled the air, "vast flights of waterfowl... Auks, Divers, Ducks and Wild Geese." A day after entering the fabled strait, the mariners spied, floating high above a bank of obscuring cloud, a mighty, snow-encrusted, cone-shaped mountain, still daunting and overwhelming from a distance of over sixty miles. Vancouver named it Mount Baker after his young lieutenant.

IT SOON BECAME evident that surveying the bewildering network of inlets, islands, coves, channels, sounds and straits here and farther north would have to be done from the ships' smaller boats. Although the *Chatham* was much smaller than the *Discovery*, even it was too large to safely navigate the uncharted and potentially dangerous inlets that snaked inland. Vancouver wrote that he "became thoroughly convinced that our boats alone could enable us to acquire correct or satisfactory information regarding this broken country" and quickly established a routine that would vary little for the rest of the expedition. Once the ships had found a safe anchorage, where an observatory could be set up on shore, the boats, typically under the command of Lieutenants James Johnstone and Joseph Whidbey or even Vancouver himself, would set out to explore adjacent parts of the shoreline. The small boats, carrying perhaps seventeen people each, were provisioned for a fixed period, usually ten days or a fortnight, and carried arms as well as goods for barter with any natives the crews might encounter.

It was not always a happy time for most of Vancouver's men. They bore the brunt of the work as, from daybreak to dark, they sailed or rowed small boats into every inlet and narrow passage considered too treacherous for the larger ships to navigate. Vancouver drove his men relentlessly, perhaps even cruelly in his quest for perfection, although he frequently joined them on these exhausting forays. Over three summer survey seasons the men covered more than 10,000 miles in small boats in "these lonely regions" and delineated over 1,700 miles of coastline, including the intricate, island-studded Inside Passage. On one morale-crushing foray, they rowed more than 800 miles in just twenty-three days—to cover just 60 miles of coastline.

When it rained—and it rained often—the officers slept in tents, while the men "had no other shelter but what they formed by the Boat Sails which were found very inadequate to screen them from the inclemency of such boisterous weather and such deluge of rain." By the second summer they had rigged awnings for the survey boats. There was little respite from the elements or from Vancouver's frequently rigid manner. Menzies recorded on one occasion that "the weather was now become so cold wet & uncomfortable that the men were no longer able to endure the fatiguing hardships of distant excursions in open boats exposed to the cold rigorous blasts of a high northern situation with dreary snowy mountains on every side, performing toilsome labor on their Oars in the day, & alternately watching for their own safety at night, with no other Couch to repose upon than the Cold Stony Beach of the wet mossy Turf in damp woody situations... enduring at times the tormenting pangs both hunger & thirst." On one foray, they ran out of provisions and instead ate fish and crows, augmented by wild berries and onions. Puget recorded his relief that his men "were not averse to eating Crows of which we could always procure plenty." Vancouver himself took his turn in the open boats, toiling and suffering alongside his men. He could not be faulted for shirking the difficult work.

All was not tedium, however. The men occasionally caught fresh fish in nets and routinely purchased fish from the native fishermen who rowed out to the ships and boats. Midshipman Bell recorded that "the land in the Southernmost parts of the streights was in several places exceedingly pleasant, there were many extensive plains where the soil was extremely rich and the verdure luxurious. Gooseberrys, Currants, Raspberrys & Strawberries were all tasted. Onions were to be got almost everywhere, as was also Samphire and a plant call'd by the Sailors Fat-hen, both of which when boiled eat remarkably well, the former being not unlike French Beans and the latter but little inferior to Spinach." The scenery was grand, with monstrous trees—the largest the men had ever seen—numerous mountainous islets and great snowy peaks to the east, some jutting abruptly from the water and others, more distant, soaring to more than 9,800 feet in height. Menzies poetically observed: "A traveller wandering over these unfrequented Plains is regaled with a salubrious and vivifying air impregnated with the balsamic fragrance... the softer beauties of the Landscape are harmoniously blended in majestic grandeur with the wild and romantic."

On their first foray ashore, Vancouver led a party to climb an island promontory and gain a perspective on the surrounding terrain. The spirits of the entire party were elevated by the natural beauty that surrounded them. The boat crew reclined on a gravel beach in front of a roaring driftwood fire, washing a feast of wildfowl down with grog and spruce beer. Vancouver described "a picture so pleasing it could not fail to call to our remembrance certain delightful and beloved situations in Old England." Only the young gentleman Manby had cause to complain: seeing a skunk in the foliage, he hoisted his rifle and shot it. When he rushed up to inspect his quarry, its dying twitches excreted "a discharge... the most nauseous and fetid." It ruined his clothes, so that even boiling produced no respite from the stench. Manby aside, Menzies wrote that after they returned to the *Discovery* around midnight they were "each well satisfied with the success and pleasure of this day's excursions."

The new purpose and the excitement eased some of the ill feeling and discontent within the ships' company. The men took pride in their work and enjoyed getting free from the ships even if it entailed hard work. Peter Puget had only good words to say about the behaviour of his crews during the long summer days of surveying. "It is impossible silently to pass over so hard and Labourious an Undertaking as the Duty of the Boats, without noting that indefatigable exertion and Attention that has on all Occasions been paid by the Officers under whose Direction they were conducted and also the Seamen who performed the Labourious task of the Oar. At this they frequently laboured from Morning till Night & always performed that Duty with alacrity, not even a Murmur was heard. Necessity obliged us frequently to pull till Eleven at Night, which Still made no difference in the Hour of Departure." Vancouver himself also wrote that "in the exposure of my people to such fatiguing and hazardous service, I could ever depend on their cheerful and ready obedience to the prudent and judicious directions of the officers who were entrusted with the command of these expeditions."

LATITUDE, BOTH ON land and at sea, was determined by measuring the angle of altitude of the sun. Longitude represented the distance of a position, east or west, from a standard meridian of longitude, normally the north-south line running through Greenwich in London. Because the earth is constantly spinning at a set speed, each hour of difference between local time and Greenwich time, for example, is equivalent to fifteen degrees east or west. Determining longitude was one of the major scientific problems of all time and had only been solved in principle in the late eighteenth century. The simplest solution for the calculation of longitude was to carry an accurate clock, or chronometer, set to Greenwich time and to observe the difference between Greenwich time and local time at high noon. The prototype chronometers that James Cook and George Vancouver brought on their voyages were finicky and bulky, and after years of exposure to the elements in the ship's cabin or on the quarterdeck, they lost accuracy. They were too large to take on small boat excursions and were used only at the base camps of the larger ships.

Vancouver and Whidbey therefore also relied on a far more time-consuming and delicate method of calculating longitude, which involved observing celestial bodies. After squinting through a telescope and noting the exact moment of the eclipse of Jupiter's moons at local time, they could consult a set of tables that would tell them when the eclipse occurred in Greenwich. The time difference between observing the same eclipse was translated into degrees of longitude. The earth, moon and stars of the solar system all move in relation to each other at fixed rates, and their movements could be predicted with a complicated set of mathematical calculations. When the moons of Jupiter were in eclipse or obscured by clouds, Vancouver would measure the angle of the moon against two fixed stars, consult a set of astronomical tables known as the Nautical Almanac and determine

Greenwich time. Each of these methods was reliable but painfully slow, particularly the method of calculating lunar distances, which required about three hours to calculate each point of longitude.

What distinguished Vancouver's work from the works of others was both the precision of his individual readings and the thoroughness and quantity of the readings he took in dangerous and difficult-to-measure locations. Vancouver, Whidbey and Johnstone spent thousands of hours over the years calculating latitude by the sun and then staring at the night sky through the telescope to determine longitude for the same point. The captain anchored his maps with thousands of points determined by these primitive and painstaking means and then track-surveyed to fill in the detail between the "peg points." When sketching his great chart in the *Discovery*'s cabin, incorporating the draft sketches of Lieutenants Baker and Puget, Vancouver began with such a well-balanced skeleton of astronomically fixed points that his accuracy was virtually assured.

AS THE SHIPS progressed south into Puget Sound—which Vancouver named after young Peter Puget, who commanded the first boat survey of the region—they cruised through seemingly endless layers of forested mountains that rose abruptly from the water. Some were islands; others, oddly shaped protrusions of the mainland, all garbed in a mighty green canopy of giant cedars and firs. Anyone who has sailed or ridden a ferry through these waters, can easily imagine and appreciate the challenge of not getting lost. Without charts, these early European visitors were surrounded by a maze of narrow winding inlets that were lined with snow-capped mountains even in June. They encountered a bewildering multitude of possibilities for travel in what proved to be a vast, island-studded inland sea. The likelihood of an east-leading waterway into the interior of the continent must have seemed great. This body of water was undoubtedly the source of the rumours of the Great Western Sea depicted on charts.

Seeing so much complex and intricate, mazelike coastline, Vancouver must have had to exercise tremendous willpower not to rush ahead and nose into the most intriguing and promising waterways to search for a northwest passage, rather than slowly and methodically plodding along the continental shelf, along every minute inlet, even when he could sense it was a dead end. But he had willpower aplenty and a rigid mind that in this instance was perhaps the only thing that pushed the survey forward in spite of the daunting odds against its success.

While Broughton took the *Chatham* to investigate the San Juan archipelago, Vancouver headed south through what he named Admiralty Inlet and ventured ashore to inspect a land "almost as enchantingly beautiful as the most elegantly finished pleasure grounds in Europe." He again took formal possession of the land for Great Britain, just in case it should prove valuable in the negotiations with the Spanish. During May and June teams of Vancouver's mariners in small boats scoured the outline of Puget Sound, including the future sites of Seattle and Tacoma, for evidence of a northwest passage. *Not here*, Vancouver claimed with certainty having followed every channel and inlet, a deflating prospect to all, since to have found it would have been the culmination of a centuries-long quest and would have led to the crews' eternal fame. For days at a time their solitude was enlivened only "by the croaking of a raven, the breathing of a seal or the scream of an eagle." Vancouver continued to bestow the landmarks of the region with the names of important British naval personages, family members and events. On May 29, the anniversary of Charles II's 1660 restoration to the throne from which his father had been ousted, Vancouver acknowledged his allegiances as a solid Tory and a Royalist when he proudly bestowed the name Restoration Cove on a coastal inlet.

In mid-June the two ships headed north together and anchored in Boundary Bay, near today's Point Roberts (named after Vancouver's "esteemed friend and predecessor," the previous commander of the *Discovery*) along the 49th parallel and the current border between Canada and the United States. While the men constructed a base camp and an astronomical observatory, and brewers and blacksmiths and carpenters were set to their work, Vancouver, Puget and Manby loaded the *Discovery*'s launch and set out north on one of Vancouver's most arduous and famous small-boat excursions. On June 12 they rowed past the delta of the as-yet-unnamed Fraser River—British Columbia's greatest waterway, which snakes north and east as far as the continental divide—but they were kept from shore by the spring flood and shoals. Both Vancouver and Puget recorded seeing the "two openings" of the river and the detritus, including innumerable "logs of wood, and stumps of trees"—sure signs of the outlet of a large river—but in accordance with his orders, Vancouver continued rowing north when he judged the river unnavigable to large ships. As they pressed on, they could see the expanse of the Strait of Georgia, "a Clear & uninterrupted view to the nw," which promised the greatest remaining possibility of providing access to an inland sea.

The men kept rowing north, inspecting the shoreline and entering the narrows of what is now known as Burrard Inlet, where about fifty people of the Capilano tribe paddled out to meet them and trade. Near present-day Port Moody, Vancouver recorded: "The shores of this channel, which, after Sir Henry Burrard of the navy, I have distinguished by the name of Burrard's Channel, may be considered, on the southern side, of a moderate height, and though rocky, well covered with trees of large growth, principally of the pine tribe. On the northern side, the rugged snowy barrier, whose base we had now nearly approached, rose very abruptly, and was only protected from the wash of the sea by a very narrow border of low land." Burrard Inlet is now part of the Greater Vancouver Harbour, which comprises the outer harbour, called English Bay; the inner harbour, past the First Narrows; and two arms, Port Moody and Indian Arm. On June 13, Vancouver became the first European explorer to pass through the narrows into the inner harbour around which the city of Vancouver now sprawls. He found it to be "a sublime, though gloomy spectacle." On June 14, the two boats left the inlet and continued cruising along the continental shelf, into Howe Sound and the long, narrow Jervis Inlet and other innumerable inlets and bays, despite a shortage of provisions. Vancouver's already-compromised constitution was strained to near breaking by these open-boat excursions.

When Vancouver finally allowed his weary men to row their way south to rejoin the *Discovery* and *Chatham* at Point Roberts, Puget joined Vancouver in one boat, leaving the younger midshipman Manby in charge of the other. As darkness settled over the water, Manby failed to see that Vancouver and Puget, a considerable

distance ahead in the gloom, had taken their boat on a slightly different route. Manby lost sight of them and found himself in command of
a group of exhausted sailors in darkness, without provisions or a compass. The next day they hunted a few birds and boiled up "a voracious
meal" of mussels, which were unfortunately tainted. The exhausted
men became weak and sick, and they "experienced every agony a poisoned set of beings could feel." It took another full day for most of the
men to recover. Now famished, they continued to row south, guided
by memory. They fortunately encountered a large native fishing party
and bartered some buttons from their coats for five large sturgeons.
The resourceful Manby tied the boat alongside "an immense large tree
drifting in the middle of the stream with a great part of the roots many
feet above the water." He lit the tree "with a fire capable of roasting an
ox" and cooked the fish, leaving the skeletal branches burning when
they pulled away. "My boat's crew suffered every hardship fatigue and
hunger could inflict," he wrote, before they regained the *Discovery*
on June 24 "in a deplorable state." Somehow they arrived there a few
hours ahead of Vancouver and Puget's boat.

Meanwhile, on the return journey to Point Roberts, Vancouver was
surprised to see, near the southern entrance to Burrard Inlet, on the
Spanish Banks, two medium-sized ships, smaller than the *Discovery*
and *Chatham* but twice the size of his open survey boats. As Vancouver and Puget crossed the inlet towards the ships it became clear they
were vessels of the Spanish navy. The *Sutil* was commanded by Dioni-
sio Alcalá-Galiano and the *Mexicana* by Cayetano Valdés. The ships
carried about twenty crew each and were engaged in a similar mission
to Vancouver's. They had been on the coast the previous year as well.
After a brief meeting with the Spaniards, Vancouver continued south,
intending to return in the *Discovery* and *Chatham*. On arrival, he still
was not aware of what had happened to Manby and the other boat.

Exhausted after the three-hundred-mile excursion without sufficient provisions, and worried over the fate of his men, Vancouver
exploded into fury and swore at Manby, sparing no thought for the
almost heroic travails of his junior officer in surviving a difficult situation. Manby stewed over his humiliating upbraiding, writing in his
journal "his salutation I can never forget, and his language I will never

forgive, unless he withdraws his words by a satisfactory apology." The historian John Naish writes in *The Interwoven Lives* that "it was a disgraceful scene in which Vancouver made yet another enemy and lost more face with his crew." Manby remained diligent and professional in his job, but he never forgot the injustice of Vancouver's outburst. Months later, when Vancouver, without prejudice and in recognition of his abilities, promoted Manby to be master of the *Chatham*, he wrote that it was "a situation I should have refused in England," but one he welcomed here "as it cleared me from a man I had just reason to be displeased with."

Once aboard, Vancouver quickly ordered the shore camp disbanded and the *Discovery* and *Chatham* to weigh anchor. He wanted to sail a little north to the entrance to Burrard Inlet, where he and Puget had encountered the two Spanish ships. The Spanish ships had also made contact with Broughton and Whidbey in his absence. On June 25, as the *Discovery* and *Chatham* drew near, the Spanish sailors "gave us three hearty cheers as we came up with them." The compliment was returned, and soon the Spanish commanders came aboard the *Discovery* to confer with Vancouver in his cabin, smoke tobacco and sip brandy. Vancouver learned that these small ships were offshoots of the famous Malaspina expedition and that they had already explored much of the same coastline as he had, which caused him "no small degree of mortification." But his consternation at not being first was relieved somewhat when he learned that the Spanish had not sailed into Puget Sound or the inner harbour of Burrard Inlet. Vancouver later learned that the Spanish ships were also searching for the secret northwest passage somewhere in the Strait of Juan de Fuca and that if they discovered it, their orders were to sail through to Hudson Bay or Baffin Strait and then rush south to Spain—all the while keeping the waterway a secret.

The British and the Spanish pooled their geographical information, while Alcalá-Galiano sent the British officers some milk and cabbages that he had brought from Friendly Cove. The Spanish commanders also let Vancouver know that Commodore Bodega y Quadra awaited Vancouver at Friendly Cove with three frigates and a brig of war. "Their conduct was replete with that politeness and friendship which characterizes the Spanish nation," Vancouver wrote, and the four ships agreed to work together for a while. So the four ships, two Spanish and two British, worked their way north through the Strait of Georgia. Vancouver and Puget, however, found the Spanish surveys to be far inferior to their own, partly because of the unsuitability of the Spanish ships for inshore work, and they soon left them behind. Vancouver was not eager to end his survey and rush to meet Bodega y Quadra at Friendly Cove, so he continued north. He regarded the cartographic survey as his great personal goal and wanted to complete as much as possible in the short survey season. He also expected additional instruction from the Admiralty regarding his negotiations with Bodega y Quadra to be brought to Friendly Cove on his supply ship *Daedalus*, and he did not want to arrive before the supply ship and his orders. Vancouver and the two Spanish captains agreed to openly share the results of their surveys, and Vancouver, ever an honourable man, accurately marked Spanish names on his chart when he determined they had explored the region before him. He even removed some of his own attributed names to accommodate their prior claims (although most of the Spanish names were removed from the region by the Admiralty when Vancouver's cartographic charts were set for publication years later).

THROUGHOUT THE SUMMER, Vancouver's survey crews encountered thousands of native peoples from dozens of settlements along the coast. In the first survey season alone, they travelled through the territory of several language and cultural groups and would eventually meet with peoples from all six of the prominent language groups along the Pacific Northwest coast: Haida, Wakashan, Tlingit, Tsimshian, Athapaskan and Chugach. The coast was populated along its entire length with tens of thousands of people in both large and small villages. Some of the people were merely curious, never having encountered Europeans before, whereas others were familiar with the trading process or at least with the goods on offer. Many were eager for firearms, but the trade was principally in small mirrors, beads and knives, while Vancouver's men received vast quantities of food, principally fish and berries. Vancouver and his officers were oddly slow to grasp the fact that these peoples were not the same as those at Nootka Sound, that the linguistic and cultural diversity of the coast was extraordinary. He continued to bestow English and Spanish names liberally over his great chart, completely ignoring local names and failing to mark even the locations, let alone the names, of prominent native settlements. To erase local place names was to make the region more familiar and welcoming to his countrymen. Thus Vancouver's map depicts an empty coast, uninhabited and unclaimed, as he affixed familiar European names in the first step to asserting sovereignty over the region.

By training Puget was strictly a naval officer, but the young lieutenant showed a surprising depth of insight and appreciation for cultures other than his own. In one perceptive instance he even saw similarities in the natural human tendency to vanity, likening the wild face painting of the native peoples to the makeup of "his own Fair Country women." Others on the expedition were not so generous or broadminded; Manby wrote, "was it not for the abominable train oil and paint so liberally daubed on their face and bodies, they might certainly be termed a very good looking race of people." Perhaps his sour opinion related more to the women's lack of interest in his amorous advances, which, judging from his journals, was his greatest preoccupation in every port the ships had stopped in since leaving England. Midshipman Bell wrote that "the women being the first we had seen since leaving the Sandwich Islands, had not a few attacks of Gallantry made on them by the Sailors though they were by no means inviting... the smallest degree of indelicacy towards one of these Ladies, shock'd their modesty to such a degree, and had such an effect on them, that I have seen many of them burst into tears, they would endeavour to hide themselves in the bottom of their canoes and discover the most extreme degree of uneasiness and distress."

The encounters between Vancouver's men and the local peoples were always brief and never allowed for any great chance of understanding or rapport, but they were almost universally peaceful. Vancouver, as his orders stipulated, enforced strict trading regulations between his people and the locals, to "conciliate their friendship and confidence." In the words of Puget, the local trade was conducted "with the Strictest honesty on both Sides—this however I greatly attribute to a proper treatment of these People on our Part, for we would never accept any Article till the Owner was satisfied with what was offered in Exchange." In several instances Vancouver's boat crews were beset by potentially hostile canoes of aggressive men bent on raiding the open boats for the goods so clearly on display. The survey boats were only about twenty feet long, whereas some of the larger dugout canoes were up to sixty feet long, with more than twice as many men aboard. These instances were defused by a judicious display of firepower from large guns or swivel-mounted small cannons. Midshipman Bell reported that "in one place they were met with a considerable tribe of Indians from whom he had nearly met with some trouble, but by early good management nothing material happened. After being very well treated by the Boats party the Natives seized the opportunity of their stopping at a Beach to Dinner, to attack them. They were observed to string their Bows and sling their Quivers and were making for the Wood behind the party at Dinner from whence it was no doubt their intention to fire their on them but as this was observ'd Mr. Menzies & Mr. Manby catching up their Muskets ran up and drove them back to their Canoes."

Menzies, in keeping with his official duties as naturalist, acted as one of the chief diplomats and communicators, taking advantage of the knowledge gained during his prior visit to the coast and his knowledge of the language of some of the peoples. His favourite tactic was to get people to count for him so that he could listen for similarities in pronunciation and know which other words to use. Although ethnography was part of Menzies's official duties, he was not as interested in foreign cultures as he was in foreign plants. Partly owing to his personal interests and partly to the brief encounters with native peoples, necessitated by a continuously moving survey, the anthropological studies of Vancouver's expedition did not match those of Cook or other scientific voyages of the era. Menzies did, however, amass a large collection of cultural artifacts through trade, and Vancouver's descriptions and those of several other of his officers, though scanty and incomplete, remain useful as descriptions of native cultures on the cusp of change. These windows of European description provide a great view of individual trees but never of the entire forest. Puget thought he would never "be well acquainted with their Manners and Customs."

THE TWO SHIPS continued north through the Inside Passage. The crews were hopeful and excited at the prospect of the northerly continuation of what Vancouver called the Gulf of Georgia: it would lead either to an inland sea or through to the Pacific, thereby eliminating the need to backtrack south and west through the Strait of Juan de Fuca. The *Discovery* and *Chatham* pushed ever northward through a narrow, serpentine channel that edged northwestward for over a hundred miles. Strong tides and treacherous currents, confined to an average width of only two miles, made navigating both ships safely through the waterway a tremendous feat. A small-boat expedition led by Lieutenant James Johnstone first brought news that the waterway did indeed lead to the Pacific. Vancouver called it Johnstone Strait, and the narrow channel is now known as Discovery Passage.

The channel opened around the northern tip of Vancouver Island into Queen Charlotte Sound, which proved more dangerous than the serpentine Discovery Passage. The sound was cluttered with a treacherous scattering of shoals that were highly dangerous for large ships to navigate without charts. On August 6, drifting in the dreaded fog that hovered over the water, the *Discovery* ran aground on a submerged rock. The vessel lurched dangerously in the water, and the men went flying as the ship leaned inexorably over on her side. The crew rushed to disconnect portions of the masts, and "lightening her as much as possible, by starting the water, throwing overboard our fuel and part of the ballast we had taken aboard in the spring." Nothing worked to right the ship, and soon the tide began to change. A horrified Manby recorded that "after lying upright for half an hour a terrible crash ensued which brought the ship on her broadside." Vancouver described their predicament as being "alarming in the highest degree." The ship was about to roll over. The crew could not determine if the hull had been pierced. If a storm arose, the ship was certainly doomed.

But luck held for the weary mariners, and the rising tide gently floated the listing *Discovery* the next morning, after a sleepless night for the sailors. With the *Chatham* and all the small boats rowing and set to anchors, the men toiled to right the ship and then worked through another night, until 2 AM the next day, re-rigging her. After only one more day of sailing the *Chatham* ran aground on a similar outcropping, but she was also saved after the worn-out mariners endured "the fatiguing exertions and anxious solicitude" of another night. Queen Charlotte Sound proved so dangerous to navigate that Vancouver ordered the small boats out again to search for a safe passage through the rocks. The entire episode is reminiscent of the 2006 sinking of the B.C. ferry *Queen of the North* in the Inside Passage, after it struck a small island in the darkness. The *Chatham* and *Discovery*, however, survived the calamity.

By late August the two ships had progressed north from Vancouver Island, along the continental shelf to a point midway to Alaska, when they encountered the British fur trader *Venus* out of Bengal, which brought them news. Mr. Shepherd, the captain, confirmed that the store ship *Daedalus* was awaiting them at Friendly Cove, as was Bodega y Quadra, and delivered a letter. It was sad news for Vancouver. The letter told of the death of his old friend Lieutenant Richard Hergest, captain of the *Daedalus*, as well as of the anxiously awaited astronomer William Gooch, in a melee during their stopover on Oahu, one of the Hawaiian Islands. The high spirits of the news of the safe arrival of the store ship were "soon damp'd and in no small degree" by the news of the deaths. Ominously, Vancouver sought information that would help him seek revenge. Not only was his friend dead, but Gooch's highly specialized skills were badly needed. Now Vancouver and Whidbey would continue to bear the entire responsibility of acting as the principal astronomical observers. They were already overworked. On August 17, Vancouver ordered his two ships south along the outer coast to Friendly Cove.

Midshipman Pitt also continued to earn his captain's wrath. On one occasion, the headstrong youth cracked part of the *Discovery*'s binnacle (the non-magnetic stand for the ship's compass) while "romping with another of the Midshipmen" on the quarterdeck. Vancouver ordered him flogged again. He was flogged a second time during the summer of 1792, for an unknown offence. Stubborn and inflexible,

Pitt refused to accept the authority of Vancouver to either order him around or punish him when he failed to obey those orders. His attitude was a constant source of smouldering conflict, barely repressed. The animosity between the two men continued to poison the atmosphere and undermine the congeniality of the ship's company, making it difficult to experience any pride in their shared accomplishments.

Menzies and Vancouver were also grating on each other's nerves, despite the friendship they occasionally shared in exploring native villages and the exotic shoreline. Even though Vancouver gave Menzies many opportunities to go botanizing ashore, where the latter made numerous novel scientific discoveries, Menzies had affinity for Vancouver the man but did not trust or understand Vancouver the captain. Everyone needed a break. They were all frustrated with the tedious minutiae of their daily routine, which allowed no error in conditions of incredible and constant danger. The stress was taking its toll and causing personalities to clash again. Vancouver's bursts of anger grew more frequent as the strain of his task and the difficult conditions took hold of his overtaxed mind.

By the time the *Discovery* cruised south along the final stretch of Vancouver Island's west coast and entered Nootka Sound for Vancouver's historic meeting with Bodega y Quadra, the British captain had already surveyed a large stretch, 500 miles, of coastline, which included most of present-day British Columbia's coast. He had proved the insularity of the largest island in Pacific America, had unravelled the puzzling geography of the coast and had made one major mistake that would provide fodder for his critics and alter the course of history half a century later. As he neared Friendly Cove for the first time since his youth, perhaps another thought was on Vancouver's mind: he spoke no Spanish. How was he supposed to negotiate with Bodega y Quadra if they could not communicate with one another?

A
Meeting of Minds

————◄ ◈ ►————

JUAN FRANCISCO de la Bodega y Quadra had an impressive reputation. Not only was he the commander of the Spanish Pacific squadron at San Blas, Mexico, with responsibility for the entire Pacific coast north of Panama, and a Peruvian-born aristocrat proud of his Castilian blood, but he was also a renowned naval explorer who had navigated as far north as Alaska on at least three voyages in the past twenty years. There was probably no one alive who had seen more of the Pacific coast of North America than Bodega y Quadra.

His portrait presents a sleek, manicured officer whose uniform displays adornments and stylish flourishes. Mysterious and reserved, with one eye concealed in shadows, Bodega y Quadra's head is askance, as if he viewed the world at a different angle than others did. In the background a quill and ink pot are prominently displayed, denoting him as a man of letters as well as a man of action. The portrait reflects his refinement, his distinction and the value he placed on his sterling reputation. A gentleman in the true sense of the word, he valued his education and his image. Broad-minded and intelligent, Bodega y Quadra was fashionable, curious and highly social. He was also a Spanish patriot, intent on gaining the best deal possible from the British representative sent to meet him at Friendly Cove.

Bodega y Quadra had arrived at Nootka in March and had immediately begun laying the groundwork for negotiations with the British.

He had a lot of catching up to do, because Chief Maquinna and most of his people had had little or nothing to do with the Spanish for the past three years, since one of Martínez's men had murdered Chief Callicum. Bodega y Quadra, a diplomatic man who shared in the spirit of the Enlightenment, began with a ceremonial visit to Maquinna at his grand lodge. Once he had identified Maquinna as the ranking chief of the loose confederacy in Nootka Sound, he continued to cultivate this relationship throughout the summer with gifts and additional visits, "constantly treat[ing] Macquinna as a friend, singling him out from the rest with the clearest demonstrations of appreciation." He added that Maquinna "always occupies the first place when he dines at my table. I myself take the trouble of waiting on him, of serving him with as much as he likes, and he makes a lot of my friendship and much appreciates my visits to his rancherias." The Spanish commander and his entourage visited Maquinna at various places and times, as a result of which they became friends. Bodega y Quadra received fresh fish from Maquinna at regular intervals. His use of silver plate and the formal rituals of the Spaniards' meals impressed the people of Nootka, who had their own elaborate rituals. Important native leaders shared the Spanish commander's table nightly, and they were freely invited to his house. Bodega y Quadra gave Maquinna his own bedroom to use when visiting the Spanish settlement. "I can perhaps flatter myself that since treating these Indians as men ought to be treated," he noted, "and not like individuals of inferior nature, I have lived in the very breast of tranquillity."

During the months he spent at Friendly Cove awaiting Vancouver, Bodega y Quadra sought to establish himself as the personable "big man" about town, increasing his personal power through generosity—behaviour the natives were familiar with, from their ceremonial potlatch. He was equally friendly and generous to all the ships that sheltered in Friendly Cove while his men set about building and reinforcing the settlement and fort. Far from continuing Martínez's brash and irritating harassment of non-Spanish ships several years earlier, Bodega y Quadra went out of his way to ingratiate himself with visitors and to offer them luxuries. From the small farms in the settlement he ordered that the bounty, including fresh milk, bread and produce, be shared with incoming ships. Much like Maquinna did with his people, Bodega y Quadra set about establishing himself as the big chief, sharing his abundance with the lesser mortals in the harbour. He invited the captains and officers from all the visiting ships in port to his nightly repast in his great hall ashore. All the surviving journals and logs from every ship to visit Friendly Cove during the summer of 1792 describe the Spaniard's generosity, amiability and hospitality. He made a grand impression as the public face of Spanish sovereignty and all it represented.

Bodega y Quadra also went to work interviewing Maquinna and the merchant captains about their opinions of the events involving Martínez and Colnett, and of Meares's claim to his lost property. He concluded that the series of events as described by Meares, which were the foundation of the Nootka Sound Convention, were at least partially false and probably completely so. The captains Robert Gray of the *Columbia* and Joseph Ingraham of the *Lady Washington*, both eyewitnesses to Martínez's actions against Colnett and the other British mariners, provided Bodega y Quadra with written testimony of events that was closer to Martínez's version of the incident than Meares's version and claimed not to be aware that Maquinna had sold any land to Meares. "We observe your wish to be acquainted with what house or establishment, Captain Meares had at the time of the Spanish arrival here. We answer, in a word, None." Another captain, Francisco José Viana, the Portuguese captain of Meares's *Iphigenia* in 1789, also denied that Meares had any significant establishment, factory or house when Martínez had arrived, apart from a "very small" house "made from a few boards got from the Indians, and when we sailed it was pulled to pieces." As for Maquinna, the chief denied ever selling any land, let alone the entire harbour, to Meares. All of these testimonials were as biased as Meares's original claims were, distorted by memory over time, tainted by the shifting political balance along the coast and partially contradicted by testimonials collected by Vancouver later in the summer. But the traders and native peoples now evidently felt that having the European side of the fur trade in the region controlled and managed by the diplomatic Bodega y Quadra and the unobtrusive Spanish Empire would be much better than having an unknown and potentially restrictive or difficult British agent.

WHEN VANCOUVER EASED the *Discovery* into Friendly Cove a few hours after the *Chatham* had arrived, the Spanish mariners on the small boat that sallied forth to meet them at the entrance to the sound were "ready to leap overboard for joy, for it seems that we were so long expected, that they had now given up all hope of seeing us at all this season." Vancouver sent Puget ashore to negotiate the reciprocal salute of thirteen guns before the ships entered. With this formality out of the way the *Discovery* cruised into the cove, blasting its cannons in salute.

Several Spanish naval ships were awaiting the latest visitors, outfitted for the occasion with brass guns polished, sails coiled crisply along the masts and broad pennants waving lazily from the top spar. Eighteenth-century civility was the order of the day. Anchored across the cove from each other, thirteen cannons boomed in salute from each ship. Puffs of smoke rolled across the water and echoed off the nearby hills. The mariners continued this loud ceremony for the next several weeks, saluting each other with cannon blasts as other trading vessels entered the sound and as they boarded each other's ships. "There was scarcely a day past without puffings of this kind from some vessel or another," noted Menzies, "and we too followed the example, and puffed it away as well as any of them, til at last we became so scarce of ammunition to defend ourselves... that we were obliged to get supplies of Powder from the Spaniards and Traders before we left the Coast."

A portrait believed to be of Vancouver shows a middle-aged man with elegantly arched eyebrows and a tight line to his lip. The tilt of his head suggests not arrogance but firmness and decisiveness—resolution. The hands and arms are relaxed and comfortable, yet the face holds an unnatural puffiness that is at odds with the determination in the coal-like eyes. At the time that Vancouver met Bodega y Quadra in the fall of 1792, his illness was taking its toll on Vancouver's overtaxed mind and exhausted body. The brutal season of surveying had worn the whole crew down, but Vancouver had endured the greatest stress and burden. He had deliberately delayed his meeting with Bodega y Quadra for months, hoping for additional instructions from London. The stress must have been mounting throughout the summer, always in the back of his mind, for he was not a natural negotiator, and he had few instructions to guide his first encounter with the intimidating Spanish nobleman, commander, explorer and diplomat.

While the cannons politely thundered around them, the two captains, crisply attired in full naval regalia, met each other in front of the great two-storey house in the village. Vancouver was astonished. Bodega y Quadra's great hall, far from Vancouver's rude compartment aboard the *Discovery,* was appointed like a European drawing room, with silver plates and utensils, crystal goblets, elegant tapestries and finely carved furniture. The house was planked in cedar and featured a balcony on the front upper storey "after the manner of the Spanish Houses." It contained a guard room on the ground floor, a servants' hall, kitchen, upper-storey rooms for Bodega y Quadra and several officers, and a large hall in the centre where they dined. A Spanish honour guard welcomed the two captains, who were received by uniformed officers at the door and escorted "with great attention and civility" up the stairs to the great hall. Vancouver's senior officers followed.

Bodega y Quadra had planned "a grand entertainment" for all the Spanish and British officers. When the officers were seated, the two captains raised a toast of Madeira to their respective sovereigns and entertained each other with civilized witticisms. They feasted on a dinner "of five courses, consisting of a superfluity of the best provisions... served with great elegance." The meal was served on a full set of solid silver plates. It was, Vancouver noted with understatement, a feast of a calibre "we had lately been little accustomed to." Although neither man spoke the other's language—a clumsy oversight by both governments—Vancouver was fortunate to have Thomas Dobson, a master's mate on board the newly arrived *Daedalus,* as a fluent Spanish speaker to act as interpreter. How no official interpreter could have been sent out from either government is difficult to comprehend, considering the scale of the preparations and the importance of the meeting. This first dinner, however, was all about hospitality and pleasure—business could wait. Bodega y Quadra "offered us every refreshment & accommodation that the settlement could afford during our stay at Nootka," Vancouver noted. "He begged that the Commanders and Officers might consider his House as their Home & that the oftener they came to it the more pleasure he should enjoy, & indeed his conduct sufficiently proved that this was by no means a ceremonious invitation, for his table was daily crowded with the Officers of the different Vessels that occasionally visited the Cove, & his Hospitality seemed to have no other bound."

After dinner Vancouver and Menzies were taken on a tour of the Spanish settlement. The settlement itself, in Menzies's words, was situated on "a rising neck of Land with Friendly Cove & the shipping right before if, & behind it a high Beach washed by the rude Surges of the open Ocean & along the Verge of its Bank a pleasing path was formed for walking where the mind could contemplate at ease the fretted wildness of the briny element foaming against Rocks & Shores without feeling the force of its fury—while on the other side huge Mountains presented themselves covered to their very summits with a continued forest of stately Pines whose dark verdurous hue diffused a solitary gloom—favourable to meditations." Clustered together were several houses, a barracks, a hospital, the blacksmith's and carpenter's sheds (who were "building and repairing Vessels and Houses"), fenced-in fields with European-style gardens growing "luxuriantly," in addition to "well-stocked" chicken pens. Goats, sheep and black cattle roamed at large, "feeding around the village."

"In short," Menzies concluded, "the Spaniards seem to go on here with greater activity and industry than we are led to believe of them at any of their other remote infant settlements." The tour was undoubtedly part of Bodega y Quadra's plan to appear to be in charge, to make his Spanish settlement at least as impressive as the nearby native settlements with their great cedar longhouses, to impress the British with the solidity of Spanish occupation—to make Friendly Cove something worth having. As they strolled, Bodega y Quadra casually commented on the good relations between the Spanish and the local people. He had completely erased the ill-will caused by Martínez's threats, violence and intimidation. No doubt the elaborate reception and tour were part of Bodega y Quadra's negotiating strategy, but Menzies also noted the Spaniard's "disinterested humanity which formed a striking trait in his character." Menzies gushed that Bodega y Quadra's "benevolent mind seemed wholly occupied in contributing to our entertainments & amusements." Far from being an adversary, the Spanish commander seemed to be their ally, about to hand over to them this thriving idyllic outpost.

One of the distinguished guests at Bodega y Quadra's table during Vancouver's first meeting was Chief Maquinna. When the *Discovery* first entered the harbour, Maquinna and some of his men had rowed out to meet the incoming vessel to present himself to the new British leader, the man who was supposed to be assuming power from the Spanish and therefore very important to the chief. But Vancouver's men failed to recognize him as a chief and had rudely prevented him from boarding the ship. Although Bodega y Quadra explained the situation to the aggrieved chief, Maquinna was still put out by the indignity. Pondering the situation, Bodega y Quadra suggested to Vancouver that the two of them pay a visit to Maquinna at his home in the nearby village of Tahsis. Maquinna agreed, and the next day a large group of British and Spanish officers accompanied their commanders in four boats sailing up the inlet. The journey to Tahsis was to be a state visit.

The European visitors camped on a nearby beach the first night, and the following day they were ushered into the great cedar hall by a procession of local dignitaries. Inside the dim, smoky, high-ceilinged structure they were shown benches newly covered in "rich furs and clean Mats." There were speeches and gift giving. The Europeans were astonished when Maquinna continued to bring out gifts by the armload, distributing them with great ceremony to his people until he, according to Menzies, "with respect to riches was brought almost upon a level with the poorest of his Tribe." During a potlatch, power and prestige were bestowed, and dignity was gained, by the distribution of wealth. Robin Fisher, author of *Vancouver's Voyage*, writes that "Vancouver and Bodega, as the representatives of Britain and Spain, haggled over land at Nootka as if they owned the place," apparently unconcerned that the real power was held by, and their presence was tolerated by, the ranking chief of a people that had inhabited the region for four thousand years. Meanwhile, as Fisher observes, neither group was particularly aware that it was "a pawn in the internal politics of Nootka Sound." By accepting Maquinna's hospitality, the visitors were, in terms of the local tradition, accepting his bounty and therefore acknowledging his superior status over other chiefs. Maquinna's authority was greatly enhanced by his relationship with the European leaders, just as they benefited from his generosity.

Before the feast, further entertainment was scheduled. There was dancing, warrior manoeuvres and an impressive show with actors in costumes representing Europeans "armed with Muskets & Bayonets, others were dressed as Chinese & others as Sandwich Islanders armed with clubs and Spears; the rest were equipped either as Warriors or Hunters of their own Nation." Then Maquinna himself, while wearing a mask, danced for the assembled dignitaries with "great agility... repeated and universal plaudits." Although Vancouver was always diplomatic and respectful of his hosts, and particularly so of Maquinna (perhaps taking his cue from Bodega y Quadra), he later wrote that he found Maquinna's dance to be "ridiculously laughable." Vancouver was then, according to Menzies, "anxious to shew them a specimen of our English capering" and ordered some sailors to "dance a Reel or two to the Fife."

Appetites whetted, they feasted on porpoise and tuna stew, boiled whole in a giant trough, "entrails and all... with a mixture of Water, blood and fish Oil, & the whole stewed by throwing heated stones in it." While Bodega y Quadra, Vancouver and the officers supped off of the Spaniard's fine silver plates on European fare, transported from Friendly Cove especially for the occasion, the natives gathered about the cedar trough with large shells "scooping it up & devouring it with relishing appetites." Over wine after dinner, they conferred about coastal geography and the fur trade, and in a speech the Spanish commander revealed to Maquinna that he intended to depart Nootka and leave the control over trade to the British, specifically Vancouver. Maquinna was annoyed and distressed at this news. He had invested time and energy in cultivating Bodega y Quadra as a friend and ally, and he felt his efforts to boost his prestige and authority by associating himself with the charismatic and respected Spanish leader were wasted. Vancouver was still an unknown, and so Maquinna began working on the British captain, perhaps a little too obviously,

for Vancouver later remarked of Maquinna's flattery that "very little dependence... is to be placed in the truth or sincerity of such
declarations."

Maquinna had grown wealthy and powerful by manipulating the
trade and pursuing a policy different from that of other chiefs. The
historian Yvonne Marshall has studied the responses of several important native leaders to the arrival of European fur traders in the late
eighteenth century, contrasting in particular the approaches of Chief
Maquinna and Chief Wickaninnish. Maquinna was head of a confederacy of peoples along the central west coast of Vancouver Island
rather than an absolute ruler. "Maquinna wisely chose to draw trading vessels to Nootka Sound by providing them with a safe, hospitable
environment in which to trade and reprovision." Nootka Sound, ironically, was not as good a region for sea otters, so Maquinna's plan was
to make Nootka Sound a friendly and peaceful port for ships to rest,
visit and trade. Stability was his trump card over other regions, such
as south at Clayoquot Sound, where Chief Wickaninnish pursued a
much more aggressive policy of intimidating, enforcing a monopoly
over trade with European vessels and attempting to obtain his own
European ship by force, to do his own trading with China.

The next morning, on the return journey, Bodega y Quadra asked
Vancouver to name some prominent landmark, a headland or an inlet,
for both of them jointly. Vancouver later chose the huge island he had
just sailed around and named it Quadra's and Vancouver's Island.
This rather unwieldy name remained in use until the mid-nineteenth
century, when it was shortened to Vancouver Island. At Friendly
Cove, after Maquinna and "a large concourse of Natives" arrived by
boat, Vancouver ordered a grand fireworks display in front of Bodega
y Quadra's manor house. Menzies recounts that "the Natives afterwards amused us in the Governor's house with a Specimen of their
singing and dancing & capering till they were perfectly tired, consisting of such uncouth attitudes & gestures as are not easily described—
but which they performed with great glee & good humour till late in
the evening & then retired very orderly to rest."

All was not so orderly among the British sailors. An American
fur trader anchored in the harbour was manufacturing and secretly

selling rotgut liquor to the British sailors, who consumed it in addition to their regular rum ration. Their rowdiness, not surprisingly, was much increased at night, followed by a dereliction of duty during the day. When Vancouver uncovered the illicit trade, he was furious, but he managed to control his temper, perhaps under the calming influence of Bodega y Quadra, or fearing a loss of dignity in front of such a distinguished person. Instead of raging at his sailors or taking action himself, Vancouver sent a note to the Spanish commander politely asking him, as the authority in the harbour, to put a halt to the bootleggers.

But the pleasantries belied the importance of the ongoing discussion: the two European leaders, while enjoying the hospitality of the local ruler and people, were verbally sparring to determine the political future of Pacific America. The Nootka Sound Convention was a broad general agreement, and Vancouver and Bodega y Quadra, although they had different conceptions of their responsibilities, were to settle some of the convention's specific terms. While their ships were snugly sheltered in the peaceful cove, the two captains pleasantly debated the details and delicately haggled over the specific requirements of the agreement—exactly what property was to be returned to Britain and where the northern boundary of Spanish sovereignty would lie. Neither Britain nor Spain actually intended to exercise the sovereignty they were haggling over in the traditional sense, for they were not interested in establishing power over native peoples, but were negotiating for the right to govern the behaviour of other European nations and colonies or ex-colonies—in Spain's case, the right to control the other nations that were frequenting the region, and in Britain's case, the right of European ships of any nationality to frequent the coast without interference from other European ships or troops. This haggling among themselves, as nations with ocean-going ships, was a global extension of their domestic internecine power struggles.

Bodega y Quadra's negotiating strategy and tactics had been developed in Madrid and Mexico before he left to take up his post in Friendly Cove in the spring. Spanish policy towards Pacific America had taken a shift under the new leadership of the viceroy of Mexico, Conde de Revilla Gigedo. He was keenly interested in the region and in maintaining Spanish control over it. One of Revilla Gigedo's first acts was to send a naval expedition under Francisco de Eliza y Reventa, who fortified Friendly Cove at Nootka Sound with permanent structures and surveyed the coast as far north as Alaska, although not very thoroughly. After the Nootka Sound Convention was signed, Revilla Gigedo was instructed to establish exclusive Spanish territory at the Strait of Juan de Fuca with a border running due north from the western entrance of the strait to "Cook's River" (Cook Inlet) at approximately 60 degrees, thereby giving to Britain exclusive control over all of Nootka Sound but preserving the vast inland territories of western North America for the Spanish crown—and, crucially, making the Strait of Juan de Fuca Spanish territorial waters. At the time the extent of the inland sea was still unknown; perhaps it even went as far inland as New Mexico, in which case having marine access to it would be invaluable to the Spanish. In expectation of the success of these diplomatic schemes, in the summer of 1792 Lieutenant Salvador Fidalgo had sailed into Neah Bay, just east of Cape Flattery, and founded a small Spanish community named Núñez Gaona. Bodega y Quadra and Revilla Gigedo hoped that the garrison outpost of Núñez Gaona would form the northern boundary of Spanish sovereignty along the coast. Maintaining the garrison and village at Friendly Cove was too expensive and ill-suited to the Spanish mission model. Thus Bodega y Quadra, armed with his depositions from the fur trade captains who had been present in Friendly Cove during the fateful summer of 1789, had solid evidence to support his position and must have felt confident of persuading Vancouver to agree to his proposal for settling the question of the border.

Vancouver was not so fortunate. When the *Discovery* first sailed into Friendly Cove, he eagerly collected the mail from the *Daedalus* hoping for updated instructions regarding his diplomatic duty and obligations, for information to guide his discussions with the Spanish commander. He was disappointed to find nothing other than a nearly year-old letter from the Admiralty and a copy of a letter from the Spanish Conde de Floridablanca, the Spanish first minister, instructing the Spanish governor to cede all the British buildings and land in Nootka Sound "which were occupied by the subjects of that sovereign in April 1789." Vancouver's letter instructed him to present to the Spanish representative a copy of this letter and officially receive the land back from Spain. The British government evidently felt it was a mere formality and thereby left Vancouver in a difficult position—his counterpart was intelligent and well informed about the history and his government's position, whereas Vancouver was completely cut off from communication with his government and had no idea that he was supposed to be haggling over the location of an international border for Pacific America.

A few days after Vancouver arrived, Bodega y Quadra sent him a letter outlining the Spanish position and claiming that Meares's story was false. Meares had never obtained any land from Maquinna, and no substantial British buildings had ever existed; therefore, Bodega y Quadra, as the Spanish representative, had nothing to formally transfer to Vancouver. He then made an offer that shocked Vancouver: Britain and Spain could settle their differences immediately by establishing the international boundary at the Strait of Juan de Fuca, in accordance with his pre-arranged plan, for the border to be located at Cape Flattery (coincidentally, not so far from the present boundary between the United States and Canada). Spanish sovereignty over the territory between California and the new boundary, Bodega y Quadra suggested, would be still intact, and the British, Americans and Russians could do as they wished with the territory farther north. He would hand over to Vancouver all of Friendly Cove, including all the newly constructed buildings, gardens, livestock and fortifications, and the handsome manor house within which he had so recently hosted Vancouver and his officers. He would then transfer his own headquarters to Núñez Gaona.

Vancouver replied with a polite note declining the offer. Not only had he received no instructions or orders authorizing him to open negotiations concerning the sovereignty of the coast, but the proposal seemed like a poor deal for Britain and ran against his interpretation of the Nootka Sound Convention. He pointed out that according to the convention, exclusive Spanish sovereignty was to extend only as far north as Spaniards had already settled along the coast—that is, only as far north as San Francisco.

Evidently the two governments misunderstood the aim of the negotiations, one believing the matter was settled and the other seeking to
gain better terms at the meeting. Vancouver, essentially abandoned by
his government, could only abide by the terms of the original Nootka
Sound Convention and was not even aware of what he was supposed
to do with Friendly Cove once the Spanish handed it over to him—
although he may have suspected that the plan was to found a convict
colony here, as had recently been done in Australia. He replied to
Bodega y Quadra that he had no power to open discussions and that
any Spanish settlement at Neah Bay would have to be open to ships
of both nations because it lay north of territory already occupied by
Spain at the time of the Convention.

The negotiations progressed slowly because every communication
had to be translated through the only bilingual person on the coast.
Over three weeks and after a dozen letters and several personal discussions, Bodega y Quadra revealed that he was not prepared to yield
the port at Nootka Sound unless Vancouver acknowledged Spanish
sovereignty from California to the Strait of Juan de Fuca, something
Vancouver felt he was unauthorized to do. Faced with Vancouver's
obstinacy and repeated claims that he had no power to make a deal,
the Spanish commander then offered to yield to the British only the
actual spot of land upon which Meares's shed had been built—a tiny
patch of low-lying beach, cut off from the Spanish village at high tide,
triangular in shape, hemmed in by bluffs and only about 330 feet
long—which Vancouver dismissively called a "small pittance of rocks
and sandy beach" and the sailors jokingly referred to as the "British
territories." For the British flag to flutter over the patch of beach while
the Spanish flag proudly flew over the nearby handsome settlement at
Friendly Cove would have been undignified. Despite these weeks of
discussion, and hindered by their limited negotiating authority and
translators, the British and Spanish commanders could not come to a
consensus. The two captains amicably agreed to send the matter back
to their respective governments for renewed discussion. They both
knew how close to war their nations had come over this wild coast,
and neither wanted to be the one responsible for an escalation of the
acrimonious dispute.

Vancouver, while not a master negotiator and hindered by a lack of communication with his government, sensed that Bodega y Quadra was trying to have him agree on Britain's behalf to a settlement that ran counter to the spirit of the Nootka Sound Convention. He would not be the man responsible for that, no matter how friendly and flattering the Spaniard was and no matter how civilized the settlement in Friendly Cove. Acutely aware that his every action would be scrutinized and that any failure would be attributed to him, Vancouver knew full well the value the government had placed on the matter. He wrote long dispatches to senior members of the Admiralty and government, including Evan Nepean, secretary of the Home Office, Earl of Chatham and Lord Grenville, outlining Bodega y Quadra's negotiations, providing a detailed map showing the tiny patch of beach that had been offered, and defending his decisions. "I was still left totally in the dark what measures to pursue," he remarked.

Vancouver had expected further instructions, and he was vexed and annoyed not to have received any—for good reason. Vancouver has come under some criticism over the years for not being a strong negotiator, but it is hard to see how he could have turned the situation to Britain's benefit. Indeed, by not making any agreements, Vancouver effectively thwarted Spain's plan to extract from him the concession of Spanish sovereignty north of San Francisco. Still, when Philip Stephens, secretary of the Admiralty, heard of Vancouver's decision months later, he was mildly disappointed that Vancouver had not accepted the proffered beach, at least as a starting point. "All that We are really anxious about in this particular part of the Business is the Safety of our National honour which renders a Restitution necessary. The extent of that Restitution is not of much moment..." One wonders why no instructions to this effect were ever forthcoming to Vancouver.

Could it really have been an oversight not to have presented Vancouver with detailed instructions to guide his actions at Nootka Sound? Officials in the British government had perhaps realized the insubstantiality of Meares's testimonials, that the entire pretext for the Spanish Armament and the Nootka Sound Convention was a sham, and may have hoped that the issue of sovereignty would be settled quickly by Vancouver and the matter closed to further scrutiny.

British officials did not want to have the sordid truth of Meares's fab-rications exposed. Vancouver may have even sensed a trap—that the lack of communication was intentional, because he was being set up as a scapegoat for the collapsing deck of cards that was the Nootka Sound Convention; that if he made a mistake in his dealings with the Spanish, blame for the whole problem could be pinned on him. He wrote a letter to Nepean, along with instructions for the letter to remain private, "excepting my conduct should fall under that censure as to require such Vindication as is here pointed out." In the letter Vancouver pointed out that this beach could not "possibly be consid-ered as the districts or parcels of Land &c intended to be ceded to me on the part of His Britannic Majesty. No—there can be little doubt I should either have proven myself a most consummate fool or a trai-tor to have acceded to any such cession without positive directions to that effect."

Vancouver feared that the current stalemate was a result of his lack of sufficient diplomatic skill, "which a life wholly devoted to my profession has denied me the opportunity of acquiring." But one must remember that Bodega y Quadra was checked just as effectively as he had checked Vancouver. There was no winner or loser in the meeting of minds in Nootka Sound in the summer of 1792. Lesser men would have reverted to posturing, threats and bluster, but for Vancouver and Bodega y Quadra, polite and "civilized" negotiation was the only hon-ourable path.

Near the end of September, Vancouver sent Zachary Mudge, first lieutenant on the *Discovery*, back to London on the tiny China-bound Portuguese trader *Fenis* with copies of all his communications with Bodega y Quadra and asked for further instructions. Mudge also brought with him a packet of plants from Menzies to give to Banks, as well as another long letter from Menzies detailing all the events of the summer. Several months later Lieutenant Broughton, com-mander of the *Chatham*, crossed overland from Monterey and took a ship to London carrying similar messages and dispatches. Mudge and Broughton arrived within a month of each other, in the summer of 1793, to find that France had declared war against Britain and Spain. In Europe, negotiations over Pacific America continued, but on the other side of the world, Vancouver was never informed of any of these developments—nor did he receive any further instructions clarifying his situation. He operated completely in the dark. His questions were left unanswered for years.

ON SEPTEMBER 22, nearly a month after their meetings began, Bodega y Quadra left Vancouver behind, hoisted his ships' sails and set off for California. Nootka Sound would remain a Spanish port open to all ships, and a new governor would arrive shortly. Vancouver lingered for another month, erecting an observatory ashore to astronomically fix their position (and producing calculations that he humbly suggested were more accurate than Cook's). He was also making some changes in the expedition's personnel.

The surgeon Alexander Cranstoun was finally to be invalided home aboard the *Daedalus* at the end of the season. Vancouver prevailed upon Menzies to officially assume the position of surgeon, complete with additional pay and responsibility. Accepting the position would place Menzies more directly under Vancouver's control. Menzies felt that the request was delivered "with a degree of earnestness that I could not well refuse." If he refused, Vancouver said, he must put his refusal of the post in writing. Seeing that most of the crew were healthy and that each ship already had an able assistant surgeon, Menzies accepted. His position in the ships' company was protected in that he reported to Banks and was not directly under Vancouver's command—but now, should the situation ever arise, he would be considered a member of the *Discovery*'s company and part of the overall command structure, with Vancouver as his senior officer. It was a post Menzies would come to regret.

Vancouver appointed Lieutenant James Hanson of the *Chatham* to command the supply ship *Daedalus*, replacing the deceased Richard Hergest. Peter Puget was promoted to first lieutenant of the *Chatham*, taking Hanson's position, and then to commander, after William Broughton left a few months later. It was a remarkable series of promotions for one so young who was not an aristocrat. Thomas Manby, despite Vancouver's unjustified upbraiding at Birch Bay months earlier, likewise was singled out for promotion to master of the *Chatham*, a great responsibility for a young officer. When he was not ill or angry, Vancouver was a calm and professional judge of ability. He held no grudge against those who proved themselves—his temper flared quickly and violently but burned out just as quickly.

Before they sailed from Friendly Cove, Vancouver was also approached by the captain of a British trader with an unorthodox request. Some of his crew had kidnapped two young women from one of the Hawaiian Islands. Now his ship was heading back to Britain, and he needed to return the women to their home. Would Vancouver perform this service? Perhaps with some misgivings, Vancouver agreed. He need not have worried.

Vancouver's ongoing quarrel with Midshipman Thomas Pitt had not diminished during the summer. One evening Pitt had transgressed a serious navy protocol. Feeling tired, he lay down on his coat for a while. Unfortunately he was supposed to be on watch in the forecastle. When his name was called from the quarterdeck, the response was silence. The officer yelled again, louder, finally rousing the drowsy lad. Sleeping on watch was a serious offence, showing an incredible lack of a sense of responsibility and potentially endangering the entire ship. Although Pitt and a witness denied that he had been dozing, Vancouver without further investigation charged him with neglect of duty. Knowing full well the seriousness of the charge, anyone accused of it would have denied it. Vancouver ordered Pitt to be locked in irons for ten days, in the dank, vermin-infested gaol, along with two common sailors.

As the *Discovery* and *Chatham* cruised south to San Francisco and Monterey, where he had arranged a further meeting with Bodega y Quadra, Vancouver became more aware of the confusing geographical tricks of the coast and decided to investigate the river that Gray had told him about in May. Although initially he had dismissed Gray's notions as unimportant, now the possibility that he had missed a significant river or inlet seemed less fantastical and more important. What if Gray had found the great river of the west? The *Discovery* and the *Chatham* anchored just off the terrifying breakers at the Columbia's bar on October 19. After making two attempts to cross the turbulent breakers, Vancouver wisely decided not to press the *Discovery* and ordered William Broughton to take the smaller *Chatham* and navigate the river.

Broughton eased the *Chatham* about a hundred miles along the broad, forest-lined waterway and ordered his boat to the shore at a point opposite the place where the Willamette River disgorges into the Columbia. He clambered up the loamy bank and officially announced that the river and all the surrounding lands were now the possessions of "His Britannic Majesty." Vancouver, sacrificing his usual generosity for political expediency, wrote in his journal that "no other civilized nation or state had ever entered this river... it does not appear that Mr. Gray either saw or was ever within five leagues of the entrance."

But Gray, despite Vancouver's uncharacteristic insinuation, had sailed his ship up the Columbia first. After his meeting with Vancouver in the spring, Gray had quickly led his ship back to the Columbia. On May 12, 1792, his ship lurched over the breakers and entered a mighty river flowing from the east, from the mountainous heart of an unmapped land. No European yet knew what lay between the Mississippi River and the Pacific coast, but in the coming years the quest for a cross-continental link would drive the agents of Britain and the United States into the interior of the distant domain. Gray lingered around the river's mouth, trading with the Chinook people for a few weeks before heading west across the Pacific with a shipment of furs. He carried with him information that later provided a geographical focal point for the westward-looking Republic.

TEN

An End
and a Beginning

— ◆ —

WHEN THE FIRST European explorers cruised the coast of California in the sixteenth century, perhaps 300,000 people from more than thirty tribes and six distinct language groups inhabited the region, which ranged from the temperate coast to the arid oak-covered central valley, to the eastern mountains and the deserts of the southeast. Several sixteenth-century Spanish conquistadors had ventured north into California searching for gold, but when they failed to uncover anything of value they turned their attention elsewhere. Voyages of exploration were also cursory and brief. In 1542 Juan Rodríguez Cabrillo captained the first voyage to sail north from Mexico to some point north of San Francisco. The English adventurer Francis Drake sailed along the coast in 1579 and named a beautiful port, possibly present-day San Francisco, Nova Albion and claimed it for England. Although the exact purpose and extent of Drake's voyage remains a mystery, a recent book by the historian Samuel Bawlf has mustered evidence that the explorer may have sailed as far north as southern Alaska while searching for the Northwest Passage.

The handful of other ships that ventured north along the coast likewise left no lasting trace or evidence of their presence. Not until 1697 did the Jesuit missionary Juan María de Salvatierra found a mission in southern Baja California. Others followed, but Spanish colonial development of the region was slow despite official claims that it belonged to New Spain. It was Franciscan monks such as Junípero Serra, with government support, who continued to increase Spanish presence in the region, setting up missions at San Diego in 1769 and Monterey in 1770. These were small religious outposts with several monks and soldiers. Although their main objective was to convert the native peoples to Christianity, these missions also strengthened Spanish territorial claims to the region. By the 1790s twenty-one established missions ranged along the coast from San Diego to Sonoma. Along with four presidios, or military outposts responsible for the meagre defence of the region, they constituted the entirety of the Spanish presence. By the time of Vancouver's voyage, the Spanish presence in California was unnoticeable outside of these tiny missions and the four understaffed presidios with their small surrounding towns, and it had little tangible impact on the hundreds of thousands of native people. Spain's was a token presence, organized principally to establish a precedent of historical occupation.

Vancouver had no knowledge of the extent of Spanish colonization in California, but obtaining this information was part of his objective in visiting the colony. His orders called on him to assess the significance of the Spanish settlements in Pacific America and to forward his observations to his government. He arranged to meet Bodega y Quadra in Monterey, where he hoped to receive dispatches from his government that would direct further negotiations and resolve his diplomatic impasse with the Spanish nobleman. While his crews were dreaming of Hawaii, sun, relaxation and the pleasure of consorting with friendly women, Vancouver was, as usual, planning to squeeze in some additional work before spending the winter there. He was particularly interested in Hawaii's political fate and had ambitious plans for his sojourn there.

But once again, Vancouver the perfectionist failed to perceive the exhaustion of his crew—or perhaps he placed their needs second to the objectives of his voyage. Instead of sailing directly for California and Hawaii, he ordered the continuation of the running survey of the west coast south from where they had started in the spring. After departing the mouth of the Columbia River, the *Discovery, Chatham* and *Daedalus* were beset by a series of vicious storms that tore at the sails, soaked the sailors with freezing rain and battered the ships. Damp, cold, hungry and exhausted, the men were soon suffering from scurvy. Fortunately, Menzies was able to defray the more debilitating symptoms with regular doses of concentrated lemon juice. Although buffeted by storms, the voyage was yoked to the task of continuing the coastal survey. The six-hundred-mile voyage to San Francisco consumed more than three weeks. The only distraction from the dreary routine and the lassitude of illness came from the enlivening presence of the two pretty Hawaiian girls who strode the deck during good weather.

Vancouver led his ragged ships into San Francisco Bay on November 14. They were the first non-Spanish ships to enter the port. Midshipman Manby excitedly recorded that "the whole country was variegated with enlivening verdure, large herds of cattle were grazing in every direction, and our brother adventurers were galloping over the hills, mounted on excellent horses." They soon discovered that Bodega y Quadra had particularly requested that the governor of the small settlement give them "every accommodation the Settlement afforded." Unfortunately, the settlement consisted of "two mud houses"—one for the governor and the other for about forty married soldiers.

Bodega y Quadra evidently did not appreciate that Vancouver may have had espionage as one of his objectives, or he did not believe there was anything to be gained that was not already common knowledge, and the British were warmly welcomed. For ten days they were feted with dinners and social gatherings and given horses for riding in the countryside. The officers were ungainly on the horses, but the two Hawaiian girls took to them "with as much ease and apparent satisfaction as if they had been brought up or accustomed to such a mode of conveyance from their infancy."

The high pommel of his Spanish saddle caused Vancouver great inconvenience on one expedition to visit a mission in the countryside, and he uncharacteristically downed several drafts of grog to ease his aching body. "Those who limped the most laughed at their own pains and gave mirth to the rest," he recorded. At the mission they feasted on beef and mutton as well as fresh fruit and vegetables, and the ever-roguish Manby was delighted to find that the young female natives at the nearby mission of Santa Clara "loitered round the woody recesses for the sake of meeting us... and practised every alluring attitude to be taken notice of." Menzies was delighted to collect new plants in the beautiful landscape that Manby described as "the most commodious in the world" with "natural beauties which exceed any in the known world." There was something for everyone in California, and the semi-holiday was a break from the tedium, danger and stress of the journey south. After ten days the ships hoisted sails and pushed farther south to Monterey, expecting to continue the holiday.

Monterey, the principal Spanish settlement in California, was a pleasant two-day voyage south from San Francisco. Arriving at the small community of several hundred inhabitants, Vancouver and his men from all three ships were given a warm reception by Bodega y Quadra, and they resumed their social life. Still, no new dispatches had arrived for Vancouver, burdening him with the anxiety of continuing uncertainty. Bodega y Quadra, however, did not seem to notice and was as hospitable as ever. He lavishly provided for all their needs during their stay in Monterey, refusing payment. (Vancouver was later to learn that Bodega y Quadra had paid for it all personally, not from government funds.) He hosted banquets, nightly entertainment including bullfights, dances, hunting trips, horseback excursions into the countryside and, as Menzies recorded, "whenever we went out in this manner Sr. Quadra's Plate & Cooking Equipage &c travelled with us, so that we had always the luxury of dining off Silver, & on the best of every thing he could afford."

The loquacious Manby continued to be mightily impressed with California, claiming that "the Great beauties of this part of California certainly exceed any in the known World, few of our Noblemans estates can equal the plains Woods and Lawns here to be met with." He was not quite so enamoured with the "Mexican Spaniards," whom he described as "without exception, the most illiterate beings in the universe... Like all ignorant people, they are much addicted to jealousy, never suffer their wives to move from the house or suffer a stranger to enter it, and what is worst of all, the brutes beat their females without mercy." Not for Manby the discreet observation.

One night, Vancouver and his officers were invited to a dance at the governor's house, where, as Menzies recorded, the local ladies staged a "Spanish exhilarating dance, the Fandango, a performance which requires no little elasticity of limbs as well as nimbleness of capers and gestures... They traverse the room with such nimble evolutions, wheeling about, changing sides and smacking with their fingers at every motion: sometimes they dance close to each other, then retire and approach again, with such wanton attitudes and motions, such yearning looks, sparkling eyes and trembling limbs as would decompose the gravity of a stoic." So enthused was Vancouver with the performance that he clapped and urged the two Hawaiian girls to display their own dances for the assembled crowd. But the Spanish ladies became offended, perhaps thinking that he was mocking them, or annoyed at the competition for the men's attention. They coolly departed.

Vancouver was much taken by the charms of his two young Hawaiian charges, complimenting the younger Tymarow on her "sensibility and turn of mind, her sweetness of temper and her complacency of manners." During the voyage from Nootka, both young women had demonstrated an ability to amuse through their witty songs "to commemorate the events of the voyage." They sang, according to Menzies, with "mirthful derision" of the filthiness of the northwest coastal peoples, joked at the stuffy conventions of the Spanish, "and even their friends on board were brought under the lash of their sarcastic verse."

Vancouver lavishly distributed trade goods and wine to the missions in a spirit of generosity and to reciprocate for Bodega y Quadra's goodwill. On December 10 he ordered an evening of fireworks, a novelty never seen before by most of the Spanish inhabitants but an event to which his crew was growing quite accustomed. The event was marred by much imbibing by the British sailors, and Menzies noted that "some little altercations took place amongst ourselves which was not so pleasant, and certainly showed the Spaniards the characteristic of English sailors who on these occasions are apt to quarrel with their best friends." No doubt the lash was liberally ordered for these transgressions. Drunkenness was one of the persistent and recurring issues that drove Vancouver to extremes in dealing with his men during the voyage. He could not abide a lack of control or disobedience of his orders: for example, an armourer named George Rebold was flogged ten times during the voyage for variations of the same offence.

While repairs to the ships were progressing, Vancouver was holed up in his cabin, preparing copies of all his charts, dispatches and correspondence to be sent back to London. He selected Lieutenant Broughton as the courier for this valuable information because he was second in command and "had been privy to the whole of my transactions with Senr. Quadra at Nootka; and whose abilities and observations would enable him... to satisfy the Board of Admiralty on many points of inquiry, for which it was impossible I could provide in my dispatches." Bodega y Quadra graciously offered to allow Broughton to accompany him in a Spanish ship to San Blas and then to travel overland across Mexico in order to board a ship to Europe.

While events in Pacific America were not universally pleasant, the holiday in California aside, they were calm in comparison with events on the other side of the world. France's revolution, in its infancy when Vancouver departed Britain, had transformed the nation and was set to transform Europe. The National Convention had declared the monarchy abolished and France to be a republic, and King Louis xvi and Marie-Antoinette would soon be guillotined; Austria and Prussia had invaded France in the start of the two decades of war that would pit Britain and Napoleonic France in a global struggle for supremacy. No one in California knew anything of these momentous distant events, which would alter the course of their lives. Life—languid, humid and relaxing—went slowly on in Monterey, but the most important task in the world to Vancouver, and so recently one of the most important developments in European international affairs, had been eclipsed.

Unbeknownst to the weary voyagers anchored in balmy Monterey, another, more personal, development was about to occur. One individual would learn of the event more than a year later, in the spring of 1794, but others would not hear about it until the ships returned to Britain more than two years later. It involved midshipman Thomas Pitt. On January 19, 1793, the senior Thomas Pitt died while on a trip to Florence. As the eldest son, the younger Thomas Pitt became, without knowing it, the Right Honourable Lord Camelford, Baron of Boconnoc, Peer of the Realm, controller of mighty estates in Cornwall and Dorset that generated an annual income of at least £20,000—a staggering sum, equivalent to millions of dollars today. Hundreds of servants, their job to fulfill their master's every whim without question, maintained numerous chateaux and mansions for Pitt's exclusive pleasure. These properties were furnished with priceless antiques and silver and gold plate of far greater value than that so generously supplied by Bodega y Quadra. When Pitt returned to London, he would assume his hereditary place in the House of Lords. In Britain, there was scarcely anyone to whom Pitt would be expected to lower himself to associate with socially. Commoners might step aside and tip their hats when he strode down a street, or furtively cast a glance at him, perhaps feeling a mixture of awe and resentment when he alighted from his gilded carriage. As well, in July 1792, Pitt's younger sister Anne had married William Wyndham, Lord Grenville, the home secretary, one of Vancouver's political masters and a close ally of the prime minister. For now, though, the tall, sunburned midshipman Pitt stalked the decks of the *Discovery*, getting into mischief and casting disdainful glances at his domineering commander.

Vancouver maintained his dislike of Pitt—nothing had occurred to change his opinion—and was annoyed at Pitt's poor performance as a senior midshipman. In the postscript to a letter to Nepean on January 18, a letter that took more than six months to reach London, an exasperated Vancouver finally hinted at the continuous trouble he was having with the recalcitrant midshipman. "Nor can I at last avoid saying," he wrote, "that the conduct of Mr. T. Pitt has been too bad for me to represent in any one respect." For the habitually laconic captain—who used understated words like "very unpleasant" or "severe" or "great surprise" to describe his shock at seeing the entire ship swamped in a terrifying storm—to even mention Pitt's transgressions in a letter to his superior indicated that Pitt's insolence and disregard of duty must have been extreme and enduring. His sneering, disrespectful nature was one of the hot buttons for Vancouver that, combined with the stress of command, the captain's underlying illness and the ominous abandonment by his government, was slowly unhinging Vancouver.

The recently promoted Manby, now master of the *Chatham*, wrote a letter home to a friend at this time that opens another window into the state of affairs on board the ships. "Good health continues in our little squadron," he wrote, "though I am sorry to add not that fellowship which ought to subsist with adventurers traversing these distant Seas, owing to the conduct of our Commander in Chief who is grown Haughty Proud and Insolent, which has kept himself and Officers in a continual state of wrangling during the whole of the voyage." Manby said that he would never forgive Vancouver, and he never did. Vancouver's irritation was primarily with the midshipmen, the young gentlemen raised to expect deference and not accustomed to having their ambitions or desires thwarted. Vancouver's trusted ship's master, Joseph Whidbey, later remarked about Vancouver in veiled language that "I never knew him [to] put a favourable construction on any part of the follies of youth."

Menzies too took the opportunity to send his own dispatches to Banks with Broughton. By the end of the season, Vancouver and Menzies, despite having an otherwise congenial relationship, were communicating only by letter regarding the plant frame on the quarterdeck. It wasn't working as Banks or Menzies had hoped, and Vancouver was partly to blame. "I have not been able to get plants to succeed," an irritated Menzies wrote to Banks, "for if it is uncovered in rainy weather to admit air, the dripping from the rigging impregnated with Tar & Turpentine hurts the foliage and soil—and if the Side lights are opened Goats—Dogs—Cats—Pigeons—Poultry &c. &c. are ever creeping in & destroying the plants." But the bulk of Menzies's communication was a sprawling complaint that Vancouver had not promoted his friend Johnstone to the command of the *Chatham* but had instead chosen the younger Puget, despite unofficial instructions to promote Johnstone. Menzies felt that Johnstone should have received the promotion. "For besides his being equally capable to Command her, his long experience & great knowledge of this coast in general, and of Marine Surveying in particular of which the other knows little or nothing, should give a decided preference in his favour." The next year, Vancouver did promote Johnstone.

After nearly two months at Monterey the ships were repaired and reprovisioned, and it was time to push on to Hawaii. Vancouver ordered the *Daedalus* across the Pacific to Port Jackson, Australia, with cattle and sheep that Bodega y Quadra had provided. It was to rendezvous with the other two ships in Friendly Cove in the fall of 1793, carrying a year's provisions for the survey expedition. Restocked from the stores of Monterey, the *Daedalus* sailed at the end of December 1792. The *Discovery* and *Chatham* departed January 15, in the company of three Spanish ships that were heading south. At sea, but before they parted company, the senior British and Spanish officers gathered in the cabin of the *Discovery* for a lingering dinner that did not wrap up until "a late hour," after much toasting to each others' health and success. They gave three cheers and went their separate ways. Bodega y Quadra had less than a year to live, and Vancouver would never enjoy the Spanish gentleman's company again. This occasion was also the last time Vancouver and his mariners enjoyed a friendly reception in the ports of Spanish America.

SPANISH CHARTS OF the time clearly showed a cluster of small islands off the coast of California, midway to Hawaii, on the same parallel of latitude. They were called the Los Majos islands, but no one could clearly say who had first sailed there. Nor could anyone give a description of them. Spanish ships had been sailing between Mexico and the Philippines for a couple of centuries, but on a different track. The Spanish officers at Monterey told Vancouver they believed the islands were chimerical, the product of wishful thinking and fantasy. Vancouver was intrigued. He wanted to locate these semi-mythical Spanish islands and to settle any lingering doubts that they represented an early Spanish discovery of Hawaii that predated Cook's discovery in 1778. Setting out west for the Hawaiian Islands, the *Discovery* and *Chatham* spent a month at sea, where "dolphin and bonetta were seen daily" following the ships. Vancouver ordered his ships to track back and forth, Cook-style, in the path of the supposed islands. Despite what Manby termed "indescribable caution," they failed to locate even a hint of the Los Majos islands.

In the absence of additional historical records, it is impossible to know for sure whether the Los Majos group was indeed the Hawaiian Islands. Strong currents could have distorted the calculations of early navigators. In any case, any Spanish contact with the Hawaiian

Islands that predates Cook was not lasting or permanent. Vancouver himself offered no official opinion on the matter, but many of his officers, including Puget, Manby and Menzies, believed the two to be the same. At the time, the question was not merely one of curiosity; Vancouver had political ambitions for Hawaii that did not allow for disputed claims of first discovery.

The *Discovery* and *Chatham* sighted the coast of Hawaii on February 12, and here the two ships separated. The *Chatham* turned south and the *Discovery* north to encircle and survey the island, with plans to meet at Kealakekua Bay. The day before they entered the bay on February 23, Kamehameha, king of the island of Hawaii, rowed out with an entourage to meet the *Discovery* and came aboard to negotiate the ceremony for the official welcome for the following day. In the great cabin, the king displayed his prowess at eating. While the officers observed in stunned amazement, he feasted on "a roasted dog, two fish and a calabash full of taro pudding... in a few minutes the whole of the dog was devoured. The fish each weighing half a pound, followed the dog, altho' they were in the same state as when taken from the water, scales, gills and garbage." Manby recorded that "his feeding actually disgusted us and the quantity he consumed would have been a profusion for three moderate men. He particularly enquired if King George lived as well as he did."

Now about forty years old, the physically powerful ruler, Hawaii's most famous and powerful king, had mellowed from the time Vancouver remembered him, fifteen years earlier. During the past decade Kamehameha had subdued and conquered the big island through both diplomacy and military conquest. He was a grand strategist and was in the process of conquering the neighbouring islands of Maui and Molokai, while the kings of Oahu and Kauai were preparing to challenge him for power. It was a volatile and unstable political climate. Although Vancouver was only planning to stay here until the end of March 1793, he had a great deal of work planned: his ships would chart some of the coastline, he would attempt to bring political peace to the warring factions and negotiate some form of cession or political subordination of the islands to Britain—and he would bring to "justice" those who killed his friend Richard Hergest and the astronomer William Gooch the previous year.

Vancouver's visit got off to a rousing start with the state welcome by Kamehameha. Early in the morning, the crews on the British ships noticed a great number of canoes congregating along the beach, with more paddling into the bay from all around. By noon the surface of the water was entirely covered—"a complete platform." The British sailors were shocked. Manby recorded that "the number of people then afloat could not be less than thirty thousand. The noise they made is not to be conceived. Everybody loudly speaking and being assisted by the musical cries of some score of hogs and pigs absolutely stunned us on board." Finally, a great procession of canoes in a V-squadron formation headed out to the *Discovery* for the official royal welcome. The largest canoe sported thirty-six paddlers, bearing Kamehameha in a brilliant yellow-feathered robe, their paddles dipping in perfect unison. The king's entourage circled the ships several times before stopping abruptly alongside the *Discovery* so that Kamehameha could climb with dignity to the deck where Vancouver waited. The magnificently attired warrior-king then made a great speech of welcome with "a princely air of dignity."

It was a grand and impressive spectacle. The king and Vancouver touched noses in the customary token of friendship, and then Kamehameha presented his kingly gift: eighty large hogs, cages of fowls and innumerable baskets of fruits and vegetables, including taro, yams, breadfruit, melons, plantains, bananas, coconuts and sugar cane. Vancouver in turn offered many small gifts, including four head of cattle transported from Spanish America—gifts from Bodega y Quadra, which he presented to the king with the hopes that the herd might prosper. After inquiring about the health of King George, particularly if he held a grudge for Cook's murder, Kamehameha presented Vancouver with his yellow-feathered robe as a gift to be presented to the English king "as it was the most valuable present he could send him, being the only one of its kind at these islands and the richest Robe of any of the Kings of Owhyee ever wore... It should not be put about any person's shoulders till it was delivered to King George in Britannee." It was the beginning of a long and fruitful relationship between the two men.

After enjoying the grand welcome to Kealakekua Bay, Vancouver stunned his demoralized crew with an order "forbidding all persons except Officers to go on shore but on duty." It was similar to the order

given at Tahiti and was justified on the same grounds: to prevent anyone from violating customs, laws or taboos and thereby endangering
the ships. Not all were pleased. Midshipman Edward Bell, clerk of
the *Chatham,* wrote: "However as I did not conceive that my situation in the Ship brought me under these Tyrannical Laws, more than
Mr. Orchard [clerk of the *Discovery*] who I observed was a free man.
I attended not to the order, nor did Mr. P [Puget] extend it to me."
Vancouver also ordered all midshipmen to be confined to their ships
unless accompanied by an officer—a highly unpopular restriction on
the actions of these haughty, impetuous youths, who were expecting a
longer leash on the palm-studded beaches of paradise. Bell wrote in a
letter home that "Captain Vancouver has rendered himself universally
obnoxious by his orders not only in the present instance to the Young
Gentlemen but at various times to all ranks of Officers in the two Vessels under his command." There was much grumbling and many sul-
len glances. But even Pitt, perhaps remembering the events at Tahiti
the previous year, did not transgress the captain's edict. Hawaiian
women were allowed on board at certain times, but the men were not
allowed to leave freely.

Midshipman Manby, now an officer after being promoted master
of the *Chatham,* seems not to have worried about the order, gloss-
ing over it in his journal. He certainly did not gloss over the crowds
of canoes that swarmed around the ship, however. Each canoe was
"freighted with the choicest part of the creation, the female sex. It is
them alone," he mused philosophically, "that can harmonize the soul,
banish the sorrows from the mind and give to mankind true felicity…
happiness is incomplete without them… Our bark instantly became a
scene of jollity and all was pleasure and delight." Not for the austere
commander these sentiments; his official journal mentions nothing of
frivolity and amusement and dalliance. It dwells heavily on responsibility, fear of violence and concern for the health of his crew. Such is
the nature of command.

In the following days, Vancouver and his men were constantly
asked for firearms and even faced a generalized refusal to trade
unless weapons were on offer. Vancouver had to announce that he
had been placed under a taboo not to sell weapons; he refused to

trade weapons on principle. Menzies, apparently agreeing with his commander, wrote about "the destructive weapons that have been so industriously dispersed among them and which serve to stir up their minds with a desire of conquest, ruin and destruction to their fellow creatures." There was little evidence of destruction and ruin in Kealakekua Bay, however, and for the next several weeks the *Discovery* and *Chatham* anchored in the bay within sight of the spot where Cook had been killed years ago. But Vancouver was an excessively cautious man. Still anxious about the incessant clamouring for guns, which the islanders wanted to use in their internal political struggles, he was mindful of the potential for violence. For the next two weeks, the planned duration of their stay, "the Field pieces...got upon deck... & about forty stand of small arms were kept loaded under a sentinel's charge on the quarter deck."

But these defensive measures proved unnecessary. Relations between the hosts and visitors was unmarred by any tension or quarrel as the British mariners repaired and cleaned their ships, mended tattered sails and collected provisions for the next leg of the journey. Menzies went on a few botanical forays inland through "dark ravines and foaming cascades" and "foliage that charmed the eye, whilst their branches formed complete parasols. The woods were every where intersected by well beaten paths that made travelling easy and the various enchanting scenes which were continually attracting the attention of the party gave a zest to their trip they spoke of with raptures." During the visit, Manby delightedly noted that the decks of both ships were "covered with lovely women. Every tar folded in his arms youth and beauty," except during several priest-proclaimed taboo periods, during which "our female friends instantly left us, with many invectives against the barbarous custom that would now confine them to their habitations." Even the men stationed on shore, who were working on an observatory that Vancouver needed to determine their longitude, enjoyed the free-flowing customs of the Hawaiians. The "considerate king supplied the astronomers with a large house about sixty yards from their residence where they might entertain their female friends and observe the beauties of Venus whilst the other planets were obscured by clouds."

When the ships were ready to sail on March 7, Kamehameha invited the officers and crew to view an impressive "sham battle" as a final entertainment. Two opposing groups of players enacted a battle, "making the most hideous faces imaginable," Manby observed. "In my life I never saw such a distortion of countenances and conceived it impossible that a human being [could] draw their features into such a variety of forms." The warriors danced, gesticulated and flung their spears, which, even blunted, "brought blood and tore pieces out of several of their bodies." King Kamehameha himself joined the battle, his muscular form leaping and dodging spears with great dexterity. "Few of his subjects equaled him in his warlike exploits, as his strength enabled him to throw his javelin an amazing distance." After the battle, some of the principal combatants and chiefs joined the officers for a tumbler of grog while Vancouver ordered a grand fireworks display for the thousands of onlookers gathered along the beach. "Balloons, flower pots, roman candles, mines and water rockets were alternately set off to the wonder and admiration of all." The display went on for over an hour, lighting up the star-studded sky. Apparently the fireworks had the desired effect. Manby's somewhat biased interpretation was that "they could only express the inferiority of Owyhee and praise the prodigies of Britannia."

On board the *Discovery* Vancouver hosted a final meeting of dignitaries, in which he sought for one final time to preach the benefits of peace and to voice his support for reconciliation among Hawaii's warring factions. For eleven years after the death of King Kalaniopuu in 1782, warfare had disturbed the peace of the islands as the king's heirs and successors struggled for supremacy. Aided by guns received from the overwintering fur traders who had been frequenting the coast of Pacific America in the past several years, the hostilities in Hawaii had grown increasingly violent. Neither faction could actually possess the territories it conquered, so the war dragged on. Vancouver, a warrior himself and an officer in the navy, harangued Kamehameha (apparently without irony) about the evils of war and "the continual state of warfare that had so long disgraced their islands; without any other motive that could be urged as an excuse for despoiling each other's lands, or destroying their fellow creatures, than a wild and inordinate ambition to possess themselves of each others territories, which experience had shown them they were incapable of retaining after conquest." If only Vancouver could have presented his impassioned speech to the gathered monarchs of Europe, then embarking on what was to be nearly two decades of war for the conquest of the continent and beyond.

Although no large-scale invasions of neighbouring islands in the Hawaiian group had occurred for nearly two years while the factions regrouped and rebuilt their societies, standing armies faced each other on Hawaii and Maui, each anticipating the sudden attack of the other. Kamehameha cited the untrustworthiness of his rival Kahekili as the reason for the constant martial vigilance and then attempted to enlist Vancouver as an ally in his struggle for supremacy. Had not Vancouver's people, Richard Hergest and William Gooch, been murdered on the orders of Kahekili's own brother while the king observed from a distance? Could Vancouver not exact his personal revenge while aiding Kamehameha? Vancouver countered by suggesting that the king place his territories under the political dominion of Great Britain. Kamehameha assented to this proposal, on one condition: that Vancouver leave an armed ship and some guns behind permanently to guard against the possible military incursions of his enemies. How could his people, Kamehameha asked, "fight with firmness for their Country, if they had imprudently given it away to those who would not protect it?" Although Vancouver does not even mention this first attempt to secure the political dependency of Hawaii in his official journal, Manby in his wry and well-grounded manner observed that "this considerate reply totally put a stop to any further proposals."

Loaded with produce and "every kind of refreshment" and with the decks alive with more than 150 grunting hogs—a fond parting gift from the king—the *Discovery* and *Chatham* hoisted sails and silently slid out of the bay. There was much sadness at this departure; Manby shared the sentiments of many when he wrote that "our decks fill'd with moisten'd eyes. The pleasing girls of Owyhee bidding adieu to the men they had attached themselves to. General sadness prevailed throughout and for my part, I felt it exceedingly... Of all sights that soothe any soul to pity, nothing so effectually does it as a woman in tears." He was considerably more cold-hearted with regard to his own female companion, Macou'ah, who "had been weeping all the morning": "We parted. I was glad she was gone." There were only a few brief stops before the dreary, sodden coast of Pacific North America drew them back.

On March 10, the two British ships crossed the short distance to Maui and cruised into Maalaea Bay, which was "high and rugged, with frequent mounts of cinders caused by volcanic eruptions." Vancouver wanted to meet Kahekili, the rival of Kamehameha, to lay his plans for peace before this king, too. He met with a familiar refrain from Kahekili: that Kamehameha and the chiefs of Hawaii could not be trusted to uphold such a bargain. As Vancouver toured the land, the evidence of warfare was around him. Hogs were scarce, because most had been killed during the last invasion, and fields and irrigation trenches were destroyed. Kahekili agreed to consider the matter of peace and vowed to plan for Vancouver's next visit to Hawaii, when perhaps the captain could ferry him across to Hawaii and vouch for his safety while he negotiated.

On Maui, Vancouver also wanted to do something about his dead friend, Hergest, and the astronomer, Gooch. Although the rumour was that Kahekili was at least partly responsible for the death, Vancouver discounted it. Kahekili had already executed three of the men responsible and admitted that three or four others remained free. Vancouver wanted them captured. Kahekili's brother boarded the *Discovery* to sail to Oahu to help apprehend them. Manby, true to form, was more concerned with the "beauteous objects of exquisite form, of elegant features... ten thousand exertions did I vent on the dawning day that compell'd me to break from the arms of these bewitching girls, so lovely and endearing..." The *Chatham* had sustained damage to her hull that was best repaired in Nootka Sound, and Puget ordered the ship to proceed ahead of the *Discovery*, first for a little charting on the north coast of Molokai, then on to Friendly Cove to await the *Discovery*.

The night before the ships departed on March 17, Kahekili, his brother, their wives and other lesser chiefs spent the evening in Vancouver's cabin aboard the *Discovery* feasting and talking. They continued with their party even when Vancouver made a great show of being tired and lay down to sleep on his cot. Early in the morning, one of the Hawaiian girls that Vancouver had not yet returned to her home shyly shook Vancouver awake to inform him that one of her prized ribbons had been stolen. The groggy commander snapped awake, his anger kindled by a wrong done to one of his young charges. The pleasant sojourn in California and the stress-free time in Kealakekua Bay seemed to have defrayed Vancouver's illness and shortness of temper, but his temper returned with a vengeance this morning. He avoided any mention of his outburst in his official reports and journal (as usual), but Menzies, who was on hand to witness his captain's rage, was not so circumspect. Interrogating his guests, Vancouver "put himself in such a passion and threatened the chiefs with such menacing threats that he terrified one of them out of the ship with great precipitation. The king, in particular, came running into my cabin before I knew anything of the business and instantly jumped into his canoe through the porthole and paddled hastily to the shore." Although the other guests were not so quick to flee the ship, Vancouver's outburst put a sad conclusion to a visit of "utmost tranquillity" and threatened to undermine his diplomatic ambitions.

On March 20, the *Discovery* anchored at Waikiki Bay to capture Hergest and Gooch's renegade killers. The men were lured onto the *Discovery* under a pretense, then grabbed and imprisoned. After a brief inquiry, Vancouver concluded they were the guilty ones and gave them over to the local chiefs for execution. On a large canoe off Waikiki Beach, they were shot in the head. Vancouver was a potentially useful ally, especially since he made known his intention to return the next year, and the chiefs were eager to secure his goodwill by complying with his demands. It is likely that the men selected for execution were not in fact the guilty ones but chosen from a random selection of troublemakers. Curiously, the number selected for execution was equal to the number of British mariners killed the previous year. Vancouver was satisfied with the punishment because the men had been accused by their own neighbours and executed by their own chief. He then ordered a fireworks display, which "to many created more terror than admiration."

Just before the *Discovery* sailed from Oahu to Kauai on March 29, Vancouver ordered Whidbey to explore and survey an unusually large bay that had been described to him by a local chief. He was not too impressed because of the sand bar blocking the entrance; the bay was later called Pearl Harbor. As a final act in Hawaii before sailing across the Pacific, Vancouver requested that the local chief grant some land to the two young women he had carried from Friendly Cove. The chief agreed, and the women were dropped off on Kauai because their home island of Niihau was suffering a devastating drought. True to his word, Vancouver did look out for their interests, securing small estates for both of them, and in his own name, so that the ladies could live as his tenants without fear that their land would be repossessed. The happy pair, loaded with presents, watched from the shore as the *Discovery* pulled away into the distance. There were times when others considered the captain unbalanced or cruel, but this surely was not one of those times.

{ ELEVEN }

Hawaii,
Alaska and Illness

———— ◆ ————

T HE *CHATHAM* HAD a remarkable run, crossing the
Pacific Ocean from Hawaii to Vancouver Island
in only twenty-eight days. It battled heavy squalls,
hail and sleet. At one point the crew went for days without warm food
in the pitching seas, and the shifts were dangerously overworked
when they finally reached Nootka Sound on April 15. After recovering
from their ordeal, Puget and his officers struck up a congenial relationship with the new Spanish governor, Salvador Fidalgo, "a man of
learning, science and great abilities." Although Fidalgo had increased
the fortifications at Friendly Cove, which was busy with mostly American traders, he was as friendly and hospitable as Bodega y Quadra
had been the previous year. He urged the officers to share his house
and table nightly and to freely visit the settlement. One night he
also lamented to Puget that his men were out of tobacco and suffering from scurvy after the dreary and miserable winter. Puget happily
offered fresh food and tobacco from the *Chatham*'s supplies to the
Spanish mariners and garrison. He also came to the aid of a horribly
scurvy-ridden American fur trading ship, in which many sailors had
already perished. The feeling of goodwill spread throughout the tiny
community. Manby wrote that "every Spaniard with a Grateful Heart,
acknowledged us their deliverers from the jaws of Death."

Puget ordered the *Chatham* beached in order to start repairing
her mangled hull and copper sheathing, and the grateful Spanish

sailors pitched in. The local people were likewise friendly and helpful, bringing fresh game and fish and vegetables. Chief Maquinna made frequent visits to the cove and always brought more food with him as gifts. The congenial atmosphere and budding friendship between these erstwhile antagonists was hampered only by the lack of a common language. Manby wrote of their conversation that "Nootka lingo forms the greatest part." As they gesticulated with signs and rough translations, Fidalgo would "slap his forehead, shrug his shoulders and exclaim '*Diable!*' What a pity; what a misfortune it is," Manby continued, "that so many languages should prevail on this little world. 'Tis burlesquing the planet, and I dare say the inhabitants of the moon are more sensible."

Manby never seems to have lost his energy and humour. His eyes strayed to the native maidens, whom he thought were "very liberal with their favors and by no means as bashful as on our last visit." On one occasion he writes of how he had persuaded an endearing young woman to wash the grease and ochre from her body using a basin with soap and warm water. Although Manby abhorred the grease, he found the women—his real interest in every location he visited—to have "pretty figures with rosy cheeks, sparkling eyes and two inviting lips, on which the glowing kiss of delight never fail'd to banish in the gulf of oblivion of every danger and distress attended on a voyage round the world." Like Manby, the officers and crew of the *Chatham* enjoyed a pleasant time while waiting to rendezvous with the *Discovery* for the season's work.

The *Discovery*, meanwhile, was having a long and dangerous voyage across the Pacific. The ship had sprung a leak and battled terrifying storms as it lurched northeast before finally limping into a small bay in northern California, far south of Vancouver's preferred destination. Then it battled contrary winds for two more weeks as it struggled north to Nootka Sound to rendezvous with the *Chatham*. The *Discovery* arrived at Friendly Cove after a voyage of fifty-one days to find that the *Chatham* had departed north two days earlier heading towards the second agreed-upon rendezvous point. The friendly Fidalgo was readying to leave, because the new governor, Ramón Saavedra, was due to arrive soon. Vancouver collected from Fidalgo letters sent to

him from Bodega y Quadra and from Viceroy Revilla Gigedo, but ominously none had come from his own government. Weary though his
crew must have been, and with the *Discovery* battered, he stayed only
two days until ordering the ship, on May 23, to rush north to catch the
Chatham.

The two ships fortunately were reunited at Restoration Bay and
continued their survey of the serpentine maze of inlets and islands
from where they had left off the previous year. Vancouver knew that
annoying and tedious though it was, the survey must be thorough to
be accepted as disproving the existence of a northwest passage. The
coast they were about to survey was one of the most complex shore-
lines in the world, comparable in intricacy only to that of southern
Chile and the fjords of Norway. The innumerable islands, deeply
indented mainland shore and steep mountains, coupled with treacherous currents and rainy and foggy days, conspired to make this part
of the survey even more difficult than the previous year's.

The pattern of the survey was the same as during the previous
summer. The larger ships established bases to calculate longitude
and latitude, collect wood and fresh water, brew spruce beer and
catch fish, while the smaller boats rowed the winding coastline. They
braved powerful eddies, flood tides and channel surges, as well as hidden jagged rocks and dangerous anchorages. Finally, they suffered
through one of the worst seasons of bad weather of the entire voyage.
The seemingly endless and undoubtedly frequent chilly rain, fog and
wind sapped their strength and morale. Manby recorded that, for one
long stretch, "the sun during the whole time had not once beam'd on
us his cheering ray. No view offer'd to gratifie the imagination... creating a weighty atmosphere and perpetual rain." On another occasion
the men on a boat foray ate tainted mussels and became violently ill;
one man died.

The reaction to the now dreary and monotonous wilderness was
shared by nearly all the men. As Robin Fisher wryly notes in *Vancouver's Voyage*, "Even Restoration Cove, the first anchorage of the summer, was named for the anniversary of the restoration of Charles II in
1660 and not because it provided Vancouver with a restoration of spirits." Only Menzies continued to be inspired by the rugged grandeur.

In a letter to Banks, he inquired if he could be the medical officer for any new colony or settlement along the coast. "I continue daily, with much delight, augmenting my knowledge and collections of the Natural History of this Country which keeps my mind in a continual scene of amusement."

Certain troublemakers had not curbed the behaviours that so irritated Vancouver: disobedience, open insolence and drunkenness. Flogging and other punishments continued to be administered with regularity. In June 1793, for reasons unspecified, Vancouver stripped Pitt of his acting rank of master's mate. The facts are unclear, but the demotion probably stemmed from an incident in which Pitt traded a set of pistols for some pieces of copper from the ship's armourer. What possible use the copper would be on the wild coast of northern British Columbia is unknown; perhaps Pitt thought of using the valuable metal to barter with local peoples. In any event, Vancouver ordered the pistol set tossed overboard, the armourer flogged and Pitt publicly chastised. Around this time Pitt wrote a letter home (a letter that did not reach London for nearly a year), complaining of brutality at the hands of Vancouver and other officers and wishing that he could abandon the survey. Pitt was not the only one feeling crushed by his duties. By this time the voyage had finally broken Vancouver's constitution as well. With stress piled upon stress, and crushed by the appalling weather, the captain now spent all his time aboard the *Discovery*. He was now too ill to command the survey boats personally, so Johnstone, Whidbey and Puget took over this job.

A few weeks after the only survey party Vancouver actually led entered at a cove near Bentinck Arm, having surveyed the inlets in Dean Channel, another famous explorer visited the same spot. Alexander Mackenzie, a fur trader of the upstart North West Company of Montreal, which was then challenging the Hudson's Bay Company's monopoly, had descended the Bella Coola River from the interior and reached the coast on July 20, 1793. The local people told Mackenzie of a large boat containing people who looked like him and who were called "Macubah" and "Bensins," probably Vancouver and an unknown seaman. They also vaguely mentioned violence, but neither Vancouver nor any of his officers note it in their journals. Two days later, Mackenzie inscribed in red ochre on a large rock near Elcho Harbour: "Alexander Mackenzie, from Canada, by land." Searching for a northwest passage from the interior of the continent, Mackenzie succeeded in reaching the Pacific. But the route was so dangerous and difficult that it certainly was of no commercial value, and he had to be content with being the first European—probably the first person—to cross the entire continent by land, as he preceded Lewis and Clark's more southern transcontinental trek by more than a decade.

Dangers existed beyond tricky geography along the northern coast. The native peoples here were "more daring and insolent." On one occasion in August there was "an unprovoked attack on the boats" on Vancouver and his men by Tlingit warriors. When they landed their boat on a beach, he was initially unconcerned when five Tlingit canoes also pulled up nearby. The large group of Tlingit sauntered over, began to steal objects from the survey party and appeared "inclined to be turbulent." Realizing the danger too late to back away safely, Vancouver wrote that "our situation was now become very critical and alarming." As he and his men clambered into their boat, a warrior lunged and stabbed a sailor in the thigh with a spear. Another sailor was attacked, and yet other Tlingit warriors grabbed muskets from the bottom of the boat—whether for theft or to attack, no one knew. Vancouver yelled to Puget, in the other boat, for the guns to be fired. Ragged shots cut through the thick fog as the oarsmen in Vancouver's boat pulled mightily away from the shore. The confrontation left at least six, perhaps as many as a dozen, Tlingit dead on the stony beach.

Vancouver was greatly distressed by the encounter and the bloodshed. He wondered if it was he who had offended the Tlingit or if their greed was to blame for the altercation—or indeed, whether he and his men were scapegoated for the actions of others, likely rapacious fur traders. Perhaps the Tlingit were responding to "injuries they have sustained from other civilized visitors," he mused. Describing violent and aggressive fur traders as "civilized" seems an oxymoron, but Vancouver used the term frequently not as a pejorative but as a literal distinction between those who lived in cities and those who did not. In any case, he had a somewhat myopic view of theft and trespass. The two "worlds" having no understanding of each other's customs or languages, any encounter between them risked violence as a result of misunderstanding or insult. Vancouver and his crew, and all the fur traders, perceiving a wild "empty" land, freely chopped wood, took fresh water, hunted animals and fish, collected plants and berries and generally did as they pleased. Even though Vancouver disapproved, Menzies was curious about native burial sites and was interested in collecting human bones. Were the European visitors not stealing from local peoples and violating their sacred places? What if the coastal peoples had been sailing along the coast of Britain, France or Spain and behaved in this way?

VANCOUVER WAS EXHAUSTED and ill when he reluctantly ordered an end to the season's surveying. "The boisterous state of the weather, the advanced season of the year, and the approach of long dreary nights, left me doubt concerning the measures that ought to be now adopted." He ordered the retreat at Cape Decision near the end of September, satisfied that he had put an end to the talk of an inland sea or a northwest passage and the claims of "other pretenders to a prior knowledge of these regions." Against the backdrop of two years' experience on the coast, Vancouver then wrote optimistically of his belief that next year's survey "would be attended with less disappointment and fatigue."

The *Discovery* and *Chatham* returned south to Friendly Cove in October. Vancouver heard from Governor Ramón Saavedra that no new dispatches had arrived for him and neither had the *Daedalus* been sighted. He dallied only three days, looking forward to respite in the milder climes to the south and perhaps a resumption of their pleasant sojourn in California. The two ships sailed on to San Francisco, arriving on October 21 to hear disturbing news: the king and queen of France had been beheaded, and all of Europe was in turmoil. Here Vancouver also learned that the stay in California was not to be pleasant. José Joaquín de Arrillaga, the new acting governor of Monterey, had issued orders that the ship-weary British sailors were not to set foot in Spanish California. Vancouver could come ashore, perhaps accompanied by an officer or a midshipman, but the others were to remain on the ship. One can imagine the British crews glumly staring at the bountiful land, remembering last year's celebrations of feasting and horseback riding as Bodega y Quadra's honoured guests. The governor's unfriendly sentiments were not shared by the other residents of Spanish California. The Franciscan fathers, remembering Vancouver's past generosity, visited the ship bringing fresh beef and "a supply of Vegetables such as greens Radishes Pumkins Water Melons & a parcel of hazel nuts, together with a basket of pears & peaches." It did not go far, divided among hundreds of men who dreamt of fresh food.

The *Daedalus* joined them at sea en route from New South Wales with another year of provisions, and the three ships pressed on to Monterey. Arrillaga did not relent in his demand that the British remain on their ships, even while he offered some provisions and help in repairing the ships. All requests for food or aid, he decreed, were to be presented to him in writing, and he would consider the requests as time permitted. Arrillaga feared that Vancouver would discover the extent of Spanish military weakness and report on it. Perhaps the governor's fear was not entirely unfounded. Vancouver's officers took special note of the Spanish military preparations, and Puget wrote notes speculating on how a small party could seize the forts and gun emplacements. Vancouver himself wrote, "should the ambition of any civilized nation tempt it to seize on these unsupported ports, they could not make the least resistance." Spanish claims looked good on the map at the negotiating table, but they were quite flimsy on the ground. The governor grudgingly offered Vancouver a small patch of turf for use in transferring supplies, but the space was adjacent to the abattoir and stank of decay. Offended and annoyed, Vancouver ordered the departure of all three ships after only a few days. They continued south and put into port in San Diego, where they were pleasantly surprised to receive a friendly welcome—in defiance of the Arrillaga's orders. Here they learned the sobering news that Bodega y Quadra was inland, dying of an unknown sickness, and was unable to visit them. Vancouver compiled a great packet of dispatches, reports and nautical charts to be forwarded overland to London, and the ships set off to survey the coast of Baja California before crossing to Hawaii.

After hearing of the tumultuous events in Europe, however, Vancouver's men were even more impatient with their survey. Knowing that other postings in the navy were now likely, they resented being trapped on the far side of the world. Science, diplomacy and exploration were no longer so interesting when a war was being fought. The crews had already been away from Britain, their friends and their family longer than those on any of Cook's voyages had been, and they had been continuously working for longer than any other sailors in the Royal Navy. Now they were missing out on a chance for action and promotion, merely to continue this monotonous, hazardous and unpleasant task on the far side of the world. Vancouver wrote in a letter to his London agent that his men were "greatly mortified at our present detention from a more active station, which would be more congenial to our wishes than remaining here in a state of unpleasant inactivity."

The strain of the rebuff and their inhospitable treatment by the governor in California weighed heavily on the weary men. They were aching for a chance to go ashore and relax. Arguments, forgotten for months, resurfaced once again. Menzies and Vancouver fought over the plant frame on the quarterdeck; Menzies wrote a formal letter of complaint to Vancouver, keeping a copy to forward to Banks. Coolly and impersonally, Menzies outlined the problems caused by Vancouver's deaf ear to his requests and how his valuable work as a naturalist was being hampered by Vancouver's inattention. He added, in a postscript for Banks's exclusive viewing, that Vancouver was "passionate and illiberal in his abuse." Menzies was at least partly correct: Vancouver could not care less if fowls had gotten into the plant cabin, or if the plants had not been watered properly. He was impatient and irritable from illness and stress, and he still had received no new orders from his government.

Another shadow, however, hung over the ships' company—one that was not a direct result of the unexpectedly cool reception in Spanish California or the unsettling news from home. At some unspecified date during the summer, young Pitt had finally provoked Vancouver into an act of violence that would seal both their fates. It was a familiar scenario. Some copper sheets belonging to the ship went missing, and Vancouver could not learn who had taken them. The boatswain was accused of the deed. When the man was being flogged to determine what had happened to the copper, he cried out in pain: "Oh Mr. Pitt how can you see me thus used." Vancouver, "perceiving that Mr. Pitt had taken the copper," ordered the boatswain cut down from the mast and young Pitt tied to it to receive the lashes instead. Menzies recorded cryptically in his journal: "punishments of a very unpleasant nature." But now it was not Midshipman Pitt whom Vancouver had ordered to be publicly flogged; still unknown to them all, it was the Right Honourable Lord Camelford, Baron of Bocannoc, who was tied to the mast.

At Monterey, Vancouver made a fateful decision. He would send Pitt to Port Jackson in New South Wales, Australia, on the supply ship, from whence he could make his own way home. When the *Daedalus* sailed from Hawaii on February 8, 1794, Pitt and two other midshipmen were on board. Vancouver would be free of him and his insolence and pranks at last—or so he thought.

THE VOYAGE FROM California was swift and uneventful, and the *Discovery*, *Chatham* and *Daedalus* drew near to the east coast of Hawaii. On January 8 they had sailed into the heavily populated Hilo Bay to pay their respects to King Kamehameha. The king approached them in a grand ceremonial canoe and clambered nimbly aboard the quarterdeck, giving an astonished Vancouver a hearty embrace. The surf here, however, was too rough for the large ships to anchor safely, and Vancouver urged the king to move to Kealakekua Bay on the far side of the island. But the king demurred: Hilo was more suited to his relished sport of surfboarding, and it was where most of his people lived. Only after Vancouver suggested that the king was being unfriendly did Kamehameha relent and move his court to the sheltered side of the island.

The three British ships anchored in Kealakekua Bay and settled in for a pleasant six-week sojourn. "Many of our friends, particularly of the fair sex, lost no time in testifying the public sentiment in our favour," Vancouver wrote in his circumspect manner. No doubt the loquacious and refreshingly candid Manby had more to say about their welcome, but unfortunately no record of his survives of this second visit to Hawaii. The mariners feasted on hogs and fresh fruits, drank clean, fresh water and began to unwind. As in the previous winter, the balmy climate and friendly reception in Hawaii soothed frayed tempers and sweetened the sour atmosphere on the ships. Vancouver and the officers stopped quarrelling and violent punishments decreased, as did the behaviour that provoked them. Vancouver's illness retreated, and his energy and enthusiasm returned.

Vancouver had plans for his visit beyond relaxing. He immediately consented to help Kamehameha construct a thirty-six-foot schooner for the king's "warship" and set his carpenters to help the single American carpenter the king had already engaged. They laid the keel on February 1, and work progressed quickly under the skilled eyes of Vancouver's men. Vancouver donated all the metalwork, canvas, rope and masts to outfit the ship, which he named *Britannia*.

Meanwhile, Vancouver and his officers noted the absence of Kamehameha's queen, Kaahumanu, whom they all remembered fondly from the previous year. Kamehameha grew annoyed when asked about her, but Vancouver later learned that the two were estranged because the king suspected his queen of being overly familiar with a lesser chief. Vancouver had a suspicion that Kamehameha was trapped by propriety and was thus unable to bring her back without losing face. He made inquiries. He met Kaahumanu's father, who assured Vancouver that his daughter desired a reconciliation, and so after discussing it briefly with the king they worked on a plan together. Vancouver let it be quietly known that when Kaahumanu and some of her female companions and family were invited to the *Discovery* to receive gifts, Kamehameha could also come aboard, as if by accident, at the same time. The meeting would appear to occur by pure chance. Kamehameha agreed to board the ship only if he could be assured that he would be favourably received by his estranged queen, so Vancouver and the king devised a scheme that Vancouver would send a present ashore after he met the queen and determined her intentions. Kamehameha received the "present" from Vancouver and then, according to plan, made a great show of being annoyed by the meagreness of the gift. He rushed into his canoe and was quickly paddled across the water. Kamehameha burst into the cabin to confront Vancouver and acted startled to see Kaahumanu, who stood shyly with her eyes downcast. Vancouver grabbed his hand and joined it to hers, and soon they were hugging and talking again, apparently with tears of joy. John Naish writes that "Vancouver, having successfully managed a denouement which was reminiscent of a scene from one of Shakespeare's Comedies, joined in the general merriment and set the wine-a-flowing."

Vancouver did not help with Kamehameha's ship and developed a sly scheme to reconcile the king with his estranged wife purely for his own amusement. He had plans of his own. But just as he manipulated Kamehameha to further his own plans to end the ongoing civil war in the Hawaiian Islands and bring the islands over to Britain, Kamehameha sought to use his relationship with Vancouver to bolster his own power and prestige. According to the young yet insightful Puget, "If his Majesty can under the Cloak of Princely Liberality monopolize the Articles of Traffic, it will not only serve himself in that particular, but be the means of giving him additional Consequence." Vancouver again broached the subject of the war and the possibility of Kamehameha formally aligning himself with Britain. He had given up on his plan of trying to reconcile the warring factions and was probably too closely associated with Kamehameha to have any credibility with the others, anyway. Apparently he was persuasive enough in his arguments that Kamehameha called for a grand council of all the principal chiefs of the island to hear the arguments for and against such a move. While Vancouver awaited the arrival of the chiefs from all around the island, and while carpenters laboured on Kamehameha's warship *Britannia,* he allowed Menzies and Baker to engage in some volcano-climbing, knowing that they would miss the important assembly.

"WE FOUND THAT the natives regard volcanoes as the habitations of evil spirits," wrote Menzies. "When any-wise enraged, [they] throw up fire and hot stones; and to appease their wrath, they conceive it necessary to make some offering to these demons by throwing cloth, hogs, and vegetables into the volcano." None came empty-handed to the volcano, and Menzies and his party were "earnestly requested to leave something too, which we did, such as nails, beads, and pieces of tape, that greatly pleased them, and they seemed to think that such offerings would be highly acceptable to these demons." Menzies and Lieutenant Baker had hiked to the 8,269-foot summit of Hualalai, the mountain nearest to Kealakekua Bay, in mid-January soon after arriving in Hawaii. Now in mid-February they were ascending a greater peak, the famous volcano Mauna Loa.

At 13,677 feet above sea level, Mauna Loa is the world's most massive volcano and surely one of the most fascinating natural wonders Menzies and the others had ever seen. Menzies, Baker and three others of the ships' company had spent several days hiking along the lower reaches of the mighty volcano, starting out with a crowd of curious onlookers whose numbers dwindled as the temperature plummeted during the ascent. One morning they awoke covered in frost, and most of the Hawaiians refused to go farther. Once they passed the vegetation level they slogged, shivering, ever upward through snow. With the temperature at 33°F, right at the freezing mark, they huddled around a small fire made from their walking sticks and nibbled their remaining provisions: a few coconuts, some chocolate and a fair bit of rum. They "could not sleep much nor was it to be expected." By this time some of them were already suffering blinding headaches, nausea, exhaustion and dehydration, brought on by the high altitude.

Awaiting the first rays of the sun, Menzies had time to contemplate their unusual predicament—freezing on a tropical island. He was amazed to have gone from tropical heat and dense vegetation, through barren rocky scrub and dried fissures from lava flows, to freezing snow in a few days of walking. "At this time," he wrote, "so many thousand feet high, reclined on the hard rock for our bed with no other shelter than the grand canopy of heaven, our minds very variously occupied sometimes meditating on the dreadful consequences of a snowstorm coming on whilst thus situated and at other times contemplating the awful and extended scene around us, where the most profound stillness subsisted the whole night, not even interrupted by the least chirp of a bird. The moon rose out of the sea at an immense distance and her orb appeared uncommonly large and brilliant... [It] led the imagination to the utmost stretch."

After a suitably subdued and hasty scramble to the rim of the crater on February 16 to view the rim's snow-encrusted, black jagged rocks and the cindery mass in the caldera, the weary party, now with only a few coconuts remaining for food and low on water, stumbled down the precipitous incline, shivering from the cold. When they reached the previous night's campsite they were stunned. A campmate who had elected not to venture to the summit with them had fled down the mountain, taking all the rum with him. "It sounded like the knell of death on us," Menzies wrote dispiritedly. Another brutal day of stumbling brought them down to a lower-elevation encampment at ten in the evening. It was, Menzies wrote, "the most persevering and hazardous struggle that can possibly be conceived." The small party had ascended the greatest mountain volcano on the islands, with Kamehameha's approval. It was the first recorded ascent of that peak, possibly the first ascent ever. It was certainly the highlight of Menzies's island excursions, a feat he proudly recalled years later and, despite the hardship and danger, a blessed opportunity to be free of the ship and the scrutinizing eyes of the captain.

Vancouver himself was not present for this first recorded climbing of Mauna Loa. He was busy with other work: laying the foundations for the greatest diplomatic coup of his voyage and for his life's most unusual and little-known accomplishment.

THOUSANDS OF PEOPLE were gathered for the grand concourse of chiefs, and Vancouver politely received each of the dozens of ranking chiefs, including an older warrior, Papeah, who claimed to be the man who stabbed Cook. Papeah still displayed scars from the battle and was honoured and respected for the deed. The pride would seem incongruous or ill-placed, considering that Vancouver had been present all those years ago for that very battle and that he was here now to persuade the chiefs to cede their land to the same nation for which Cook sailed. But the two sides held no hard feelings, and the grand concourse began with plays, sporting games, dances, performances and much feasting and greeting of old comrades. Vancouver added to the festivities by arranging a spectacular fireworks display from his dwindling supplies.

Peace and war in the islands were the great topics of discussion. In addition to having their own internal conflicts, the islanders were coming to grips with the effects of the frequent visits of European and American ships. Many, perhaps most, of these ships' captains and sailors were interested in nothing other than a quick profit: some were violent, some kidnapped women (only to throw them overboard later), some cruised off in the night without repaying debts, while others sold low-quality merchandise, including guns of such poor craftsmanship that they exploded in the face of the first person to fire them. The islanders were increasingly unable, because of inferior technology, to police their own waters. They had no authority over the well-armed ships anchored offshore that chose to act criminally. Essentially they found themselves defenceless against aggressive or hostile armed Europeans and Americans. Many of the chiefs felt that a protecting power would help them keep control over their own affairs.

Apart from the mutual respect and friendship between Vancouver and Kamehameha, cultural similarities attracted the islanders to Britain rather than to the United States. Both Hawaii and Britain were monarchies, whereas the United States was a democratic republic, a governing structure that made no sense and was perhaps even feared by the upper classes. In turn, Vancouver and other British mariners admired the culture of the islanders, comparing it favourably with that of Europe. One hierarchical class-based society recognized and saluted the other. Vancouver had witnessed first-hand the absolute power of the rulers of Hawaii. One day, while playing together, a low-born boy injured the son of a chief; the boy's eyes were jabbed out. He was left blind and alone for two days, before being strangled to death for the offence. Although Vancouver could not have known it, this incident would prove to be an apt metaphor for his future unravelling. He was soon to feel the power and retribution of his own hereditary aristocracy.

Kamehameha, the seven principal regional chiefs of Hawaii and Vancouver's senior officers gathered in the cabin of the *Discovery* on the sultry evening of February 25. Kamehameha rose, and the group fell silent as he prepared to speak. He began with a lengthy preamble detailing his relations and friendship with "his good, faithful Brother King George." He listed all the presents given to him by Vancouver, "the Agent or representative of said brother," and highlighted the political advantages that would arise from a stronger political affiliation with Britain and her powerful king. Foremost among these advantages was the ability of the Hawaiians to defend themselves against the increasing numbers of foreign ships arriving at the islands. Another chief spoke about the need for conquering Maui and said that the military force provided by Britain would certainly help in this conquest. Another chief, Keeamoku, asked, as related by Menzies, "what advantages were they to gain by this cession of the island. Would the King of Britain fight their battles & defend their plantations? Would he leave a Vessel at the Island to guard their Coast from invasion? Or would he give them arms and ammunition to defend themselves & their property? If he would do either of these he said he should readily give his consent." Others also spoke, all favourable to the proposal.

Kamehameha pointed out the ship now under construction in the harbour under Vancouver's guidance and claimed that it "would be the means of defending the Island & overawing their enemies from further attack." He then made his proposal to give up the island to Britain, and they unanimously voted in favour, and, according to Vancouver, "acknowledged themselves to be subjects of Great Britain... They were no longer *Tanata no Owhyee*, the people of Owhyee; but *Tanata no Britannee*, the people of Britain." A crier shouted the news from the *Discovery*'s deck to the great congregation of canoes, while Puget rowed ashore to plant the Union Jack and take formal possession of the island. The ships fired their guns in commemoration, and Vancouver presented Kamehameha with a copper plaque detailing the ceremony.

Numerous historians have pointed out that Kamehameha and his chiefs certainly held a different view of the ceremony than did Vancouver and his officers. What the king and chiefs wanted was protection from other European and American visitors and military help in their civil war. Even Vancouver noted that they all repeatedly stressed that "their religion, government, and domestic economy was noticed; and it was clearly understood, that no interference was to take place in either." Clearly the Hawaiians viewed the agreement as one that created the relationship of a protectorate rather than being a true cession of sovereignty.

A week after the ceremony, on March 3, Vancouver bid farewell to Kealakekua Bay for the final time. The *Discovery* and *Chatham* weighed anchor and sailed off into "a serene, tranquil ocean, fanned by a gentle breeze." The decks of the ships were crowded with more than a hundred hogs, a final parting gift from Kamehameha, and below decks the ships were well stocked with fresh fruit and vegetables. Before leaving the islands altogether Vancouver wanted to finish his partial nautical survey of the islands he had missed so far, so the ships spent two weeks cruising the remaining uncharted coasts of Maui, Oahu and Kauai. They visited the two young women they had left behind the previous year, and Menzies reported that the women had astutely given away most of the gifts they had received from Vancouver and the officers, "by which means they became respected for their generosity and now lived comfortable and happy." All was apparently good on Vancouver's Hawaiian estates, where the women lived. In his idle moments, perhaps Vancouver imagined returning as the governor of the newly ceded island group.

THE *DISCOVERY* AND *Chatham* sailed directly to Cook Inlet, Alaska. Vancouver's plan was to start as far north as they planned to go, at 60 degrees latitude, and then work their way south to Cape Decision, their completion point from the year before. Vancouver was already convinced that they were not going to discover any great inland seas or a northwest passage south of the Arctic. He had seen too much of the coast to believe it would magically change, and he was running out of unexplored space for any waterway to exist other than in Cook Inlet. His depressing realization was shared by the officers and crew. Certainly they had done good work from a scientific and perhaps diplomatic perspective, but they had not made a great geographical discovery that would ensure their fame and careers. They were able to suppress their natural anxiety and curiosity about European affairs while they were in Hawaii, on light duty and with plenty of recreational opportunities, but sailing north again to the cold, drizzly coast for yet another season of monotonous and tedious survey work was not inspiring or morale boosting. What of the war in Europe? How fared the Royal Navy? What opportunities for advancement were slipping by while they wasted their time charting this final bit of coast in the freezing north—claimed by the Russians anyway and certainly of no immediate value?

The one flaw in the plan of starting in the north in early April was the weather. Although Vancouver had visited Cook Inlet before when sailing with Cook, that visit had been during late May and June, and he was unprepared for the freezing cold of April. In the North Pacific the "climate began to assume a degree of severity that was new to us... the mercury stood at the freezing point, and for the first time during the voyage the scuttle cask on the deck was frozen." The men, so used to the heat of Hawaii, suffered pitiably to now be exposed to the cold. By April 12 they sighted land but were then buffeted by a storm bringing frost and snow. The two ships carefully picked their way through ice floes and giant tides that threatened to grind the hulls of the ships apart. They sailed up Cook Inlet as far the large ships could safely go and then sent out the crews in the smaller boats for one last, slim chance of glory. If a northwest passage existed at all, it would be here. Whidbey spent two days rowing up the waterway, surrounded by ice-encrusted, malevolent-looking peaks that "appeared to form an uninterrupted barrier." The waterway was blocked. Vancouver was a little perturbed to find that "Cook's River" was indeed an inlet, noting that if Cook had spent only one more day exploring it they all could have been spared a great deal of discomfort. The ships continued plodding south through chunks of ice, carrying out their "very irksome and tedious task."

The boat crews, led by Puget, Johnstone and Whidbey as in the previous year, slowly worked their way into every major inlet and around every large island. They briefly encountered many native groups from several cultures. All the local people were familiar with the Russian traders and knew Russian words. Puget concluded that they were controlled by aggressive Russian traders who employed them as hunters and treated them as serfs, indentured under the threat of violence. In the past decade Russian traders had constructed permanent trading posts in the region, including at Cook Inlet and Prince William Sound, and they were making trading voyages even farther south. Vancouver visited several tiny outposts and found them filthy and stinky, little more than clusters of rude log huts, and did not linger long. Approaching one hut on a muddy footpath, his nose was assaulted by "a most intolerable stench, the worst, excepting the skunk, I had ever the inconvenience of experiencing." As the crews entered the territory of the Tlingit once again, the encounters became more strained, and they feared violence similar to that of the year before. On several occasions they narrowly avoided attack only by quick thinking and defensive precautions. Vancouver and his senior explorers, Whidbey and Johnstone, had no inclination to shoot people.

The men had to contend not only with the harsh weather but also with their master's increasingly erratic behaviour. The melancholy weather and the tedious minutiae of his task again took their toll on Vancouver's overtaxed body and mind. Surging from extreme to extreme, seemingly without reason, his moods became a matter of grave concern for his officers. Wild bouts of uncontrolled fury were followed by days of listless torpor, in which the captain morosely stared from the deck of the ship at the passing land. Menzies, who recorded that he had "constantly prescribed for Capt. Vancouver himself since we left England" (what, he does not tell us) was disturbed by his captain's response to seemingly insignificant events, such as the theft of a trinket from the ship by a visiting chief that drove him into a passion. But Vancouver never considered halting the expedition on account of his own health—he would rather have died on the job than have failed to complete it.

Near the end of the survey, however, Vancouver was clearly ill. One day, after weeks of monotonous convalescence aboard the *Discovery* while the charting continued in the smaller ships, he became agitated and restless, and he set out in a small boat to join his men. He was forced to return after only a few hours, "seized with a most violent indisposition, which terminated in a bilious colic, that confined me for several days to my apartments." It was his final effort at surveying away from the *Discovery*. Much of his time thereafter was spent laid up in his cabin. His illness now left him plenty of time to reflect on his life, and he developed a yearning for home, a nostalgia for the halcyon days of his youth in Norfolk. His mind drifted to the ones he loved. While standing at the deck of the swaying ship in the drizzle, exposed to the periodic squalls, looking out over the shadowy shore in the distance, grey and desolate, he pulled from his memory names important to him. A curious collection of place names dot the fjords of southern Alaska—the long and winding Lynn Canal after his native town, the nearby Point Bridget after his mother, Point Mary after his older sister. And, with a grandiose flourish of Vancouver's pen, the "panhandle" of Alaska became New Norfolk, now populated with landmarks honouring villages and friends from his homeland.

On the rolling sea just off the present-day British Columbia–Alaska border, Vancouver, undoubtedly ill and driven by little more than willpower, completed his hydrographic survey and appropriately named his final anchorage Port Conclusion. It was August 19, 1794—two and a half years and three survey seasons after he began his cartographic quest to chart Pacific America. Before departing for home, the weary mariners held a special celebration, with "a double allowance of grog... for the purpose of drinking His Majesty's health." The men continued the celebration when the officers had retired, laughing with "no small portion of facetious mirth" about their four-year April Fool's joke, scouring the coast for the mythical Strait of Anian. Proving that the strait did not exist, however, was almost as important as finding where it might have been; there could be no more speculation. Vancouver was pleased, writing that his survey would "remove every doubt, and set aside every opinion of a north-west passage..."

After years of meandering through the mist, the weary mariners, in dilapidated boats, had mapped most of the major inlets and waterways of Puget Sound and the Strait of Georgia. They had proved that Vancouver Island was indeed an island and established that "Cook's River," which even the vaunted explorer thought might lead to a western or polar sea, was in fact an inlet. Vancouver had solved the puzzle of the complex and deceptive continental shoreline and plotted everything on his great chart. When Charles Wilkes resurveyed Puget Sound for the U.S. Navy in 1841, he was amazed at the accuracy Vancouver had achieved under such adverse conditions and despite his failing health. Well into the 1880s Vancouver's charts of the Alaskan coastline remained the accepted standard. His surprisingly accurate chart of the vast stretch of previously obscure shoreline, a long, tortuous and confusing line from Oregon to Alaska, was sent off to the Admiralty in London. The coast of Pacific America was no longer *terra incognita*—it was a place on a map. North America now had a shape.

THE *DISCOVERY* AND the *Chatham* cruised into Nootka Sound for one final visit in early September. They met the new governor, José Manuel de Álava. Although friendly and hospitable, Álava had no news or instructions for Vancouver. But he was expecting his own documents for the negotiations, and he suggested that Vancouver stay as his guest until they arrived. In the meantime, Vancouver and Álava hosted Maquinna aboard the *Discovery* in a manner "suitable to his rank," and they were in turn invited to the chief's great cedar home for a celebration. The time passed smoothly and without incident, but the men were driven nearly mad with impatience to return home as they worked to repair the extensive damage to the ships. By mid-October there was no word, and Vancouver reluctantly ordered the ships to sail on to Monterey. At Monterey there were also no instructions from the British government.

Over two and a half years had passed since Vancouver had had any communication from home. Had the messages been lost or captured? Perhaps the silence was the result of an oversight, and his work was being praised and applauded in the highest circles. How could it not be so, considering the difficulty of Vancouver's task and his thoroughness in completing it? The uncertainty continued to gnaw at his gut, destroying whatever remained of his constitution and feeding his anxiety and fear in the quiet nights.

The hated governor Arrillaga was no longer in charge in Spanish California, however, and once again the British ships were welcomed hospitably. They purchased fresh food, rode horses, went hunting and explored on shore. Vancouver promoted Manby from master of the *Chatham* to lieutenant of the *Discovery*—a great promotion for one so young, but Manby left no record of whether he had finally forgiven Vancouver for his outburst years earlier. In early December the ships put to sea for the home voyage, leaving the Nootka Sound Convention unresolved. They celebrated Christmas, their fourth away from home, off the coast of Panama. The men were issued extra rations of grog, with which they toasted the memory of Bodega y Quadra and Kame-hameha, the two great leaders who had hosted them so generously, and without whose help their task would have proved impossible.

As they continued south along the western coast of South America, scurvy appeared in the crew. Even with additional citrus rations, the cases grew more numerous. On March 25, 1795, Vancouver decided to put into Valparaiso, the first European-style city the British sailors had seen since leaving Cape Town more than four years earlier. While the men recovered from scurvy and repaired their once-again storm-battered ships, Vancouver, Puget, Menzies and several other officers accepted an invitation from the governor to visit Santiago. Horses and an escort were provided for the journey. The leading citizens received them with great honour and hosted them in fine rooms, with good beds and plenty of delicious food. They enjoyed two weeks of social-izing, parties, dancing and dinners before reluctantly returning to the coast. But Vancouver's health had again deteriorated. After the fete in Santiago the captain was "in a very feeble and debilitated state," and he could not stay on board the ship because it was too uncomfort-able. He went ashore while others supervised the work on the ships, strengthening them as best they could for the terrifying voyage round Cape Horn.

Still battered, leaky, with tattered sails and rotting ropes, the *Discovery* and *Chatham* rounded Cape Horn and, for the first time in over four years, departed the Pacific Ocean. They entered the Atlan-tic Ocean on a course to South Africa in quest of news and supplies. Surely, a hero's welcome awaited them.

PART IV

In the most FAITHFUL MANNER

TWELVE

Powerful Enemies

——◄ ◈ ►——

PORT JACKSON IN 1794 was a ramshackle outpost of tiny wooden houses, perched precariously on the rim of the vast, untamed hinterland of the Australian wilderness. Convicts shuffled by under the watchful eyes of their jailers while Aborigines squatted in the dust in the scorching heat. The young Lord Camelford strolled down the beach. He was both confused and pleased with the knowledge of his father's death. He had never been overly intimate with the man, but his father had left him with something very valuable indeed: the means of revenging himself against the man who had wounded his pride, humiliated him and tarnished his honour. When he returned to Britain he would assume the mantle of nobility and tour his grand estates, but for now the raw-boned, sunburned youth contented himself with scheming for a chance to regain his home while proving his abilities as a navy officer. He would not return home in professional disgrace, a disgrace brought on by what he believed were George Vancouver's unjust, tyrannical actions. He knew that Vancouver's official reports could seriously impede if not entirely derail his career in the Royal Navy, regardless of his social rank; the navy had its own code, which sometimes transcended class and privilege. Lord Camelford would somehow have to prove that his poor record reflected Vancouver's resentment, envy and animosity rather than any failings of his own.

Thomas Pitt made his way north from Australia through the archipelago of southeast Asia, the East Indies, perhaps by catching rides on a series of merchant ships. Eight months later he was on a ship bound from China to India, where his great-great-grandfather had first made the family fortune with the East India Company. At the Dutch port of Malacca he spied the British frigate *Resistance*, commanded by Edward Pakenham. Pitt charmed his way to a position aboard the forty-four-gun ship, and after a few weeks, before the end of December 1794, while the *Discovery* was cruising south from California on the home voyage, he had already been promoted to acting lieutenant. Pakenham was apparently much taken with the young officer, writing to the Admiralty that Pitt was "a most promising Officer, every way qualified for Promotion, and bids fair to prove a credit to the service." Pakenham urged Lord Grenville, Pitt's brother-in-law, to press for the lad's official promotion and wrote to Pitt's mother praising his abilities and maturity. Either Pitt was exerting extreme self-control, forcefully checking the impulsive arrogance, disobedience and temper that so infuriated Vancouver, or Pakenham sought to use Pitt's connections to further his own station—or both. In any case, after a year on the *Resistance*, Pakenham urged his new third lieutenant to leave his post, claiming that there was no possibility for his further promotion in the Indian Ocean squadron.

The twenty-year-old Pitt, now the possessor of more personal riches than the combined assets of his entire ship's company, then purchased a small ship, the *Union*, hired twenty men to crew it and set off west on a further adventure en route to home. The *Union* was a poor purchase. Aged and waterlogged, it soon sprang several leaks. Days of round-the-clock pumping kept the sinking scow afloat until the crew sighted land on the horizon. As the ship's timbers warped and burst in the surf, Pitt ordered his men to launch the small boats just before the *Union* slid under the waves. The exhausted party rowed all day and night, pulling up on the beach of Ceylon after midnight. Here they remained for a month, until February 1795, when Pitt sailed in the East India Company frigate *Swift* across the Arabian Sea, arriving at Suez in mid-April. From there he ventured overland on camel to Alexandria and then chartered a boat to Venice.

While in quarantine in Venice Pitt wrote two letters that outlined his dual passions: promotion and revenge. To his mother, he exhorted: "for God sake make haste to get me the Rank of Post Captain that I may not throw away any more time… all depends upon the present moment." He desperately wanted the status of a senior rank in the navy and believed that such a rank could be secured by his mother. He also wrote to his old captain, Vancouver, in a lordly and arrogant tone, demanding that Vancouver meet him in Hamburg on August 8, 1795, for a duel. Listing the ignominies he had suffered at Vancouver's hand aboard the *Discovery,* Pitt then threatened Vancouver: "Be assured Vancouver all this will not do, things have gone much too far and the result of an obstinate refusal will only be the heaping of reiterated disgraces on your head." Only by accepting the duel, he claimed, could Vancouver salvage "the few surviving remnants of your shattered character." As an afterthought, Pitt then enclosed a draft for £100, "which you are at liberty to make use of in defraying the Expenses of your journey."

ROUNDING CAPE HORN, the *Discovery* and *Chatham* battled terrifying snowstorms, mountainous waves and ferocious winds. Their aging sails tore, their rotting ropes split and their sodden wooden planks sagged, stretched and leaked. Passing into the Atlantic Ocean, the imminent danger passed, and on June 8, 1795, Vancouver ordered the *Discovery* to leave the *Chatham* behind because she was sailing too slowly. But as had happened on several past occasions, when the *Discovery* reached the island of St. Helena off the west coast of Africa on July 2, the *Chatham* was there, snugly anchored and patiently waiting. Whether it was deliberate or not, the *Chatham's* erratic sailing speed was undoubtedly exasperating for Vancouver.

Before sailing into port at St. Helena, Vancouver issued an unpopular directive collecting all the journals, log books and drawings of all "the officers, petty officers and gentlemen on board the *Discovery*." Although for reasons of national security this was not an uncommon naval practice, Vancouver was met with stony and barely veiled hostility. These were personal accounts, written in hard conditions during years of loneliness and isolation, and many crew members had dreams of publication, fame and money from their literary works, for which there was usually a great demand. Vancouver merely followed orders to collect these writings, but he still bore the brunt of the men's disappointment. The men grumbled, but the material was delivered; all were aware of Vancouver's sudden, seemingly uncontrollable bursts of fury, his intolerance of any questioning of his command and his inflexible, literal-minded nature. They may have suspected him of slowly going mad, swinging as he did from genial and hearty to morosely moody to raging and irrationally angry. Surely, they thought, a more rational or humane commander would have found some way around the tedious orders of the Admiralty. Menzies, who had suspected this order would be forthcoming, begged to keep his journal until the completion of the voyage, and Vancouver easily granted his request. Menzies, however, had other plans. Months earlier, as the ships were anchored in Valparaiso, he had written another letter to Banks outlining his version of the events of the voyage and adding that "when the Journals of the Voyage &c. are demanded by Captain Vancouver, I mean to seal up mine, & address them to you, so that I hope you will receive them."

At St. Helena, Vancouver reported to the governor and discovered that the war between Britain and France had broadened to include Holland. During the previous winter, French troops had conquered the country and captured the Dutch fleet that was iced in at Texel. Britain declared war. Not long after Vancouver heard this news, from the masthead the lookout spied an unsuspecting Dutch merchant ship approaching. Vancouver ordered the *Discovery* ready for action, and the battered survey ship sallied forth to capture the heavily laden *Macassar* without a fight. The crew were all cheerful at the prospect of prize money, but seventeen men had to be moved from the *Discovery* to sail the new vessel, leaving the *Discovery* shorthanded for the final voyage home. After a few weeks of repairs to get the ships seaworthy again, the *Discovery* and *Chatham* departed for home on separate courses. The *Chatham* sailed to Brazil first, with dispatches to a British force then preparing to sail and capture Cape Town, while the *Discovery* rushed to catch up with a north-headed convoy for protection in case it met French privateers.

The loss of seventeen men to the prize ship made sailing the *Discovery* much more difficult. On July 28 Vancouver was shorthanded and ordered the sailor who was tending to Menzies's plant frame to regular duties on watch. When a storm blew in, the sailor was ordered aloft by the ranking officer on deck. The frame was left uncovered, and the plants were drenched and flooded, ruining some and seriously damaging others. Menzies was devastated, for he had issued strict orders to replace the glass cover of the frame during any storm. He stalked onto the quarterdeck and confronted Vancouver, demanding that the man be punished. Vancouver, however, heard the case and, finding that the man was obeying the orders of a senior officer, ordered no punishment. Menzies was furious; he challenged the captain publicly and loudly.

A public challenge on his quarterdeck was the one thing sure to unbalance Vancouver. He "flew into a rage" and ordered Menzies to be placed under arrest until he could convene a court martial for "great contempt and disrespect." Confined to his cabin, Menzies wrote a letter to Banks that was sent off as soon as the convoy sailed to the west coast of Ireland, on September 13, 1795. He painted Vancouver as an irrational tyrant and suggested that "I trust you will have the goodness to inform their Lordships, in my vindication, that the alleged complaint for which I have been put under arrest by Captain Vancouver, has wholly arisen from his own proceedings." Banks, who had never received a report favourable to Vancouver during all the long years of the voyage, brooded over what course of action to take.

Vancouver, perhaps sensing trouble, issued a written request to Menzies demanding his journals. Menzies's original orders for the voyage were to deliver his journals and drawings to Joseph Banks and the secretary of state rather than to the Admiralty. The intractable Scot, angry at his commander while under arrest and facing court martial for the earlier incident on the quarterdeck, yet secure in the support of Banks, reasoned that Vancouver had no right to his writings. If Menzies ever regretted accepting his appointment as the *Discovery's* surgeon, he did now. In taking the post, he had become a regular member of the ship's company and subject to Vancouver's orders. But Menzies was not one to give up easily. He claimed that Vancouver referred to him as the surgeon, and he would certainly deliver the sick book and related material on the health of the crew; but his other written material and drawings pertaining to the natural history he would keep to give to Banks. Vancouver, not unusually, was enraged, but he had urgent dispatches to deliver to the Admiralty. He handed command of the *Discovery* to Lieutenant Baker and rushed off to London, "not however without emotions... natural on parting with a society with whom I had lived so long, shared so many dangers."

The *Discovery* and *Chatham* arrived home in London by mid-October to little fanfare, and the crews were paid off by the end of the month. The war with France was the only item of interest, and as a result the only public mention of Vancouver's great voyage and all its incredible accomplishments was a short paragraph in the *Annual Register* and a few lines in other papers. No great tour and lecture circuit, no rounds of fashionable drawing rooms, no lionizing editorials. But anonymity and the lack of recognition for his accomplishments were mild responses, compared with the treatment Vancouver would receive in the coming year.

He spent the weeks until November 3 wrapping up the affairs of the ships—finalizing the records, cataloguing the remaining stores and paying off and transferring the crew to other ships and positions. He fought for the interests of his crew, arguing for their promotion and settling outstanding grievances and legal matters. On November 4, he was placed on half pay and lingered in London for two months before moving to Bristol Hot Springs, in January 1796, hoping to recover his health at the resort. He wanted "to take advantage of the salubrious air, and waters of this place... I hope to establish the foundation of a perfect cure." But his health, so fragile and erratic during the final years of the voyage, degenerated rapidly once he had discharged his official responsibilities. He was soon in "a very debilitated state," and his brothers held little hope of a full recovery. While Vancouver's mind cleared and his tendency towards erratic rages abated along with his anxiety, his physical state worsened. Weakness, aching joints, loss of appetite, nausea and vomiting rendered him unfit for travel and allowed him little pleasure or enjoyment. No longer needing to remain in control of his ships, he began to slide into his illness. Once he was able to let go of his responsibilities, illness latched on with vigour and drained his vitality. Soon the captain was little more than a husk of his former self.

He requested permission from the Admiralty to use his and his officers' journals and drawings made during the voyage to prepare a published account of the great expedition. He also asked for a reimbursement of the expenses incurred in producing engravings for the final work, a request that was held up by bureaucratic stalling. Moving to a stone cottage in the village of Petersham, a few miles up the Thames, Vancouver settled down to complete the final, sedentary portion of his work—to produce a clear record of his incredible voyage so that it would not be lost to history. His financial situation was his one great worry: he had received no official pay since December 1790 and was not about to receive any soon. And the prize money due from the capture of the *Macassar* was held up in a legal dispute over the distribution of the substantial proceeds. No record exists of why Vancouver's pay was withheld, but the delay certainly caused him great hardship. He was living on savings and on borrowed funds against the security of his pay. Soon his creditors began to hound him, and he desperately sought advances from his London prize agent to meet expenses. Menzies, in contrast—whose salary, at Banks's urging, was more than double Vancouver's captain's salary during the voyage—had already received all his back pay and expenses, as had all the other officers.

Vancouver had been settled in Petersham for only a few months when Thomas Pitt's condescending and threatening letter challenging him to a duel arrived in the summer of 1796. Although rumours had circulated in London, within certain circles, that a challenge was forthcoming, Vancouver knew nothing about them until he read the letter. He was in no condition to travel—nor was he strong enough for a duel, even if he had been inclined to accept Pitt's call for satisfaction. Fortunately the letter was delivered to him after August 8, the date Pitt had stipulated for the engagement. But this unnerving incident would not be the end of their turbulent relationship.

Vancouver still believed that normal bureaucratic channels and procedures would deal with his legitimate concerns regarding Pitt's instability and aggression. He composed a letter in response to Pitt's and directed it to Camelford House in London rather than to Hamburg, wherein he asserted that Pitt's actions alone had resulted in the punishments and that a captain was not accountable "in a private capacity to answer for his Public Conduct in his official duty." Furthermore, Vancouver wrote, if Pitt wanted to pursue the matter he would be "willing to submit the Examination of his conduct to his Lordship's further satisfaction to any Flag Officer of His Majesty's Navy." He received no reply from the agitated youth. Lord Grenville, Pitt's brother-in-law, was aware of the developments and intervened to try and halt a scandal, but he was too late. As soon as Pitt set foot in London, he dashed off in a coach to Vancouver's home in Petersham. He pounded on the door with his fist and lunged into the entry when the door opened. He demanded a duel immediately, as they were now "two men face to face," and roared his fury over Vancouver's calm attempts to refute the accusations and extricate himself from personal responsibility for his professional conduct. Pitt, according to Vancouver's sworn testimony, growled that he had "thirsted for [Vancouver's] blood and that the idea had kept him alive" in the years after he was sent home. Vancouver somehow was able to shut the door on him, but not before Pitt spoke his final threat: he would get his satisfaction from Vancouver in a duel, somewhere, somehow.

In this militaristic age of the Napoleonic wars, refusing a duel—sometimes known as a trial of honour—could be construed as an act of cowardice or weakness, or even an admission of guilt. Vancouver, as a senior naval officer concerned with his reputation, wanted to make sure that his refusal of Lord Camelford's demands would not prejudice him. He spoke to several highly placed individuals, including the fair-minded Lord Grenville, all of whom advised him not to answer personally the demands for satisfaction arising from his professional actions. Vancouver carefully wrote out another refusal to duel, again offering for any flag officer to be the adjudicator of their dispute. On September 8, Vancouver's brother Charles delivered the note to Camelford House. He was met by the young lord, who sneered, was wild-eyed and shook with suppressed rage. Claiming that Vancouver was a cowering "Poltroon," Pitt vowed to wait for him in a coffee house and insult him publicly. If Vancouver refused to join him in combat like a gentleman in order to defend his honour, then he "should meet him, box it out, and try which was the better man."

Suspecting that Pitt was serious, Vancouver approached Lord Grenville, who despite his close relationship to the Pitt family (having married Thomas's younger sister Anne), remained one of the few powerful men who would treat Vancouver with respect. Grenville agreed that Lord Camelford was wild and unpredictable, although he refused to hear Vancouver's defence of his actions against him on the *Discovery* and suggested that Vancouver apply to the court for protection against the dangerous and violent Lord. On September 20, Charles and the ailing George Vancouver swore jointly to the truth of the series of events leading up to Pitt's final threat. Their lawyer, J.A. Park, advised them that because Lord Camelford was a peer of the realm, their case would be presented not in the usual straightforward fashion but in person to the Lord Chancellor, Lord Loughborough.

The next day the two brothers set out from Vancouver's lodgings at 142 Bond Street for Lord Loughborough's house in Bedford Square. By ill luck, or more probably as a result of information from spies employed by the wealthy lord, when Charles and George rounded the corner onto Conduit Street, there was Lord Camelford, waiting across the street in the company of two companions. Decked out in full naval regalia, Pitt strode directly across the street and raised his cane to strike Vancouver so that he would be insulted and goaded into accepting a challenge. As Pitt lunged forward, Charles leaped in front of his invalid brother, slammed his fist into Camelford's shoulder and grasped at his collared throat to keep him away. Camelford turned his attention to Charles, attacking him as he was hauled off by the crowd. Then Camelford lashed out with his cane while the debilitated Vancouver weakly parried the blows, until the crowd restrained the furious lord. Camelford threw off the restraining hands, swore he would attack Vancouver whenever he encountered him and then levelled a sneering challenge to Charles as he retreated through the crowd of onlookers.

As the crowd dispersed, the two brothers collected their wits and slowly went on their way to Lord Loughborough's residence, where they presented their case. Then they went to swear their affidavit in the presence of a notary. Lord Loughborough sent a note demanding Lord Camelford's presence the next morning. That night, however, an account of the day's events appeared in the *Herald,* including the assertion that Vancouver had been attacked with a series of blows by a "Lieutenant" for declining a duel of honour. An infuriated Charles Vancouver composed a refutation to the biased and incorrect report, and it appeared in the *Morning Chronicle* on September 22. Charles's letter set out the facts and background of the dispute, including Lord Camelford's punishment for misconduct as an officer on the *Discovery*. Meanwhile, however, the Lord Chancellor had met with the wild-eyed and trembling Camelford, calmed the young lord and informed him that he must put up a £5,000 surety to keep His Majesty's Peace, with an additional £5,000 to be supplied on demand by two guarantors, Lord Grenville and another companion. As soon as Charles's refutation appeared in the *Morning Chronicle,* one of Lord Camelford's cronies delivered it to the Lord Chancellor and received the right to print a public defence because Charles's account had been published after Camelford had agreed to his surety for good behaviour. Charles was to blame for fanning the flames of the dispute, judged Lord Loughborough.

"The power of coffee-house scandal when manipulated by members of the establishment," observed the historian John Naish, "was every bit as powerful then as the sanctimonious power of journalism today." During the following few weeks the papers were filled with personal anecdotes of Vancouver's nastiness, and puns, jokes and stories appeared that ridiculed Vancouver as a coward for refusing to duel Camelford. It was a campaign "clearly inspired by Lord Camelford's friends," writes Nikolai Tolstoy in his biography of Camelford, *The Half-Mad Lord.* Vancouver should change his name to "Rear-cover," claimed one paper. "Captain Vancouver says that Lord Camelford cannot *write.* He must, however, acknowledge, that the young Nobleman can *make his mark,*" the *True Briton* declared. It also claimed two days later that Lord Camelford had a power to rival the first lord of the Admiralty, for "he has made Captain Couver *a yellow rear*" (yellow for coward; yet also an allusion to the rank in the Royal Navy of yellow rear admiral, the next promotion Vancouver might strive for). One other much-discussed rumour was that there was a failed mutiny aboard the *Discovery*. Vancouver had no hope of being portrayed in a fair or compassionate light. He became a laughingstock, and worse was to come.

On the morning of October 1, 1796, the public was treated to a satirical cartoon by the famous political caricaturist James Gillray, the most prominent and popular caricaturist of the day. The sketch, titled *The Caneing in Conduit Street,* was mockingly dedicated "to the Flag Officers of the British Navy." Gillray painted the terminally ill Vancouver as a cringing, grossly overweight, incompetent, corrupt coward. A heroic Lord Camelford boldly cries: "Give me satisfaction, Rascal! Draw your sword, Coward. What you won't?—why then take that Lubber! & that! & that! & that! & that!" He raises his cane to deliver a thrashing to a blubbering Vancouver, who is crying out for protection from his brother and the Lord Chancellor.

The drawing prominently hints at references to the numerous unsavoury rumours about the voyage that were clearly well known in London society. The action takes place in front of a shop called "The South Sea Fur Warehouse," listing for sale "Fine Black Otter Skins," in reference to the unsubstantiated claim that Vancouver engaged in the illegal private trade of government goods. He looks foolish, decked out in a ceremonial feather cape captioned "The Present from the king of Owyhee to George III, forgot to be delivered"—a reference to another rumour. A long scroll coils from Vancouver's pocket, detailing his alleged misdeeds as captain, including: "List of those disgraced during the voyage—Put under arrest—all the ship's Crew—Put in irons, every Gentleman on Board—Broke, every man of honor and Spirit—Promoted, Spies, etc." Under Vancouver's foot lies a trampled pamphlet emblazoned with the words "Every officer is the Guardian of his own Honour." Two dirty-looking children laugh in the background.

Gillray's famous caricature was a complex and nuanced attack, calculated to ridicule Vancouver and place his voyage in an unflattering light. That Gillray had access to so much information on such short notice reveals just how well known the titillating and lurid details of the internal conflicts of the voyage were in London by the fall of 1796. Whether Pitt paid for Gillray's services, or whether he was intuitively responding to the tenor of upper-class gossip, is unknown, but Gillray's lampoon certainly had a devastating impact on Vancouver's career, legacy and health. The smirking rakes of the coffee-house and private-club circuit chatted away, producing new grist for the rumour mill. Vancouver became a laughingstock; the only thing the public knew about his voyage was that he had punished some aristocratic midshipmen, had allegedly stolen goods and was corrupt and cowardly for refusing a duel of honour over his misdeeds in the king's service.

Now Vancouver rose each day to read the papers in horror. Wherever he went, people stared. How could his long years of punishing, dangerous and dreary service to his country be so ridiculed and misconstrued? He sought Lord Grenville's support in publishing a defence of his actions but was rebuffed—Grenville would offer unbiased advice and guidance, but he would not put his name on it, and he did not want to hear either side of the dispute. Grenville's prime concern was to avoid a public scandal that, however it played out, would surely be humiliating to both sides. He was married to Pitt's sister, so it was a personal matter, and it was understandable that he might want to keep it as quiet as possible. Compounding the problem for Vancouver was the fact that his long years of service in Pacific America had prevented him from building a network of supporters and patrons. At one point, a few months after his return and before Camelford's assault, he wrote in a personal note to Lord Chatham of being "as it were insulated, from all connections with persons of consequence" with "no friend in power." Even his old commander Sir Alan Gardner, who had been instrumental in securing command of the *Discovery* for him in the first place and who was still in an influential position in the Admiralty, never rose to his defence. Most likely his mind had been poisoned by years of Banks's informal talk within his upper-class peer group or by the fact that his nephew, Robert Barrie, who was a midshipman on *Discovery*, disliked Vancouver and had become a close companion of Pitt's.

Vancouver no longer had any supporters in the upper echelons of British society, and the nature of his conflict precluded any from rushing to his defence. There appeared to be a consensus on Vancouver's performance, and who was to challenge it? Pitt's conflict with Vancouver had raised the issue of duty and class in the Royal Navy. What right did Vancouver, a middle-class upstart, have to flog a young member of Britain's leading political family and to punish other midshipmen of noble birth? He was caught in a clash within the Royal Navy between officers of merit and officers of privilege—if Vancouver been of higher social standing, he would not have been criticized for disciplining an obnoxious midshipman like Pitt. On land Pitt towered over Vancouver in status, but shipboard he was supposed to be subservient to a man he considered his social inferior.

On October 1, the day after *The Caneing in Conduit Street* was printed, Pitt was ordered to join the seventy-four-gun frigate *London* at Portsmouth and cruised to the West Indies, giving Vancouver some respite. When he returned several months later, however, Pitt continued to harass Vancouver's brother Charles, accosting him in an optical shop and insulting him, challenging him to a duel and denouncing him as a coward in public on numerous occasions throughout 1797, until he was thankfully sent off on another voyage.

JOSEPH BANKS WAS also slyly interfering in Vancouver's work and life. Soon after the ships had arrived in home waters and Banks had read Menzies's final letters, he set to work behind the scenes to engineer Vancouver's disgrace. For years he had been feeding the salacious shipboard gossip that Menzies had been sending him to the curious in the powerful echelons of the governing elite, including the navy. Now he began writing letters on Menzies's behalf to high officials such as Evan Nepean, the new secretary of the Board of the Admiralty, the Duke of Portland, the new secretary of state succeeding Lord Grenville, and the Earl of Chatham, the First Lord of the Admiralty. Banks successfully argued for Menzies to be released from custody and allowed off the ship. Menzies's collections and botanical papers were unloaded from the ship and delivered directly to Banks. Vancouver was pressured to withdraw his request for a court martial—a simple task, since Vancouver never held a grudge and Menzies had apologized to him for the incident. Banks then secured Menzies's journals for himself, shutting down Vancouver's request. He argued that Menzies should continue to receive his large salary while preparing his journals to Banks's satisfaction but was unsuccessful. Menzies, not phenomenally wealthy like Banks, needed an income, so he returned to work fumigating hospital ships and then joined the *Princess Augusta,* on which he worked for many years as a surgeon. Banks then began soliciting support to blend Vancouver's and Menzies's accounts of the voyage together for final publication, thereby cutting Vancouver out of a full share of both the royalties and the fame. Vancouver challenged Banks's request and eventually received the right to publish his own account of the voyage as well as funding for engravings to illustrate it.

Not to be rebuffed easily, and further inspired by Vancouver's public ridicule from the Camelford affair, Banks dug in and began pressuring Menzies to complete his journals so that they could be rushed to publication before Vancouver's. At the request of Pitt's mother, for "the unexampled species of tyranny and cruel oppression exercised during several years by my son's wretched commander," Banks began to compile a folder of information detailing Vancouver's alleged harshness and irrational and sadistic anger towards his gentlemen midshipmen, and towards Pitt in particular. Banks had the ear of the powerful and well-connected, and he continued to tarnish Vancouver's reputation both within the navy and among other important people: Vancouver was a violent, brutal, low-class scoundrel, a man preoccupied with money and power, it was said. He may be an officer, the rumours ran, but he certainly was not a gentleman. He could be dispensed with. The establishment closed in to protect its own.

"It is hard to say what effect the Camelford affair and Banks's lobbying actually had on Vancouver professionally," writes historian Nigel Rigby in *Pioneers of the Pacific,* "but while the Admiralty accorded him the honour of promoting all those he recommended—and he was generous in his recommendations—he was certainly beset with a number of official irritations, obstructions and delays." Vancouver met with delays in getting permission to publish his book, delays in receiving answers to his questions about his supplementary pay, delays in receiving his back pay, delays in receiving his prize money—it seems too much of a coincidence that bureaucracy should have complicated every matter in his professional life, having met every minor request with obfuscation. Vancouver's treatment in the press was no less trying and was so obviously tainted by the influence of the establishment. Charles Vancouver wrote that the "public papers teemed" with "foul, false, and scandalous aspersions" concerning George Vancouver and his brothers.

Banks even secured written testimonials from several of Vancouver's shipmates to give credence to the negative rumours about Vancouver's character. Included were Thomas Manby (who despite his promotions never did forgive Vancouver for the tongue lashing), Menzies and, surprisingly, Joseph Whidbey, Vancouver's shipmate and companion for more than a decade. According to Menzies, Whidbey was "the chief confident of C. Vancouver most part of the voyage." Whidbey turned against his one-time friend in condemning Vancouver's treatment of the young aristocrat and his command in general. "If such a construction as *Purloining* is applicable to the cutting up of an Iron hoop," he wrote jocularly, "I am afraid there are few Officers in the Navy that are not guilty of Purloining." Banks later sponsored Whidbey as a Fellow of the Royal Society.

Vancouver may have expected Menzies to provide Banks with damaging negative reports of his activities—they had had several public quarrels over the years—but with Whidbey, his assistant and survey companion for much of his naval career, the betrayal was complete. Vancouver knew he would never receive another command, even if he overcame his illness. In the social and political climate of eighteenth-century Britain, where respect, status and power were based on parentage rather than ability, Vancouver could never triumph over such powerful enemies. All that remained for him was the publication of his journal, his one chance to set the record straight.

Some form of clandestine hearing or investigation into the scandalous rumours about the voyage and Vancouver's behaviour may have taken place. It was not a court martial or court of inquiry, and no records of it survive apart from Vancouver's reference to it in his letters to his brother and agent. Nearly all mention of Pitt is mysteriously absent from surviving journals of the *Discovery*'s crew. The log books that detailed every instance of official punishment are selectively miss-ing key dates—between May 27 and June 10, 1793, and between August 16 and September 6, 1793. The references to Pitt and his transgressions and punishments were excised from the journals, either as evidence for an investigation or to protect Pitt's reputation from the damning records, or both. No action was ever taken against Vancouver, so the evidence must have vindicated him or showed that his discipline did not vary significantly from the naval standard for the day.

Vancouver's final year and a half was not as horrible as his first year after returning from the voyage, but it was not a good time. His health declined rapidly after the Camelford affair, and for most of 1797 he was too weak to travel and was usually unable to leave his bed. According to his brother Charles, he suffered from "a violent inflam-mation in the stomach," a delicate euphemism for nausea and vom-iting or abdominal pains. The historian and physician John Naish, in his book *The Interwoven Lives,* gives an informed and persuasive assessment of Vancouver's illness. Unlike previous writers who have proposed problems with Vancouver's thyroid or adrenal gland as a probable source of his uncontrollable temper and debilitating illness, Naish suggests that Vancouver suffered from chronic nephritis and kidney failure associated with Bright's disease. Chronic malaria can cause renal damage, as could a streptococcal epidemic, both of which were very common on the crowded, poorly ventilated confines of eigh-teenth-century ships, particularly in the Caribbean, where Vancouver served before assuming command of the *Discovery.* Vancouver was sick and absent from his ship *Europa* on several occasions and had brought large quantities of Peruvian bark, a malaria cure, with him on his great voyage. Renal damage can "smolder on for years before causing renal failure." Other symptoms of this malady include water retention, causing pudginess—Vancouver did get quite heavy near the end of his voyage and after his return, as the Gillray lampoon so cru-elly portrayed him. "The terminal phase of his illness and the manner of his death are fully in accordance with a diagnosis of uremia due to renal failure."

As his health rapidly declined, Vancouver laboured away on his book, rarely leaving his cottage in Petersham, and arranged the engraving of the plates for publication. All the engravings were based on sketches made during the voyage. His brothers, Charles and John, rallied to his aid, helping with his work, which they believed was of great importance. They also believed that the publication of George's book would clear his reputation and perhaps even give him some of the recognition that he deserved. His name was still bandied about in the press in a negative light. But Vancouver would not live to see the final publication. He was a slow and methodical writer, inclined towards tortuous prose. The book was all he had to live for, but he became so weak that he was unable to write it himself. As he lay aching and propped up on pillows, his brother John took dictation. Vancouver's illness, distractions, worries and failing health delayed the book's publication several times.

It was a bitter time to be denigrated instead of celebrated. Vancouver had been abandoned by nearly everyone except his family, but particularly by his nation and by the service to which he had devoted his entire life since the age of fourteen. Life at sea had permanently isolated him from his family and his childhood friends, and his colleagues were all in the navy, a fraternity from which he was effectively barred by both illness and disgrace. His back pay for nearly five years of service as captain of the *Discovery* was delayed for nearly two years and amounted to the not-so-princely sum of just over £700. The prize money from the capture of the *Macassar* arrived barely in time for him to will it to his siblings. According to his brother John, Vancouver "sank into the arms of death" at four o'clock in the morning on May 12, 1798, leaving a large estate of over £5,000. Naish writes that "reading the story of the final years of this hardly known and little understood man I believe that many of my fellow-countrymen [in Britain] will find it difficult to contemplate the state of his mind and body at that time without some feeling of pity and a sense of national remorse."

When he died, Vancouver had not yet completed the final one hundred or so pages of his book, detailing the last leg of the journey around Cape Horn and home. His handwritten notes were revised by John, who had been working on the project with him for over a year. *A Voyage of the Discovery to the North Pacific Ocean and Round the World; in Which the Coast of North-West America Has Been Carefully*

Examined and Accurately Surveyed was published a few months after Vancouver's death, in August or September of 1798. It ran to nearly 500,000 words—over five times the length of an average book today. The resulting tome was a somewhat plodding but incredibly detailed account of a monumental voyage. It was illustrated with beautiful, high-quality engravings and accurate, detailed charts of what had been one of the last remaining uncharted coasts on the planet. It was not a quick read, however, and Vancouver reminded his readers that the voyage was "to obtain useful knowledge"; therefore, he wanted his book "to *instruct*, even though it should fail to *entertain*." He also took pains to defend his legacy by gently urging readers, in his introduction, to judge for themselves whether he had accomplished his goals in Pacific America. "But as I have hitherto only pointed out in general terms the outline of the intended expedition; the various objects it proposed to embrace, and the end it was expected to answer, will be more clearly perceived by the perusal of the instructions under which I was to sail, and by which I was to govern my conduct; and the reader will be thereby enabled to form a judgment, how far His Majesty's commands, during this voyage, have been properly carried into execution." With the last of his energy, Vancouver felt he had to defend his own legacy and reputation.

Joseph Banks continued to press for Menzies to complete his own journal and rush it to press ahead of Vancouver, right up until the moment of Vancouver's death. But while Banks in this instance was vindictive, petty and mean, Menzies deliberately stalled his journal work, out of embarrassment or remorse. He delayed in delivering his journals to Banks, not wanting to be the one who further humiliated his commander. He had frequently quarrelled with Vancouver, presenting the events of the voyage in a tainted and prejudicial light in his letters to Banks, but he shied from this final betrayal of the man with whom he had also shared triumphs and incredible successes and enjoyed moments of peace and comradeship.

Menzies put off Banks's urgings by claiming that he was "but a slow hand with the pen" and that his other work constantly interfered with his writing efforts. "It is what I most ardently wish," he wrote to Banks in early 1798, only a few months before Vancouver's death, "for more reasons than one, and therefore have lately applied to it very close." Incredible as it seems, Menzies was slower at organizing his journal, much shorter in length and already mostly written during the voyage, than was an incapacitated, dying Vancouver, harassed by the press and hounded by his creditors—a man so debilitated that he was confined to his bed, unable to eat, too weak at times to even lift his own pen and unable to concentrate because of constant headaches. Menzies's heart was not in it to further humiliate Vancouver.

After Vancouver died and his book was published, Banks had little further contact with Menzies. He lost interest in the journal project and, indeed, in Menzies's career. The historian, archivist and Vancouver specialist W. Kaye Lamb commented that the reason for this coolness in their relations was "Menzies' failure to complete his fair copy in time to enable Banks to embarrass Vancouver." Vancouver won at least this battle to get his book out first, although it cost him his remaining health, if not his life. Oddly, much later in Menzies's long life, when he was a dignified and respectable London physician, the passing of time may have eased his feelings of resentment and ill-treatment. He claimed then, highlighting Vancouver's accomplishments and their shared adventure, that "those books that Vancouver wrote—strange that he could put so much of himself into the printed page. He was a great Captain."

THIRTEEN

Sovereignty
and Fate

◄ ◆ ►

O N JANUARY 11, 1794, about a month before Vancouver put Pitt on the *Daedalus* and sent him
home from Hawaii in disgrace, British and
Spanish negotiators concluded their final meeting in Madrid. Representatives of the two powers appended their signatures to a historic
document, the "Convention for the Mutual Abandonment of Nootka."
As far as European interests were concerned, Friendly Cove would
become a free port, and Spanish and British citizens were forbidden
to construct permanent buildings or fortifications. Most importantly,
Britain and Spain agreed to defend the port from claims of sovereignty or dominance by any other power. Neither nation would own
Friendly Cove or Nootka Sound or claim exclusive sovereignty over
the coast, and neither would permit claims of sovereignty from Russia or the United States. A new set of agents were commissioned to
travel to Friendly Cove and complete the formalities. On March 16,
1795, when the *Discovery* and the *Chatham* were visiting Valparaiso,
only three months after they had departed Spanish California, José
Manuel de Álava, the Spanish governor of Friendly Cove, and Lieutenant Thomas Pearce of the Royal Navy sailed north from Monterey
to Friendly Cove. They disembarked from their ships for a few days,
conducted interviews, raised and lowered the British flag and gave to
Maquinna official documents, outlining their agreement, that he was

to show to future traders. Álava then ordered that the Spanish fortifications be removed and stowed the valuable items in his ship, and the
foreign powers departed, leaving Maquinna and his people to stare at
the retreating vessel. The fur trade would continue, but the imperial
wrangling had ended. Spain's northernmost outpost in Pacific America was officially abandoned. The Spanish village was soon plundered
by the local people and replaced with traditional lodges.

With the Nootka crisis effectively resolved and the interest of
European nations focused on the war in Europe rather than sover-
eignty over a distant coastline, British and Spanish interest in Pacific
North America diminished. But Vancouver's voyage established precedents and set in motion events that would change the vast region.
The political future of three European empires, the new nation of the
United States, the not-yet-created country of Canada and hundreds
of thousands of indigenous peoples from Hawaii to Alaska to British
Columbia, owe their current political affiliation, for better or worse,
to Vancouver's decisions during his great voyage. Spain never again
extended a colonial presence north of California after being checked
by Vancouver's refusal to acknowledge Spanish sovereignty at Friendly
Cove. Russian expansion south from Alaska was deterred because
of the provisions of the Convention for the Mutual Abandonment of
Nootka. Throughout the 1790s, British merchants increasingly were
at a trading disadvantage with Americans, not only because of the
greater distance they had to travel but also because of the wars with
Napoleonic France between 1793 and 1815. As Britain pressed mariners from the merchant marine for service in the Royal Navy, American entrepreneurs moved in to fill the void and virtually monopolized
the Pacific coastal trade. It was only Vancouver's historical legacy that
stood as a bulwark against American political claims to the entire territory from California to Alaska.

In the mid-nineteenth century, the dispute over sovereignty in
Pacific North America was between the United States and Britain.
The British were anxious to hold the Columbia River, the artery of the
fur trade west of the Continental Divide and part of the current state
boundary between Washington and Oregon. They proposed extending the border along the 49th parallel west to the Columbia River and

then following the Columbia to the sea. To the American negotiators, who had their eye on the large, deep harbours of Puget Sound (the first viable harbours north of San Francisco), this proposition was clearly unacceptable. But in 1818, weary from years of inconclusive conflict during the War of 1812, neither the British nor the Americans were willing to press their claim to the land on the far side of the Continental Divide. So they agreed to jointly occupy the region, deferring more complicated, and politically charged, questions to the future. (The terms of the Anglo-American Convention of 1818 were reaffirmed indefinitely in 1827, with the provision that either country could cancel the agreement with one year's notice.)

In 1819 Spain and the United States signed the Adams-Onis Treaty. The United States acquired the territory of Florida from Spain for $5 million, and as part of the deal the Spanish ceded all Spanish territory north of California, (north of the 42nd parallel), however ill-defined that territory may have been. Russia, in two separate treaties, with the United States in 1824 and with Britain in 1825, bowed out of the region (but retained the right to trade), agreeing to a southern boundary for Alaska at "54-40." Old Oregon, now understood to be the territory west of the Rocky Mountains, north of Spanish California and south of Russian Alaska, became a political no man's land, jointly controlled by Britain and the United States and open to settlement and commercial development from both nations. The joint occupancy agreement provided security for Canadian fur traders to keep moving west, knowing that they would not be entering the domain of a foreign power. When the Hudson's Bay Company established a new trading fort along the Columbia River in 1825, Sir George Simpson named it Fort Vancouver. "The object of naming it after that distinguished navigator is to identify our claim to the Soil and Trade with his discovery of the River and Coast on behalf of Grt. Britain." The vast territory, however, remained the domain of the native peoples and fur traders until the 1830s, when the first wagon trains began rolling west along the Oregon Trail.

With the ominous words "Fifty-four Forty or Fight!" presidential candidate James Polk won the 1844 U.S. election, disrupting the joint occupancy accord in Oregon and sparking one of the most boisterous and potentially violent disputes of the mid-nineteenth century. While Congress debated claiming the entire Pacific Northwest and using force to back up its claim, both Britain and the United States began preparing for war. The epic migration of settlers to the Oregon Territory in the 1830s and early 1840s compelled the two nations to stake claims in the remote region. The British pointed to the coastal explorations of George Vancouver and the presence of the Hudson's Bay Company, while the Americans based their claims on the discoveries of Robert Gray, who first sailed up the Columbia River, and the epic overland trek of Lewis and Clark. Vancouver's *A Voyage of Discovery* and his collection of nautical charts were the only accurate source of geographical information available to the negotiators on both sides of the dispute. At the time, the only European "government" in the region was run by John McLoughlin of the Hudson's Bay Company, whereas the vast majority of white people living there were American citizens. For years the Hudson's Bay Company conducted its affairs with the assumption that the territory south of the Columbia River would eventually go to the United States while that north of the river would go to Britain, and it managed the fur trade accordingly: greedily plundering the southern region while preserving the northern portion for later.

When an American cattle rancher named Ewing Young died without a will, the colonists needed a set of laws to dispense with his estate. Whose laws? What country did these people live in? A pending war with Mexico averted the crisis when the United States backed down from its claim of "Fifty-four Forty or Fight," not wanting a war on two fronts. The British did not want a war over a distant land either, especially when at least one British naval commander, John Gordon, did "not think the country worth five straws." When the majority of the citizens in the territory took a primitive vote in favour of joining the United States, Britain agreed, in 1846, to extend the border along the 49th parallel to the coast, through the Strait of Juan de Fuca and around Vancouver Island. The historian Bern Anderson wrote in *Surveyor of the Sea* that "without the solid foundation of Vancouver's monumental work as a base for the British position, however, it is conceivable that the northern boundary of Oregon might have been fixed at latitude 54–40 North, and Canada today would have no Pacific shores." The cumbersome name "Quadra's and Vancouver's Island" was replaced with the snappier Vancouver Island to acknowledge British sovereignty as Spanish influence and interest in the region waned. In 1849, the British Colony of Vancouver Island was created. When the terminus of the Canadian Pacific Railway was to be located in an as-yet-unnamed and non-existent city at Burrard Inlet in 1884, W.C. Van Horne chose the name Vancouver for the new settlement so that people would associate it with the British colony and give them a general idea of its location.

Just as George Vancouver placed the cultural stamp of Great Britain on the Pacific coast of North America, he left a legacy in the Hawaiian Islands. The political situation changed dramatically after he left the islands for the last time in 1794. A little over a year later, Kamehameha conquered his rivals and added the islands of Maui, Molokai and Oahu to his kingdom. A few years later he subjugated Kauai, thereby unifying all the islands under his command. Until his death in 1819, Kamehameha remembered Vancouver and remained favourable, in concept at least, to his kingdom becoming part of the British Empire. But the British government never followed up on Vancouver's diplomacy. Britain and France formally acknowledged the Hawaiian kingdom as an independent state and admitted her into the Family of Nations on November 28, 1843.

Throughout the nineteenth century American missionaries and whalers, who found the islands ideally situated as a base in the middle of the Pacific Ocean, increased their presence and influence. In 1874 the American Reciprocity Act allowed Hawaiian sugar to be imported to California duty-free while giving the United States Pearl Harbor as a naval base, integrating the economies of the two nations. After a bloodless revolution in 1893 and the creation of a short-lived republic backed by pro-American big-business interests, Hawaii became an American territory on July 7, 1898, against the wishes of a majority of indigenous Hawaiians, who favoured their traditional monarchy. Kamehameha's "ceding" of Hawaii to Britain in 1793 remains little more than a footnote in the history of the island group—although the Hawaiian flag, designed at Kamehameha's request in 1816, contains a small Union Jack, representing its historical relationship with Britain.

WHEN VANCOUVER'S RECORD of his voyage was posthumously published in the fall of 1798, it received favourable reviews in Britain in naval publications if not in the mainstream press. The *Naval Chronicle* praised it in a long review as a "naval classic" and compared it to other accounts, such as that of Lord Anson's famous circumnavigation fifty years earlier. The *Annual Register* gave it a twenty-page review that highlighted the importance of the voyage but mildly criticized Vancouver for initially missing the mouth of the Columbia River and suggested that "so might other openings equally have escaped observation." The generally favourable review concluded with a passage that would have surely caused Vancouver to fling down his paper in irritation, had he been alive to read it: "On the whole, we must be allowed to repeat, that the prospect is considerably lessened, but, that it is by no means yet proved, that a N.W. passage does not exist."

A Voyage of Discovery was an important book but not an easy read. One of Vancouver's midshipmen claimed after reading the book that "even tho. I accompanied him I think it is one of the most tedious books I ever read." Unlike most other exploration books of the era, including those of Cook and Mackenzie, *A Voyage of Discovery* was not edited for length and detail or rewritten for excitement. Although the prose is leaden in places and bogged down with details, Vancouver, without the benefit of academic education beyond the age of fourteen, wrote the entire account himself with the clerical assistance of his brother John. His accompanying charts were universally praised for their accuracy and detail. Within a few years of its original publication, his book had been published in French, German, Danish, Swedish and Russian, and a second edition was published in Britain in 1801. Oddly, though, the book was never published in Spanish, and it was not until 1986 that the Hakluyt Society published a reprint. The intervening two centuries were a dark time for Vancouver's legacy.

Vancouver's reputation in Britain never recovered from the bad publicity surrounding his dispute with Thomas Pitt and the enmity of Joseph Banks. Vancouver named nearly four hundred geographical features during his voyage, and most of those names have remained; and his name is shared by a huge island and one of Canada's premier cities (as well as an American city)—but few know anything about the man or the great voyage that inspired these place names. No biography of Vancouver was written for more than a century after his death. Some histories of the Royal Navy from the nineteenth century fail to even mention his name; others relegate his voyage to a mere footnote. When British historian Robert Kerr compiled, between 1811 and 1824, a monumental eighteen-volume comprehensive history of naval exploration and navigation, Vancouver was mysteriously absent. Kerr did not even mention the voyage or the captain, while devoting numerous pages to countless minor and insignificant adventures. He consulted with Banks on the project, and as Bern Anderson observes, "ignoring Vancouver's voyage must have been deliberate, a reflection of the antipathy of some toward Vancouver."

Banks's antipathy to Vancouver must have run deep for it to continue several decades after Vancouver's death. That he wanted not only to tarnish, but to expunge, a dead man's legacy reveals a tenacious and vengeful side of his personality. Banks was not even gracious in victory, and he remained unable to appreciate the significance or tremendous accomplishments of the voyage because of his hatred of the man. Something may be missing from the historical record that would help explain the antipathy. No doubt Vancouver also disliked Banks, taking his cue during his formative years from his mentor Cook, who resented Banks's meddling. Of all the hundreds of place names that Vancouver bestowed on the landscape of Pacific America, Australia and New Zealand, not one single feature was named for Joseph Banks. Banks's enmity towards Vancouver may have developed from nothing other than the fact that Vancouver did not show the proud lord the deference he expected—that Vancouver's dealings with Banks were "not such as I am used to receive from persons in his situation," as Banks wrote to Menzies.

Through the powerful influence of Banks and others, Vancouver's voyage and his related accomplishments were to a large extent erased from the collective history of British exploration and the Royal Navy. George Vancouver should have returned a hero, for he was certainly one of the great mariners of his age, or of any age, but the arbitrary priorities of Britain's polarizing class hierarchy denied him a fair public trial during his lifetime. He was completely forgotten by the nation he had served for his entire adult life. When George Godwin wrote the first biography of Vancouver in 1930, much of the relevant material had already vanished, having been considered unworthy of preservation. Godwin nevertheless sought to revitalize Vancouver's legacy by portraying him more as a courageous imperial agent, boldly and heroically promoting British ways and interests in the far corners of the earth. Later writers emphasized the accuracy of his charts and scientific work along the Pacific coast of North America but tended to gloss over the unsavoury aspects of his voyage. The very few relatively recent writers who have examined Vancouver and his voyage—such as W. Kaye Lamb, John Naish, Nigel Rigby and Robin Fisher—have striven to present a more balanced appreciation of his flaws and his admirable characteristics, placed within the context of his time. But Vancouver's story remains little known.

Vancouver's voyage was the last of the great voyages of discovery in the Pacific, and George Vancouver is far more important than simply as the maker of a chart of Pacific America. He was one of the key players in the epic European power struggle of the late eighteenth century, but his achievements were undeservedly overshadowed by Cook's voyages and by the drama of the Napoleonic wars. When he and his men returned home, Britain was at war with Napoleonic France, and the nation was more interested in military heroes than Cook-style scientific and geographic explorers. The historically significant outcomes of his voyage did not manifest themselves until decades after his death, and his role in shaping those events was deliberately obscured by Banks and others. Nearly every aspect of Vancouver's voyage— every decision he made during four and a half years at sea, without direction from his government—was questioned and criticized by his detractors. Because of Pitt's antagonism and upper-class snobbery, most Britons' perception of the voyage at the time was that not one single thing Vancouver did was worthy of note, that everything he did was bungled and incompetently done. They then returned their attention to the war with France.

Some of the complaints against Vancouver carried some legitimacy at the time. Perhaps he should have undertaken his cartographic work with a lesser drive for perfection. He pursued this monumental goal, a scientific and practical legacy that he rightly imagined to be his chance for historical immortality, "with a degree of minuteness far exceeding the letter of my commission or instructions; in this respect I might possibly have incurred the censure of disobedience, had I been intrusted with the most liberal, discretionary order, as being the fittest and most likely means of attaining the important end in question." He must have known that he was violating the spirit if not the letter of his orders. His superiors even anticipated his stubbornness, for in his orders they tried to draw attention to the need for haste, but he tenaciously dedicated himself to completing the nautical survey to his own exacting standards. Like a dog holding a bone, he refused to let go of his dream. But his meticulous nautical survey showed something no one was eager to acknowledge: there was no northwest passage, no great inland sea. For with all his efforts, Vancouver had discovered nothing that could help Britain defeat Napoleon. Nor was Hawaii, although strategically important as a mid-Pacific stopover, of any immediate help in the war effort.

Vancouver was accused of being weak in his dealings with the Spanish and in promoting British interests. Some claimed that he had failed in his negotiations with Bodega y Quadra and that he should have seized upon the Spanish commander's offer of an international border at the Strait of Juan de Fuca instead of dithering and sending to Britain for instructions. Perhaps Vancouver should have accepted Bodega y Quadra's deal to secure a border even though he had no directive to do so, although by making a decision of this magnitude he would also have exposed himself to the possibility of professional censure for exceeding his orders. He may have even suspected that his quarrel with Pitt would not bode well for his future and so stuck rigidly to his orders during the negotiations, to forestall criticism. Historians have confirmed the sensibleness of his decisions regarding Bodega y Quadra's proposals: the Spaniard's interpretation of the land to be returned to Britain was clearly in violation of the Nootka Sound Convention. By keeping to the letter of his orders, Vancouver at least avoided the ignominy of a politically motivated court martial.

Admittedly Vancouver should have adhered to the social mores in Britain that dictated that a troublemaker like Pitt had to be tolerated, even if it was unjust to do so. His treatment of Pitt lost him the respect of some of his men and incurred the disfavour of some influential people who were behind the scenes. Banks and Pitt had so poisoned the public perception of Vancouver and his accomplishments that facts alone were not enough to garner him any supporters. Indeed, at the time of Vancouver's return, not many people were aware of the details or accomplishments of his voyage. They were eager to find fault and thus saw his actions in a negative light.

Vancouver imagined himself to be a scientist-adventurer of the Enlightenment like Cook, but what the Admiralty wanted, or imagined that it wanted, was a decisive Royal Navy commander boldly challenging the Spanish, who were now allied with France. When Vancouver failed to live up to its expectations by not securing concessions from the Spanish or locating a viable northwest passage, the Admiralty devoted little effort to defending him against his upper-class enemies, many of whom were his superiors in the navy. Ironically, Vancouver was a true agent of empire, leaving the stamp of British culture and politics wherever he travelled. From that point of view, he carried out his orders better than the Admiralty could have ever envisioned, although they failed to realize the extent of his accomplishments at the time.

In recent years, interest in Vancouver and his epic voyage has been on the upswing. The 250th anniversary of Vancouver's birth was celebrated in King's Lynn in Britain and in the city of Vancouver, British Columbia, in June 2007. Other public events included the sailing of the tall ship *Earl of Pembroke* (similar to the *Discovery*), celebrations of British Columbia First Nations cultures, special museum exhibits and a remarkable series of paintings specific to the voyage by the marine artist John Horton. This movement is the beginning of a long-overdue recognition of George Vancouver's historical influence and of his incredible tale of eighteenth-century derring-do.

Not everyone celebrates Vancouver's voyage. His personal accomplishments in sailing vast distances into the unknown with primitive technology, and his triumph over adversity and illness, can be universally appreciated. But the future that his voyage heralded was not a cause for celebration among the native peoples of the South Pacific and western North America. Although Vancouver accomplished much in assigning nearly four hundred prominent place names along the Pacific coast, most of them still in use today, he operated with a sort of blindness as well. In stamping his and his nation's names on the coast, including those of his friends, fellow officers, family, and important naval and political figures of the era, he ignored and erased many of the existing place names that the local peoples had used for centuries. He made no effort to identify native place names, and as a result his maps fail to show *any* of the numerous native villages along the coast. All is depicted as a great empty land.

The purpose of Vancouver's expedition was to check the Spanish and secure free trade and new markets for the products of British industry, not to achieve cultural or biological dominance. Although he was relatively respectful of native customs and rights, and indeed the trade was initially mutually beneficial, those who followed him were less respectful. Vancouver would have been shocked by and alienated from our modern culture. He would have had more in common with the historical peoples of Hawaii or Pacific North America, with their cultures of self-reliance and their relationship to the sea, than to the modern multicultural metropolises that arose in the wake of his explorations.

The late 1790s were the peak years of the trade, the years when the greatest profits were made and the time of greatest cultural change for the Pacific coast peoples. For them, the trade was a mixed blessing. Before disease and violence had taken their toll, before the sea otters were hunted to near-extinction in the 1830s, and before the land was invaded by colonists, the fur trade produced a cultural flourishing. The new wealth, particularly in metal tools such as chisels, hatchets and saws, improved carving and woodworking for a people who lived amid some of the largest trees in the world. When young Midshipman Vancouver was in Nootka with Cook in 1779 he may have noticed small carved ritual poles on the beach in front of the villages, but when he came ashore as captain in 1792 he probably saw some of the earliest examples of the monumental freestanding totem poles, now over thirty feet tall and layered with the visages of beasts both grimacing and grinning. Tall poles have become a hallmark of coastal native cultures.

Would the peoples of the coast have been better off if the region had fallen under the sway of the Spanish Empire or the Russian Empire, or if either Britain or the United States had more fully dominated the area? One of these imperial powers could surely have claimed the region. Vancouver could never have imagined the changes that have since occurred in Hawaii and Pacific North America; he could never have conceived of a world in which millions of people from all over the globe live in great cities located in regions he once found sparsely populated, work on farms where he saw only an endless carpet of mighty trees and operate thousands of giant, noisy ships on waters where once the silent *Discovery* was by far the largest vessel to be found. He never imagined the forces that his voyage and his great chart would unleash. For better or for worse, his voyage was the start of the journey down a path that has led directly to the world we know.

VANCOUVER AND HIS epic voyage deserve to be remembered and acknowledged, if not celebrated, as one of the greatest naval adventures of the Age of Sail and as a testament of human perseverance in the face of almost insurmountable odds. Vancouver's story is a classic example of how messy, unfair and fickle the future can unfold, of how seemingly minor decisions can have major ramifications, and of how fate or luck play a role in determining everyone's future. How could a man who devoted his life to his country and who accomplished great things that would benefit it in the future be shunned, humiliated and driven to an early death by anxiety and worry? What does Vancouver's ignominious end tell us about our current heroes or anti-heroes, about our belief in the accuracy of our understanding of, and knowledge of, the past? Fashion and the media have as much an impact on historical legacy as an individual's actions do. Interpreting the past and researching for accuracy, often with only fragmentary documents and oblique references, is the ongoing work of historians. The lens through which we view past peoples and events is constantly evolving.

Imagine how Vancouver might have been received or remembered in Britain, and then by extension in Canada and the United States, had circumstances been different: what if he had ingratiated himself with Banks and forbore punishing the obnoxious Pitt?

Instead of having the image of an erratic, sadistic captain abusing his crew while descending into madness, instead of seeing a weak negotiator, a tedious perfectionist and a coward refusing a duel of honour, we would have a positive perspective, given the same facts. A young captain leads two ships on a pioneering voyage of discovery around the world and into dangerous uncharted waters. Almost all his men survive and return home. His men, often with the dedicated captain on board, cover more than ten thousand miles in small open boats exposed to the elements and danger. The voyage produces an impressively accurate nautical chart of over 1,700 miles of an unknown coastline, including some of the most intricate and complicated coastal geography in the world. The voyage effectively disproves one of the greatest geographical myths of the era while solidifying British claims of sovereignty against Spanish claims and laying the groundwork for the British governance of Hawaii. The intrepid adventurer sails more than 65,000 miles during four and a half years at sea—the longest circumnavigation ever by sailing ship and a significantly greater distance than Cook's second voyage—and accomplishes just as much politically and scientifically. Vancouver's success or failure is a matter of spin and perception. The truth, as ever, is slippery and elusive, and evaluating Vancouver and the accomplishments of his epic voyage is no less difficult.

Vancouver the mad tyrant was part of the myth propagated in his final years and after his death, just as the sagacious and perfectionist scientific cartographer, the charter of the northwest coast, is also part of the Vancouver myth that became popular in the twentieth century. The real Vancouver was much more complicated. He was both endearing and repulsive by modern standards and by the standards of his day. He was occasionally tyrannical and verbally abusive; yet so were many of his contemporary commanders. He was hard on himself as well as on his officers and crew, especially the young coddled gentlemen who comprised the bulk of his midshipmen's berth. Vancouver had the best interests of his crew in mind, but he acted like an overstrict parent towards his energetic and headstrong children. He kept them alive so that they would return home, even if they would have had more fun while taking greater risks. He considered one of his great achievements the fact that only six of his men died out of a crew of 170 (four drowned, one ate poisoned mussels and one succumbed to dysentery)—less than a third of the standard mortality rate even for much shorter voyages. It is probable that more of those sailors would have died if they had remained in England.

Despite his erratic temper in his final years, Vancouver was not a malicious martinet lashing and punishing his crew for slight infractions or to satisfy his own sadistic urges. The record shows that he never set his men to a task he himself would not undertake, and he worried incessantly when they failed to return from sounding forays in the deep, winding fjords. He kept them mostly free from scurvy and other shipboard diseases. From his earliest days at sea, under the tutelage of James Cook, he strove to maintain the same cool-headed presence of command, the generous awareness of the contributions of others and the meticulous observance of manners and protocol shown by his mentor. He was not always successful, and certainly he must not have been an easy man to work with, even if his finer qualities became apparent afterward. But he was fair in admitting the contributions of others and generous in his recommendations for promotions. He had a distinct lack of personal vanity. He was not always a respectful commander in the heat of the moment, but he was deeply aware of his responsibility to his men and his objectives, and later, he was deeply aware of and frustrated by his failing body and his erratic, fraying temper. If he had a major flaw, it was that he demanded of his men the same commitment and dedication that he demanded of himself—a sacrifice few were willing to make.

Epilogue

———◆———

FTER VANCOUVER'S DEATH, Thomas Pitt continued
to be a violent, arrogant and perhaps unhinged
individual. The final years of Pitt's life differed
little from his youthful days aboard the *Discovery* and vindicated
Vancouver's assessment of him. The young lord went on to become
an abusive and overbearing officer during a short and dishonour-
able naval career, in which he murdered a fellow lieutenant during
an alleged mutiny and somehow escaped punishment on a technical-
ity. His biographer wrote that he "acted at this time in a violent and
eccentric manner more appropriate to the Spanish Main a century
earlier." After several other scandals and run-ins with authorities,
he was struck from the commander's list of the navy. Pitt was widely
believed to be at least half-mad and deranged, and his notorious final
years were marked by bullying, arguing, fighting, public disputation
and sporadic violence. In 1802, in a rage of misguided passion over the
affections of a young woman, he demanded a duel with one of his cronies. Thomas Pitt was shot in the chest and killed at the age of twenty-
nine. He never matched the rosy picture painted by the press and his
supporters during his public quarrel with his old commander.

Friendly Cove and Nootka Sound continued to be the centre of
the maritime fur trade and a resting place and rendezvous for ships
for several decades after Vancouver sailed away from the coast for

the last time. Nootka Sound's decline as a safe anchorage during the nineteenth century coincided with the hunting to near-extinction of the sea otters. Friendly Cove never regained its former fame, and the fascinating history of the region has been mostly forgotten. Nothing tangible remains from its brief moment in the international limelight. With a permanent population of only two, the cove still possesses the appearance of greater significance. The shaggy branches of the mighty Douglas-fir forest hem in the remaining clearing like a wall, marking it as distinct from the dense, looming forest. One must use some imagination to picture the events that happened here, but the task is not impossible. A knowledgeable visitor, using copies of historical engravings and sketches, can identify Meares's beach, the rocky outcropping where the Spanish fort once commanded the harbour, the village sites of both the Spanish garrison and Maquinna's people. With a bit more imagination, one can picture the *Discovery,* the *Chatham* and many other ships anchored in the sheltering harbour and understand why this tiny spit of land would have been such a valuable base.

Although Friendly Cove is now a Canadian National Historic Site, it has no official interpretive centre or display to mark it as a place that was once one of the most important harbours in the world. Most visitors here—hikers returning from a multi-day trek along the western coast of Nootka Island or day visitors on a boat trip from the town of Gold River—have no idea that events here inspired one of the great epic voyages of the eighteenth century and changed not only the history of western North America but the histories of three European empires.

What happened to the dream of finding a northwest passage south of the Arctic—a notion effectively disproved by Vancouver's meticulous survey? It did not die. The famous British quest for the passage merely shifted north to the Arctic in the nineteenth century. Countless lives were consumed in trying to plow giant wind- and steam-powered ships through the ice-choked channels of the Arctic Archipelago. The passage was not successfully navigated until 1906, when the Norwegian mariner Roald Amundsen piloted his tiny vessel *Gjoa* from east to west. The passage has so far had no commercial value, but the ancient dreams of a seaway through North America continue to live in today's attempts to explore, claim and fight over the rights to the resources of this northwest passage.

The historical threads of Vancouver's life have unravelled. His reputation is improving, finally, 250 years after his birth. Yet the question arises: What do we really know about George Vancouver—not his scientific and political accomplishments, which have been unearthed and studied by historians despite Joseph Banks's efforts to conceal them—but about the man himself? He was undoubtedly brave; even his harshest critics never challenged his courage at sea. His voyages into the unknown were equalled by some, but they were never surpassed by the many globe-girdling explorers of the eighteenth century. He was a harsh disciplinarian, with a quick and furious temper, rendered erratic by anxiety and his struggle with chronic illness. He had little patience for youthful pranks or any public challenge to his authority. He loved and was loved by his siblings. He was insecure about not appearing to be infallible; he was certainly a meticulous perfectionist when it came to his survey work and the writing of his manuscript. He was not a perfect man, and he was not from a perfect age, but neither was he a mean or vindictive man. Vancouver was a complex blend of the traits, some admirable, others less so, that all human beings share. But overriding these obvious characteristics is his deep secrecy about his personal feelings and a concern that his public persona be in accord with the honour and traditions of an eighteenth-century Royal Navy officer. Pitt's public challenge to Vancouver's competence and honour while he slowly succumbed to illness, even more than the lack of fame or public recognition, must have been a most bitter and humiliating defeat for a man like Vancouver.

We will never know of his inner turmoil or emotional suffering, because he left no candid journal of his thoughts and aspirations. All we have is his detailed public account of the voyage, a handful of letters he wrote to colleagues, which contain a few veiled references to his inner thoughts, and the comments of others with whom he worked and lived. He has left much unanswered. Did he believe in God? We do not know. Did he ever have a lover or romantic feelings towards another? He must have had feelings, at least, though his professional duties left little time for a private life. What did he feel and do when he retreated to his cabin after a violent outburst? Was he as quick to forgive as he was to anger? Did he regret his temper or think it was part of his job? Vancouver will remain a somewhat enigmatic figure, despite a great ocean of details. He was certainly one of the great captains of his age, and of all time. His epic voyage to unknown Pacific America is one of a handful of truly incredible voyages in the history of seafaring, on par in its own way with the voyages of Columbus, Magellan, Drake, Bougainville and Cook. Vancouver was at heart a good man. He accomplished great things and, as our historical and cultural ancestor, he deserves a greater place in our collective memory.

Sources

‹ ◆ ›

A NOTE ON SOURCES

The ultimate job of a popular historian and biographer is to blend scholar-
ship and storytelling, to provide solid historical context and analysis as well
as a strong narrative. The challenge is to provide just the right level of detail
for average readers while faithfully adhering to the historical record. As with
most historical biographies, and indeed anything in history, this telling of
George Vancouver's story has had to rely on incomplete documentary source
material. The judgment of the author is important. Fortunately, almost all the
extant material relating to his voyage is readily available.

I have not gone through archives scouring for new documentary evidence
of Vancouver's voyage, and I have not seen the original handwritten letters of
Vancouver, Pitt, Banks, Menzies and others. Academic historians have been
doing this sort of detective and cataloguing work for decades, and a lot of these
records, including all the most important correspondence, is reprinted in full
in reliable secondary sources, such as edited or annotated reprints of original
journals and publications. Many of Vancouver's officers' journals have been
reprinted or republished in recent editions. What I have attempted to do is
place Vancouver's life and defining voyage in a broader historical setting than
previous biographies, which are all quite old and reflect the prejudices and priorities of their era. I have updated the interpretations of events to reflect contemporary thinking on issues such as the relationship between Europeans and
indigenous peoples. I have emphasized the interactions between personalities
by incorporating opinions and quotes from Vancouver's officers. And I have
tried to give the story the strong narrative drive that it deserves and that is
strangely absent in many other works on Vancouver. The story of Vancouver's

incredible life and adventures and the struggle for imperial dominance over Pacific America is at heart a human story rather than a technical story.

GENERAL SOURCES

The most important general source on Vancouver's voyage is the Hakluyt Society's annotated 1984 reprint edition of Vancouver's *A Voyage of Discovery.* Edited by W. Kaye Lamb, it includes a scholarly 256-page introduction and ten appendixes of reprinted source material originating in various archives primarily in Britain. It includes hundreds of pages of transcriptions of Vancouver's correspondence with the Admiralty, his officers and Spanish officials, listed in chronological order by name. "The primary sources relating to Vancouver's voyage of discovery are widely scattered," Lamb writes in his preface, "and I am greatly indebted to the many institutions and individuals who made it possible for me to assemble copies of virtually all of them." Without this groundbreaking scholarly work, the present biography would not have been possible.

Another important source is Vancouver's first biography, *Vancouver: A Life* by George Godwin, which also includes appendixes that reprint much primary-source material relating to Vancouver and his voyage. The most thorough and detailed recent overview of Vancouver's voyage, including the background of his key officers, is *The Interwoven Lives of George Vancouver, Archibald Menzies, Joseph Whidbey and Peter Puget: The Vancouver Voyage of 1791–1795,* by John Naish. Additional correspondence originating from Joseph Banks and Archibald Menzies can be found in the Brabourne Collection at the National Library of Australia and is available online, although deciphering Bank's spidery handwriting is incredibly difficult.

VANCOUVER'S EARLY CAREER AND LIFE

The information on Vancouver's early life is sparse but the same in nearly all secondary sources and is based on George Godwin's *Vancouver: A Life* and in Lamb's introduction to the Hakluyt edition of Vancouver's *Voyage of Discovery.* For information on Vancouver's expeditions with James Cook, see in particular J.C. Beaglehole's *The Life of Captain James Cook* and *The Journals of Captain James Cook on His Voyage of Discovery: Volume II, The Voyage of the Resolution and Adventure 1772–1775.* Material on scurvy and other diseases in the Caribbean came from Stephen R. Bown's *Scurvy: How a Surgeon, a Mariner and a Gentleman Solved the Greatest Medical Mystery of the Age of Sail* and from Sir James Watt's paper "The Voyage of Captain George Vancouver 1791–1795: The Interplay of Physical and Psychological Pressures" in the *Canadian Bulletin of Medical History.*

THE SEA OTTER TRADE AND
THE NOOTKA SOUND CONTROVERSY

The background of the Nootka Sound Controversy is covered in numerous academic books and papers. Two books in particular were of great use: *Flood Tide of Empire* by Warren Cook and *The Northwest Coast: British Navigation, Trade, and Discoveries to 1812* by Barry M. Gough. Each of these contains a thorough discussion of these events, relying on a wealth of primary sources, Spanish and English. See also Alan Frost's "Nootka Sound and the Beginnings of Britain's Imperialism of Free Trade" in *From Maps to Metaphors: The Pacific World of George Vancouver*. Meares's writings can be read in his *Voyages Made in the Years 1788 and 1789, from China to the North West Coast of America*. For the text of Martínez's report see Ray Manning, *The Nootka Sound Controversy*, and for Colnett's report see F.W. Howay's edited *Journal of Captain James Colnett aboard the Argonaut*.

VANCOUVER'S VOYAGE

The primary account of Vancouver's voyage is George Vancouver's own published work, *A Voyage of Discovery to the North Pacific Ocean and Round the World, 1791–1795*. I have relied on the Hakluyt reprint edition. Correspondence between Vancouver and others during the voyage are contained in the appendixes of this work. The journals and logs of Vancouver's key officers have also been published in recent years, in particular those of Menzies, Manby and Puget. See also the web resource *Vancouver's Letters Relating to the Voyage of the Discovery and Chatham*.

Numerous secondary chapter-length accounts of Vancouver's life and voyages have been published, far more than I have listed in my bibliography. The most complete book-length overviews of Vancouver's life and career are *The Interwoven Lives of George Vancouver, Archibald Menzies, Joseph Whidbey and Peter Puget: The Vancouver Voyage of 1791–1795* by John Naish and Bern Anderson's *Surveyor of the Sea: The Life and Voyages of Captain George Vancouver*. Robin's Fisher's *Vancouver's Voyage* contains dozens of historical and modern illustrations relating to the voyage, concentrating on Vancouver's activities in present-day British Columbia. See the *Historical Atlas of British Columbia and the Pacific Northwest* by Derek Hayes for an overview of the cartographic history of Pacific America and for several reprinted historical maps and charts.

MENZIES, BANKS AND THE CAMELFORD AFFAIR

The ongoing quarrel between Menzies and Vancouver, and Menzies's betrayal of Vancouver to Banks, is thoroughly discussed in "Banks and Menzies: Evolution of a Journal," contained in *From Maps to Metaphors: The Pacific World of George Vancouver,* by W. Kaye Lamb. John Naish also discusses in detail the strained relationship between Menzies and Vancouver in *The Interwoven Lives of George Vancouver, Archibald Menzies, Joseph Whidbey and Peter Puget: The Vancouver Voyage of 1791–1795.* Nigel Rigby likewise outlines the awkward relationships between Menzies, Pitt, Vancouver and Banks in *Pioneers of the Pacific: Voyages of Exploration, 1787–1810.*

The Camelford Affair, as it became known, is based on the established facts of the case as presented by several reliable secondary sources. In particular see Nikolai Tolstoy's biography of Thomas Pitt, *The Half-Mad Lord,* for a thorough recounting of Pitt's relationship with Vancouver during the voyage and the subsequent scandal. This work contains numerous excerpts from newspapers and from Camelford's and Vancouver's correspondence. Lamb's introduction to the Hakluyt edition of *A Voyage of Discovery to the North Pacific and Round the World, 1791–1795* also details Pitt's punishments on board the *Discovery* and the scandal in London.

VANCOUVER'S ILLNESS

Many have discussed and speculated on the nature of Vancouver's illness, including Bern Anderson in *Surveyor of the Sea* and Sir James Watt in "The Voyage of Captain George Vancouver 1791–1795: The Interplay of Physical and Psychological Pressures" in the *Canadian Bulletin of Medical History.* The most recent and, in my opinion, most authoritative and accurate discussion and assessment of Vancouver's illness is in John Naish's *The Interwoven Lives of George Vancouver, Archibald Menzies, Joseph Whidbey and Peter Puget: The Vancouver Voyage of 1791–1795.*

Selected Bibliography

Anderson, Bern. *Surveyor of the Sea: The Life and Voyages of Captain George Vancouver.* Toronto: University of Toronto Press, 1960.

Anonymous. *The Life, Adventures and Eccentricities of the Late Lord Camelford: To Which Is Added the Particulars of the Late Fatal Duel: Genuine Extracts from His Lordship's Will, &c.* Sold by R. Mace... and the booksellers in general: W. Williams, printer, 1804. Microfiche.

Barnes, Dr. Phil. *A Concise History of the Hawaiian Islands.* Hilo, Hawaii: Petroglyph Press, 1999.

Bawlf, Samuel. *The Secret Voyage of Sir Francis Drake: 1577–1580.* Vancouver: Douglas & McIntyre, 2003 / New York: Walker & Co., 2003.

Beaglehole, J.C. *The Journals of Captain James Cook on His Voyage of Discovery: Volume II, The Voyage of the* Resolution *and* Adventure *1772–1775.* Cambridge: Hakluyt Society, 1969.

———. *The Journals of Captain James Cook on His Voyage of Discovery: Volume III, The Voyage of the* Resolution *and* Discovery *1776–1780.* Cambridge: Hakluyt Society, 1967.

———. *The Life of Captain James Cook.* Stanford: Stanford University Press, 1974.

Bell, Edward. *A New Vancouver Journal on the Discovery of Puget Sound by a Member of the* Chatham's *Crew.* Edmond Meany, ed. Seattle, 1915.

Blane, Gilbert, Dr. James Lind and Dr. Thomas Trotter. *The Health of Seamen.* Christopher Lloyd, ed. London: Navy Records Society, 1965.

Bown, Stephen R. *Scurvy: How a Surgeon, a Mariner and a Gentleman Solved the Greatest Medical Mystery of the Age of Sail.* Toronto: Thomas Allen, 2003.

Colnett, James. *The Journal of Captain James Colnett aboard the* Argonaut *from April 26, 1789 to Nov. 3, 1791.* F.W. Howay, ed. Toronto: Champlain Society, 1940.

Cook, Warren. *Flood Tide of Empire: Spain and the Pacific Northwest, 1543–1819.* New Haven: Yale University Press, 1973.

Cutter, Donald. *Malaspina and Galiano: Spanish Voyages to the Northwest Coast, 1791 and 1792.* Vancouver: Douglas & McIntyre, 1991.

Dalrymple, Alexander. *Plan for Promoting the Fur Trade and Securing It to this Country, by Uniting the Operations of the East India and Hudson's Bay companys.* London: George Bigg, 1789. Microfiche, Canadian Institute for Historical Microreproductions, 1999.

Fisher, Robin. *Vancouver's Voyage.* Vancouver: Douglas & McIntyre, 1992.

Fisher, Robin, and Hugh Johnston, eds. *From Maps to Metaphors: The Pacific World of George Vancouver.* Vancouver: UBC Press, 1993.

Frost, Alan. "Nootka Sound and the Beginnings of Britain's Imperialism of Free Trade." *From Maps to Metaphors: The Pacific World of George Vancouver.* Vancouver: UBC Press, 1993.

Fry, Howard. *Alexander Dalrymple and the Expansion of British Trade.* London: Frank Cass, 1970.

Galloway, D.J., and E.W. Groves. *Archibald Menzies M.D., F.L.S. (1754–1842), Aspects of his Life, Travel and Connections.* London: Archives of Natural History, 1987.

Godwin, George. *Vancouver: A Life, 1757–1798.* London: Philip Allan, 1930.

Gough, Barry M. *Distant Dominion: Britain and the Northwest Coast of North America, 1579–1809.* Vancouver: UBC Press, 1980.

——. *The Northwest Coast: British Navigation, Trade, and Discoveries to 1812.* Vancouver: UBC Press, 1992.

Haig-Brown, Roderick. *Captain of the* Discovery: *The Story of Captain George Vancouver.* Toronto: Macmillan, 1956.

Harbord, Heather. *Nootka Sound, and the Surrounding Waters of Maquinna.* Victoria: Heritage House, 1996.

Hayes, Derek. *Historical Atlas of British Columbia and the Pacific Northwest.* Vancouver: Cavendish Books, 1999.

Howay, F.W. *The Dixon-Meares Controversy.* Toronto: Ryerson Press, 1929.

——. *Voyages of the* Columbia *on the Northwest Coast, 1787–1790 and 1790–1793.* Boston: Massachusetts Historical Society, 1941.

——, ed. *The Journal of Captain James Colnett aboard the* Argonaut *from April 26, 1789 to Nov. 3, 1791.* Toronto: Champlain Society, 1940.

Justice, Clive L. *Mr. Menzies' Garden Legacy: Plant Collecting on the Northwest Coast.* Vancouver: Cavendish Books, 2000.

Kendrick, John. *The Men with Wooden Feet: The Spanish Exploration of the Pacific Northwest*. Toronto: NC Press, 1985.

Lamb, W. Kaye. *The Voyage of George Vancouver 1791–1795*. London: Hakluyt Society, 1984.

——. "Banks and Menzies: Evolution of a Journal." In *From Maps to Metaphors: The Pacific World of George Vancouver*. Vancouver: UBC Press, 1993.

Lloyd, Christoper, ed. *The Health of Seamen: Selections from the Works of Dr. James Lind, Sir Gilbert Blane and Dr. Thomas Trotter*. London: Navy Records Society, 1965.

Manby, Thomas. *Journal of the Voyages of the HMS Discovery and Chatham, 1790–1793*. Fairfield, WA: Ye Galleon Press, 1992. Facsimile reprint.

Manning, William R. *The Nootka Sound Controversy*. Part XVI of the Annual Report of the American Historical Association for the Year 1904, Washington: Government Printing Office, 1905. Reprint: Ann Arbor: University Microfilms Inc., 1966.

Marshall, Yvonne. "Dangerous Liaisons: Maquinna, Quadra, and Vancouver in Nootka Sound, 1790–5." In *From Maps to Metaphors: The Pacific World of George Vancouver*. Vancouver: UBC Press, 1993.

Meany, Edmond S. *Vancouver's Discovery of Puget Sound*. Portland, OR: Binfords & Mort, 1957.

Meares, John. *Voyages Made in the Years 1788 and 1789, from China to the North West Coast of America*. London: 1790. Reprint. Amsterdam: N. Israel, 1967.

Menzies, Archibald. *The Alaska Travel Journal of Archibald Menzies 1793–1794*. Introduction and annotation by Wallace Olson. Fairbanks: University of Alaska Press, 1993.

——. *Menzies' Journal of Vancouver's Voyage*. C.F. Newcombe, ed. Victoria: British Columbia Archives Memoir No. V, 1923.

——. *Journal of Archibald Menzies, Surgeon and Botanist on Board Discovery* [electronic resource]. Marlborough, England: Adam Matthew Digital, 2007.

Morgan, Murray C. *The John Meares Expeditions: The Last Wilderness*. Seattle: University of Washington Press, 1955.

Naish, John. *The Interwoven Lives of George Vancouver, Archibald Menzies, Joseph Whidbey and Peter Puget: The Vancouver Voyage of 1791–1795*. Lewiston, NY: The Edward Mellen Press, 1996.

Olson, Wallace M. *With Vancouver in Alaska, 1793–1794: A Day by Day Description of the Voyage, Events, and the Places He Named*. Auke Bay, AK: Heritage Research, 2004.

Pethick, Derek. *First Approaches to the Northwest Coast*. Vancouver: J.J. Douglas, 1976.

———. *The Nootka Connection: Europe and the Northwest Coast, 1790–1795*. Vancouver: Douglas & McIntyre, 1980.

Puget, Peter. *Vancouver Discovers Vancouver: An Excerpt from the Rough Logs of Second Lieutenant Peter John Puget*. W.K. Lamb, ed. Burnaby, B.C.: Vancouver Conference on Exploration and Discovery, 1990.

Rigby, Nigel, Pieter van der Merwe and Glyn Williams. *Pioneers of the Pacific: Voyages of Exploration, 1787–1810*. Fairbanks: University of Alaska Press, 2005.

Rodger, N.A.M. *The Wooden World: An Anatomy of the Georgian Navy*. London: William Collins and Sons, 1986.

Scofield, John. *Hail, Columbia: Robert Gray, John Kendrick and the Pacific Fur Trade*. Portland: Oregon Historical Society Press, 1992.

Thurman, Michael. *The Naval Department of San Blas: New Spain's Bastion for Alta California and Nootka, 1769–1798*. Glendale, CA: Arthur H. Clarke, 1967.

Tolstoy, Nikolai. *The Half-Mad Lord, Thomas Pitt, 2nd Baron Camelford*. London: Jonathan Cape, 1978.

Vancouver, George. *A Voyage of Discovery to the North Pacific Ocean and Round the World, 1791–1795*. Four volumes with an introduction and appendices. W. Kaye Lamb, ed. London: Hakluyt Society, 1984.

———. *Vancouver's Letters Relating to the Voyage of the Discovery and Chatham* [electronic resource]. Marlborough, England: Adam Matthew Digital, 2007.

Walbran, John T. *British Columbia Place Names, 1592–1906*. Reprint. Vancouver: Douglas & McIntyre, 1977.

Watt, Sir James. "The Voyage of Captain George Vancouver 1791–95: The Interplay of Physical and Psychological Pressures." *Canadian Bulletin of Medical History* (Volume 4, 1987).

Williams, Glyndwr. *The British Search for the Northwest Passage in the Eighteenth Century*. London: Longmans, 1962.

———. *The Expansion of Europe in the Eighteenth Century: Overseas Rivalry, Discovery, and Exploitation*. New York: Walker & Co., 1966.

Wing, Robert C. *Joseph Baker: Lieutenant on the Vancouver Expedition, British Naval Officer for Whom Mt. Baker Was Named*. Seattle: Gray Beard Publishing, 1992.

———. *Peter Puget: Lieutenant on the Vancouver Expedition, Fighting British Naval Officer, the Man for Whom Puget Sound Was Named*. Seattle: Gray Beard Publishing, 1979.

Acknowledgements

———— ◆ ————

I WANT TO particularly thank publishers Scott McIntyre and Scott Steedman for the enthusiasm, faith and dedication they have shown to this project. The entire editorial, production and publicity team at Douglas & McIntyre has been a pleasure to work with, and I would like to highlight the excellent work of Jessica Sullivan, Peter Cocking, Iva Cheung, Emiko Morita and especially editor John Eerkes-Medrano. The beautiful cover image is by marine artist John Horton. Historian and geographer Derek Hayes graciously provided copies of Vancouver's maps. Thanks as always to Bill and Frances Hanna. As well, this book could not have been completed without the unflagging enthusiasm and support of my wife, Nicky Brink, who in addition to her usual contribution to the ideas and clarity of my writing also secretly arranged a trip for us to Friendly Cove in Nootka Sound. Thanks also to the Canada Council for the Arts for its generous support.

Index

Valdés, Cayetano, 133, 134–35

Vancouver (BC city), 132, 224, 229

Vancouver, Charles, 10, 208, 209–10, 213, 216, 217

Vancouver, George: appearance, 144; assessment and legacy, 3–4, 219, 221, 224, 225–33; character and personality, 176, 232–33, 236–37

Vancouver, George, before expedition: background and family history, 9–10; career choice of Royal Navy, 16–18; on Cook's second voyage, 15, 17–18, 21–24; on Cook's third voyage, 26–31; on *Courageous* (1790), 79, 88–89; on *Europa* (1784), 58–61; on *Fame* (1782), 53; home leaves, 31–32, 57–58; illness (1788), 59–60; interest in other cultures, 28; on *Martin* (1780), 51–53; navigational skills, 19, 22; proposed *Discovery* expedition (1789), 71–73

Vancouver, George, expedition leader: appointed commander, 84–85, 89; with Bodega y Quadra at Nootka Sound, 144–56; claims for British Empire, 108, 131; on coastal scenery, 128; Columbia River, 124, 125, 157–58; confrontation with Tlingit, 181–82; diplomacy with Hawaiians, 170–71, 172–74, 175, 186–87, 189–92; diplomacy with North American natives, 111, 115–16, 135–36, 148; diplomacy with Spanish, 134–35, 153, 154–55, 182–83; efforts against scurvy, 108, 110–11; Hergest and Gooch, revenge for, 174, 175; illness of, 104, 144, 180, 182, 194–95; instructions to, from government, 89–92, 120, 151–52, 153, 154–55, 156, 160, 179, 182, 184, 196; journal confiscation, 203–6; leadership style, 104, 112–15, 117–20, 133–34, 150, 156–57, 163–64, 165, 166, 169–70, 180, 184–85, 194, 203–6, 228–29, 232–33; Manby and, 133–34, 166; Menzies and, 84–88, 106, 140, 166, 184, 205–6; navigational and survey

work, 107, 126, 129–30, 131–34, 139; organization and preparation, 92–94; personnel choices, 94–98, 156–57; Pitt and, 113–15, 118–19, 139–40, 157, 164–65, 184–85; refused shore leave to crew, 112, 169–70; report to London, 155; ribbon incident, Maui, 175; sanitation orders, 104–5; Tenerife incident, 102–4. *See also Discovery/Chatham* expedition

Vancouver, George, post-expedition: Camelford affair, 207–13; character assassination, 213–16; clandestine investigation, 215–16; final illness and death, 206–7, 216–19; isolation, 212–13; remuneration, delayed, 207, 217; *A Voyage of Discovery* published, 207, 216–18; wrapped up expedition affairs, 206–7

Vancouver, John, 10, 217, 225

Vancouver, John Jasper, 9, 10, 24

Vancouver Island, *viii*, 138–39, 149, 224. *See also* Friendly Cove; Nootka Sound

Van Horne, W.C., 224

Viana, Francisco José, 143

Voyage of Discovery, A, 217–18, 219, 225

Wales, William, 17

Watt, James, 60

West Indies Station (Port Royal), 58–59

Whidbey, Joseph: background and character, 60–61; GV and, 61, 94, 111, 166, 215; on impressment, 78; as master of *Discovery*, 94; survey work, 107, 126, 129–30, 139, 176, 180, 193–94; Tenerife incident, 102, 103

Whidbey Island, *viii*

Wickaninnish, 42, 91, 149

William Wyndham. *See* Grenville, Lord

Yuquot. *See* Friendly Cove

Zaikov, Potap, 44